A PRACTICAL GUIDE TO CHILD DEVELOPMENT

Volume 1 The Child

Valda Reynolds Cert. Ed.

Joint Chief Examiner, Midland Examining Group, for GCSE Home Economics: Child Development

Stanley Thornes (Publishers) Ltd

First published in 1987 by
Stanley Thornes (Publishers) Ltd
Old Station Drive
Leckhampton
Cheltenham
GL53 0DN

Reprinted 1987 (twice)
Reprinted 1988

British Library Cataloguing in Publication Data

Reynolds, V.
    A practical guide to child development.
    Vol. 1
    1. Child development
    I. Title
    155.4   BF721

ISBN 0-85950-221-X

Typeset by Tech-Set, Gateshead, Tyne & Wear
Printed and bound in Great Britain at The Bath Press, Avon

A PRACTICAL GUIDE TO CHILD ░░░ P░

Volume 1   The Child

Also available fro ... nes (Publishers) Ltd in 1987:

Valda Reynolds   ● A PRACTICAL GUIDE TO CHILD DEVELOPMENT
   Volume 2: The Family
   ● A PRACTICAL GUIDE TO CHILD DEVELOPMENT
   Teacher's Book

Contents

Preface   **ix**

Acknowledgements   **x**

SECTION A   **Planning and Preparing for a Family**   **1**

1 The Responsibility and Value of Family Life   2
    The role of the parents   2
    When to start a family   2
    Family finance   3
    Family planning   4
    Termination of pregnancy   7

2 Pre-planned Parenthood   8
    A woman's health before conception   8
    Health hazards for both parents   9

    Follow-up exercises   10

SECTION B   **Conception to Birth**   **13**

3 Basic Physiology   14
    Female and male reproductive systems   14
    Puberty   16
    Menstruation   18
    Sexually transmitted disease   20
    Conception   21
    Infertility   22
    Artificial insemination   24
    Chromosomes and genes   25
    Twins and multiple births   26
    Blood groups and rhesus incompatibility   28
    Congenital handicap (handicap from birth)   29
    Confirmation of pregnancy   32

    Follow-up exercises   34

4 Development of the Foetus   38
    The three trimesters   38
    The umbilical cord and the placenta   38
    The amniotic sac   40
    The stages of development   41
    Changes to the expectant mother during pregnancy   44
    Complications during pregnancy   48

    Follow-up exercises   50

5	Care of the Expectant Mother	53
	Perinatal mortality rate	53
	Basic medical care	54
	Things to avoid during pregnancy	55
	Miscarriage and those at risk	56
	Caring for herself	57
	People who look after the expectant mother	65
	The antenatal clinic	66
	Diary of a pregnancy	68
	Antenatal classes	71
	Follow-up exercises	73
6	Preparations before the Birth	76
	Getting things ready for the baby	76
	Consumer advice	88
	Preparing for the birth	89
	Breast or bottle feeding	92
	Follow-up exercises	94
SECTION C	**Birth and Postnatal Care**	**97**
7	Birth	98
	The start of labour	98
	The stages of labour	100
	Pain relief during labour	102
	Special treatments and conditions	103
	Premature babies	105
	Care of the mother after birth	107
	Care of the baby after birth	109
	Follow-up exercises	111
8	Looking After the Newborn Baby	113
	Establishing a routine	113
	Relationships	115
	Special requirements of the newborn baby	117
	Follow-up exercises	135
SECTION D	**Physical Development**	**139**
9	Stages of Physical Development	140
	Height and weight	141
	Vision and hearing	143
	Teeth and bones	145
	Locomotion	147
	Co-ordination	150
	Developmental testing	152
	Follow-up exercises	154

10	Conditions for Physical Development	157
	Food	157
	Bowel and bladder training	167
	Exercise and fresh air, rest and sleep	169
	Clothing	172
	Toys and activities	179
	Prevention and treatment of illness and disease	180
	Safety in the child's environment	191
	The Green Cross Code	201
	Follow-up exercises	204

SECTION E   Intellectual Development   **213**

11	Stages of Intellectual Development	214
	Professor Jean Piaget	214
	Cognitive development	215
	Patterns of learning	216
	Follow-up exercises	219
12	Conditions for Intellectual Development	220
	The child's environment	220
	Speech and language development	225
	Toys, games and activities	230
	Safety of toys	236
	Follow-up exercises	237

SECTION F   Social and Emotional Development   **243**

13	Social Development	244
	The stages of socialisation	244
	Social behaviour and social training	246
	Toys, games and activities	249
	Follow-up exercises	250
14	Emotional Development	252
	Conditions for emotional development	253
	Emotional disturbance	255
	Follow-up exercises	257

APPENDICES   **259**

A	Professional Carers	260
B	Special Services and Clinics	261
C	Voluntary and Other Organisations	262
D	Useful Sources of Information	264
E	Further Reading	266
F	Examination Techniques	267
G	A Specimen Examination Question and Answer Scheme	268

H   Further Activities   271
     I   Nursery activity   271
     II Safety activity   274
     III Playgroup activity   277
J   Assignments   281
     Assignment I   281
     Assignment II   283
     Assignment III   285
K   How the Follow-up Exercises Link with the National Criteria
     Assessment Objectives   287

GLOSSARY   293

INDEX   299

Preface

Child development and child care courses are popular options in schools. Whether the student is aiming for an examination certificate leading to a career working with children, or simply has a natural concern with preparing for parenthood and caring for children, this interest should be provided for.

The aim of the two volumes of this book is to cover the range of information required by the various GCSE boards in their syllabuses, within the national criteria for Home Economics: Child Development; and by students taking NAMCW (National Association for Maternal and Child Welfare) and pre-nursing courses. It should also be useful for any of the Preparation for Parenthood or the Family and Community courses, in which a sound knowledge of child development is required.

The six main sections of this volume deal with the care and preparation needed before, during and after pregnancy; the development of the foetus; and the physical, social, emotional and intellectual development of the child (referred to as 'he' or 'she' in alternate chapters). At the end of all but the first chapter are follow-up exercises (sets of graded questions) and activities, arranged in order of increasing difficulty, and requiring a variety of different techniques and skills. Some of these questions are open-ended activities that demand individual research.

In the national criteria for GCSE Home Economics there is a list of assessment objectives that need to be tested in the syllabus. The follow-up exercises and activities have been linked to these objectives as a guide for teachers, and all the objectives have been covered to some degree. Appendix K gives the objectives in condensed form, together with a matrix to show which questions cover each of them. The exercises are also divided into categories, which loosely indicate the ability range they suit. Those in Category 1 are the least demanding.

Ten appendices provide a summary of services available, addresses of organisations referred to in the book and of sources of more information, and suggestions for further reading. Teachers should find especially useful the copyright-free pupil assignments and the ideas for further activities. For the guide to the important area of examination techniques and the copyright-free specimen examination question and answer scheme, I have drawn from my own experience as a chief examiner.

The glossary and index provide an explanation of unfamiliar terms and a comprehensive guide to the topics dealt with.

Some topics in this book are covered in greater detail in Volume 2, which also covers the other topics in the examination syllabuses. The separate Teacher's Book will provide useful data and answer schemes for the follow-up questions.

Most child development classes include pupils with a wide range of ability. The in-depth information given in this book is detailed enough to cover the needs of the average to high ability candidate, but the straightforward text, clear illustrations and varied activities should interest and stimulate those of lower ability.

The United Kingdom does not compare very favourably with some of the other European countries in its standards of care and understanding of the needs of the expectant mother and the child. The infant mortality rate is still too high, cases of child abuse too numerous and the number of divided families too great for us to feel complacent. It is only by educating our young people in all aspects of child development and family care that these statistics will be improved.

The book is intended as a modest contribution towards this desirable goal.

Valda Reynolds
1987

Acknowledgements

The author and publishers would like to thank the following for their help in the production of this book:

Pam Knight for the cover design.
Margaret Lanfear for typing the script.
Peter Reynolds for compiling the index and his support during the writing of the book.

and for photographs:
The Health Education Council (p. 11)
Mothercare (pp. 64, 230 (upper), 231 (lower right) and 249 (left))
Sterling Health (p. 201)
Vision International (pp. 27, 106, 110, 155 and 170).

SECTION A Planning and Preparing for a Family

1   The Responsibility and Value of Family Life

The role of the parents

Magazines, TV and newspapers will tell you that child abuse is increasing, the birth-rate is falling, there are more single-parent families and the divorce rate is rising. All this would seem to indicate that traditional family life is breaking down, but this is not the whole picture. Although there are a lot of family problems, and some of the old values are changing, marriage and child rearing are still popular.

These days it is easier for young couples to plan their family by limiting the number of children they have, and choosing when to have them. As parents, they are then more likely to be in a better position to give their children a stable, secure and loving background, so that the children can develop into well-balanced, healthy adults.

When to start a family

A responsible couple who plan to marry will discuss their plans for a family before they do so. They may seek advice from their doctor, their parents, or their religious counsellors. The Marriage Guidance Council and the Family Planning Association will give useful advice to young couples on the responsibilities of marriage and starting a family.

Study this list of things which a couple should consider and see if you can add to it.

- Do we want to have children at all? Are both of us fully satisfied with our careers, and would not want to give them up or interrupt them? Both partners must agree on this point.
- Are we both sufficiently mature to be able to accept the responsibilities of a family? If we both enjoy a full social life and have lots of outside interests, would we want to give up a lot of this to look after a baby?
- Have we both got jobs, and some money saved up? Could we lose one income and still support a family? Babies must have warmth, shelter, food and clothing, which are all costly.

- Have we got suitable accommodation? Is this accommodation secure? It is very difficult to bring up a baby in a one-room flat, and many landladies and landlords will not allow a couple to stay on when they have a baby. Can we get a council house? Can we afford to buy our own property? If we live with our in-laws will they welcome a young child?

- Are we healthy? Does our family background have evidence of any hereditary diseases? Do we smoke, drink, or take drugs? All these things can affect the health of the baby – are we prepared to take a risk?

- Are we agreed about division of labour? If the father expects to continue his social life and leave the babyminding to the mother, will she consent?

- Can we get on with each other's relations? In-laws and relations have strengthened many marriages, but they can also cause a lot of friction.

- Is this a mixed marriage, religiously or ethnically? If it is, can we each accept the other's ideas, and agree on how to bring up the children?

- Do our ideas on bringing up children coincide? A lot of trouble can occur when parents do not have the same views on important issues such as discipline, feeding, education, etc.

These are some of the matters which a young couple should discuss. If they have different ideas about a lot of them, it would be better for them to wait to start a family until they can agree upon these basic issues.

Family finance

Money is an important issue when deciding the best time to start a family. A baby does not need luxurious surroundings, but there are essential items of equipment, comfortable clothing and suitable food to be provided. There are ways of obtaining things quite cheaply, such as buying them second-hand (for example, from jumble sales), or making them at home, but to prepare adequately for a new baby can cost several hundred pounds.

Here are some examples of where the money goes:

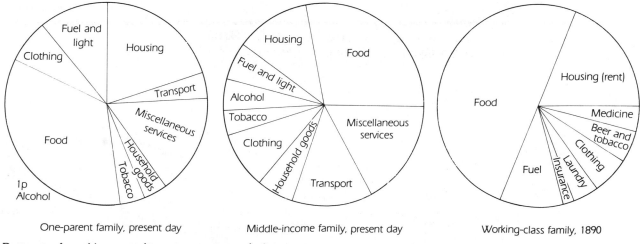

One-parent family, present day   Middle-income family, present day   Working-class family, 1890

Patterns of weekly expenditure: pence in each £

3

Discussion points

What do these figures show you?

Compare the budget of the middle-income family with that of the one-parent family.

What were the priorities of working-class families 100 years ago?

Family planning

Many couples decide to wait a few years before starting a family so that they can provide a comfortable home and have some savings and perhaps a few labour-saving devices, such as a washing machine, fridge and vacuum cleaner, which help with the extra work a baby brings. They must therefore consider the various methods of **contraception** (birth control).

The aim of contraception is to prevent the sperm from the male fertilising the egg (ovum) in the uterus (womb) of the female (see p. 21). There are several ways that this can be done, and it is sensible to get expert advice from the start.

No method of contraception is 100 per cent perfect, but some are more reliable than others. Advice may be sought from several sources, such as:

- the family doctor
- the health visitor
- the Family Planning Clinic
- books and magazines.

Contraceptives are reasonably reliable, in theory, but when people get careless or do not use the device correctly the reliability rate goes down. It is irresponsible for young people, experimenting with sexual relationships, to have sexual intercourse without taking any precautions. An accidental pregnancy can be a disaster for the mother, the father and the unwanted baby.

Methods of contraception

Method	Description	% of couples using method*	
		Popularity	Effectiveness (in theory)
Oral contraception (the pill)	*A set of pills only available on prescription. The combined pill must be taken one each day for 21 days, starting on the fifth day after menstruation (see p. 18) begins and ending on the 25th day. During the gap when the pill is not taken, bleeding takes place.*	58	99
	The combined pill contains two hormones, oestrogen and progesterone, which control the reproductive organs to prevent ovulation. The minipill contains only one hormone, progesterone, and is a useful but slightly less effective alternative for women who cannot tolerate the combined pill.		
	A very safe method, but not recommended for women with high blood pressure, those who are overweight and those suffering from certain medical conditions.		

*Source: UK Family Planning Clinic figures, 1983

(continued)

Method	Description	% of couples using method*	
		Popularity	Effectiveness (in theory)
The intra-uterine device (IUD) or coil	A small piece of shaped plastic or copper which is fitted inside the uterus with a special plastic inserter. This must be done by a doctor. A small thread is left so the woman can check that it is still in position.	16	96–98
	A safe method, but it can cause bleeding and discomfort in some women. It must then be removed and another method used instead.		
The condom or sheath	A thin sheath of rubber which is rolled on to the erect penis before intercourse.	10	97
	A popular method as it requires no medical consultation. Reliable if carefully used, especially with a spermicide. Sheaths also provide a barrier to diseases such as AIDS (see p. 21).		
The diaphragm or Dutch cap	A rubber cap fitted by a doctor, which fits the neck of the uterus. It can then be removed and replaced by the woman. It should not be removed until eight hours after intercourse.	7	97
	Quite reliable, especially if used with a spermicide.		
Sterilisation	a) Male sterilisation – vasectomy. The sperm tubes of the male are cut and tied or blocked.	2	99
	b) Female sterilisation. The fallopian tubes are cut and tied or blocked.		
	This is a very safe method, although occasional failures occur (1 in 1000), but it usually means that the sterilised person cannot have more children. It therefore needs careful thought before seeking to have the operation carried out.		

Source: UK Family Planning Clinic figures, 1983

(continued)

Method	Description	% of couples using method*	
		Popularity	**Effectiveness (in theory)**
Spermicides	*These are available as creams, tablets or foams, and are placed in the vagina immediately before intercourse. They are not very reliable on their own, but increase the reliability of a diaphragm or sheath.*	*1*	*70*
The rhythm method, or 'safe period'	*A method used by couples who do not believe in the chemical or mechanical birth control methods. This method relies on knowing the stage when there is no egg in the fallopian tube (see p. 15). The menstrual cycle (see p. 19) must be worked out to show when it is safe to have intercourse.* *Only reliable for women with very regular periods.*	*5*	*60–65*
Withdrawal (coitus interruptus)	*A method relying on the penis being withdrawn just before the man's climax (see p. 22). Not a safe method as some semen may escape before climax, or the man may leave the withdrawal too late.*	*5*	*No figures available*
Spermicidal sponge	*A mushroom-shaped polyurethane sponge, impregnated with a spermicide cream.* *This method only became available in the UK from March 1985. It gives up to 24 hours' protection and does not need a prescription, but the failure rate can be higher if it is not used carefully.*	*Figures not yet available*	*85 (estimated)*

Source: UK Family Planning Clinic figures, 1983

Reliability of the most popular methods of contraception

	In theory	In practice
Contraceptive pill	*99%*	*90%–95%*
Coil (IUD)	*98%*	*95%*
Condom (sheath)	*97%*	*90%*
Diaphragm and spermicide	*97%*	*83%*

Termination of pregnancy

It is easy to obtain advice on contraception and carry out contraceptive methods which are very reliable. Those couples who have an unwanted baby through being irresponsible or ignorant often experience difficulties in their relationship, and problems such as baby battering and child neglect can result.

Sometimes, in special circumstances, it may be necessary for the woman to have a pregnancy terminated, but termination (abortion) should *not* be thought of as a method of birth control. Many people think that there are no circumstances in which a human life – in this case, that of the unborn baby – should be taken. It is illegal to terminate a pregnancy without medical approval, and the operation must be done by a qualified doctor. A back-street abortionist can cause death or serious illness of the pregnant woman, apart from breaking the law.

The Abortion Act (1967) states that a doctor may terminate a pregnancy provided that two doctors are of the opinion that:

- continuing the pregnancy would involve risk to the mother, or
- there is a risk that the child, when born, would suffer from a serious physical or mental handicap.

The termination must be carried out in a National Health Service hospital or an approved private nursing home; and the Department of Health must be notified within seven days.

The 'risk to the mother' of a continued pregnancy may mean physical or mental risk. Social circumstances will also be taken into consideration, such as rape, an already over-large family, poor housing conditions, or other circumstances which could mentally unbalance the expectant mother.

Comparative figures for abortions in the UK

	1969	1971	1979	1981	1983
Total number of abortions (to nearest thousand)	50 000	95 000	121 000	129 000	127 000
Abortions to single women (as a percentage of the total)	45%	47%	52%	54%	58%
Place (to nearest thousand):					
NHS hospital	34 000	53 000	56 000	61 000	62 000
Private hospital	16 000	41 000	65 000	67 000	65 000

Source: Office of Population Censuses and Surveys

These figures show a steady increase in the number of abortions from 1969 to 1981 and a slight decrease from 1981 to 1983. (Note that 58 per cent of abortions in 1983 were to single women.) Since 1979, slightly more abortions have been performed in private hospitals and clinics than in NHS hospitals.

In 1981, 197 abortions associated with German measles (rubella) took place. In 1978, this figure was 896. The figure varies from year to year (see p. 9).

2 Pre-planned Parenthood

A woman's health before conception

Once the decisions have been made about when to start a family, there are many ways in which a woman can prepare herself for what should be a happy and exciting event.

The number of babies being born with a physical or mental handicap has dropped rapidly during the past few years, owing to better medical knowledge and skills, but even fewer handicapped babies would be born if more women consciously prepared themselves for pregnancy. Pregnancy is going to be a long tiring time, with a lot of hard labour when the baby is being born. It is sensible therefore for the prospective mother to be in good health before she becomes pregnant. The following are some of the positive steps she can take to make sure that she and the baby are as healthy as possible during those important nine months.

- For general good health she needs a sensible diet, plenty of fresh air and exercise and sufficient rest.
- Weight is important. Excess weight at the beginning of a pregnancy will put strain on the heart, legs and feet as the pregnancy develops, and will be difficult to lose after the birth. Being very much underweight can cause problems to mother and baby.

  It is much simpler to increase or decrease the weight before a pregnancy begins.
- Any minor ailments such as anaemia, headaches, indigestion, etc., should be treated. A pregnant woman should not be taking drugs which could harm the baby. Women with more serious medical conditions, such as diabetes, heart complaints, epilepsy, etc., should consult their doctor *before* they consider becoming pregnant.
- Many mothers find that after the birth of their baby, their own teeth have suffered from a calcium deficiency. Before starting a pregnancy women should therefore have a thorough dental check and any necessary treatment. They should use a fluoride toothpaste to build up the enamel. Extra milk and cheese will provide more calcium in the diet to strengthen the teeth.
- During pregnancy many women have discomfort and problems with their feet and ankles, which have a lot of extra weight to bear. It is sensible for women to have treatment for corns, hard skin, or other foot problems before they become pregnant.

Health hazards for both parents

Some couples who wish to start a family are very concerned because there are medical conditions in their families that they fear may be hereditary and could be passed on to their baby. Conditions such as haemophilia, schizophrenia and some types of blindness and deafness may be inheritable, but the couple can obtain advice from their family doctor or a genetic counselling unit if they are worried about this.

Other health hazards can be avoided or treated as follows. A further list is given on p. 54.

- There is no doubt that the expectant mother who smokes is putting her own health and that of her baby at risk. Before a woman who smokes becomes pregnant she should try to give it up or at least cut down.

- No woman who has become addicted to any type of drug should become pregnant. Drugs taken by the expectant mother will pass into the developing baby and may cause the baby to be born addicted. Any woman who is an alcoholic should not become pregnant. A lot of alcohol can damage the unborn baby. Any woman who is addicted to drugs or alcohol should get help before a pregnancy is started.

- Some types of STD (sexually transmitted disease, also called VD or venereal disease) if left untreated can affect the woman's ability to conceive, and can also be transmitted to the unborn baby. Treatment can be obtained from special clinics.

- A woman who develops rubella (German measles) during the first three months of pregnancy stands a high risk of the baby being damaged. Rubella can lead to blindness, deafness, heart damage and physical deformity in the baby. All girls in the United Kingdom between the ages of 11 and 13 are now vaccinated against this disease, but it is wise for the woman who is planning a pregnancy to have a test to see that she is still immune to the disease.

- The health of the father of the child is also important. He owes it to his partner to be strong and healthy so that he can give her the support she needs during her pregnancy. If there is any chance that he may have contracted a STD, he must go to a special clinic, or his partner may also become infected. If he cuts down on smoking, drinking and excess food it will help her to do the same. The money saved will also be useful for all the things that are going to be needed.

Follow-up exercises

Category 1

1 Copy these sentences and complete them.

To prepare for a healthy pregnancy a woman should:

a) give up _____ and _____

b) plan her meals so that she has a _____ _____ .

c) check that she is immune to _____ _____ .

d) take off any excess _____ by going on a _____ , or increase her _____ if she is very much _____ .

e) think about any _____ diseases in the family and consult _____ if she is worried.

f) consult her dentist about her _____ , drink more _____ to get extra _____ and use _____ _____ .

g) not be taking any _____ which could harm _____ _____ .

2 *a)* List the ways in which expectant parents can save money when buying clothing and equipment for the new baby.

b) Copy this chart and complete it to show what checks would have to be made on things which had been bought second-hand.

	Cot	Pram	Baby clothes
Safety			
Hygiene			
Possible repairs			

Category 2

3 Why is the contraceptive pill such a popular method of birth control?

If you were a health visitor what advice would you give to a woman who was thinking of starting her first course of contraceptive pills?

4 Write a paragraph describing the home life of an average family about 30 to 40 years ago – perhaps when your parents were young.

Compare this with an average family's home life today, and make a list of the things which have brought the alterations about. The list should include education, money, changing moral values and contraception.

Activity

This illustration is issued by the Health Education Council to make expectant mothers think about the dangers of smoking.

Design a poster which you think would emphasise the dangers of smoking, alcohol or drugs during pregnancy.

SECTION B Conception to Birth

3 Basic Physiology

To understand the physical processes of conception, pregnancy and birth, it is necessary to know how the female and male reproductive systems work.

As a child grows into an adult the reproductive organs develop to make possible the bearing or fathering of a baby. This stage is known as puberty. It often starts at about 11 to 13 years, usually earlier for girls than for boys. It can be much earlier or later, depending upon the individual. Factors such as heredity, social conditions, diet and race will all affect sexual development.

Female and male reproductive systems

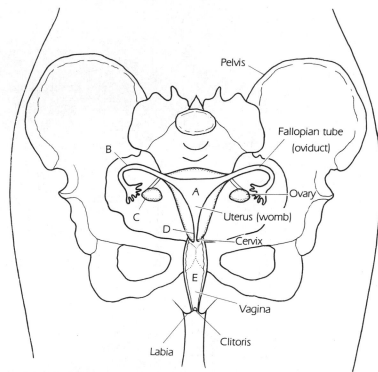

Female reproductive organs

The internal female reproductive organs consist of:

- **A** the **uterus** (womb) in which the baby grows. The uterus is a hollow, pear-shaped organ with thick, muscular walls.

- **B** two tubes about 10 cm (4 in.) long called the **fallopian tubes** (oviducts), one on each side of the uterus. The sperm swims along these to fertilise the egg.
- **C** two **ovaries**, which lie one on each side of the pelvis and are white and oval shaped. They produce and release **eggs** (ova), and also control the female sex hormones **oestrogen** and **progesterone**.
- **D** the **cervix** (neck of the uterus), which is at the lower end of the uterus. The cervix is usually closed, leaving only a small gap for the entrance of sperm, or exit of menstrual fluid.
- **E** the **vagina**, into which the cervix extends a short way. The vagina is a tube about 10–12 cm (4–5 in.) long leading to the surface of the body.

The external female reproductive organs are known collectively as the **vulva**, and consist of:

- the **mons pubis**, a soft pad of fatty tissue covered in pubic hair, which lies in front of the pubic bone.
- the **labia**, which are folds of skin enclosing the urinary opening and the vaginal opening.
- the **clitoris**, which lies between the mons pubis and the urinary opening, and is of a sponge-like tissue that is very sexually sensitive. When sexually stimulated, blood is pumped into the tissue, causing the clitoris to enlarge.

The male reproductive organs consist of:

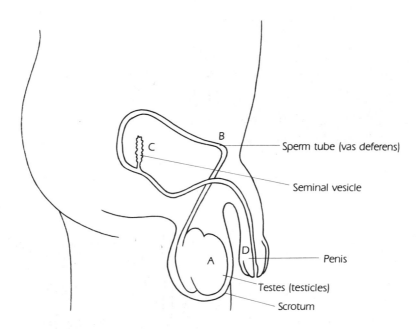

Male reproductive organs

- **A** the **testes** (testicles), which are the male equivalent of the ovaries. They are contained in the **scrotum**, a pouch of skin below the pelvis. The testes constantly produce the **sperm** needed to fertilise an egg. They also produce the male sex hormone testosterone.
- **B** the **sperm tubes** (vas deferens), along which sperm produced by the testes travel.
- **C** the **seminal vesicles**, which store and secrete **semen** (seminal fluid). The semen is a nourishing fluid which carries the sperm down the penis and out of the body.
- **D** the **penis** usually hangs limply, and is of sponge-like tissue. When sexually stimulated, blood is pumped into the tissue, causing the penis to enlarge and harden into an **erection**.

Puberty

During puberty certain physical changes occur which transform the typical child's body shape into that of an adult.

Girls

- Body hair grows under the arms and pubic hair covers the surface of the body round the vulva.
- Fat is laid down over the hips and thighs and round the chest and breasts. The breasts and nipples develop.
- A growth spurt results in increased height.
- The ovaries begin to develop ripened egg cells, which are shed every month during menstruation (periods).

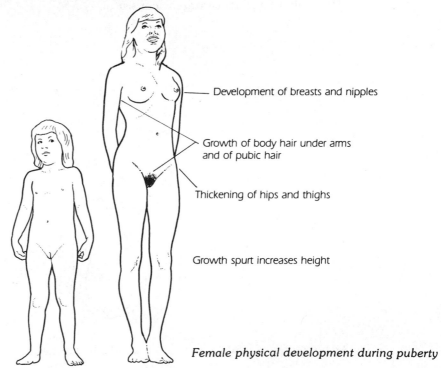

Development of breasts and nipples

Growth of body hair under arms and of pubic hair

Thickening of hips and thighs

Growth spurt increases height

Female physical development during puberty

Boys

- The penis and testes grow.
- Body hair appears under the arms and on the chest and face, and pubic hair grows round the penis and testes.
- The shoulders broaden and the muscles of the arms and chest develop. Pelvic bones grow at a slower rate, giving slimmer hips.
- Bone development makes the face less rounded and the feet and hands more angular.
- The larynx (voice box) grows larger and the voice deepens.
- A growth spurt results in increased height.

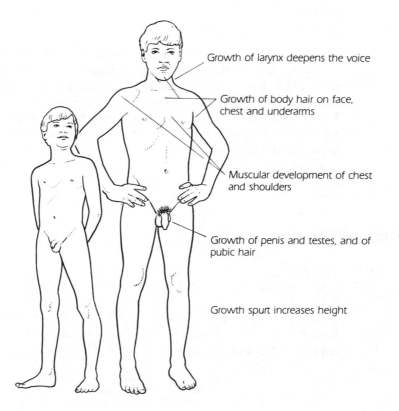

Growth of larynx deepens the voice

Growth of body hair on face, chest and underarms

Muscular development of chest and shoulders

Growth of penis and testes, and of pubic hair

Growth spurt increases height

Male physical development during puberty

Puberty in both sexes is controlled by **hormones**. These are powerful chemicals which circulate in the blood and control growth and metabolism; they are produced by the endocrine system, which is made up of various glands that each produce and secrete their own particular hormone.

- The **pituitary gland** is at the base of the brain. It produces the growth hormone, stimulates and regulates the working of the sex organs, and helps to control the other endocrine glands. It is known as the master gland.

- The **adrenal glands** lie on top of the kidneys, and secrete adrenaline when certain emotions are aroused.
- The **pancreas** produces the hormone insulin, which helps to keep the correct level of sugar in the blood.
- The **thyroid gland**, situated just below the voice box, produces the hormone thyroxin which controls the energy output of the body and the rate at which food is converted into energy.
- The sex hormones are produced by the sex glands. The female ovaries produce oestrogen and progesterone and the male testes produce testosterone.

The body cannot function correctly if the glands are not producing the correct level of hormones. Some glands depend upon others to control them, so if one gland is not working properly it can affect others.

As well as stimulating physical sexual development during puberty, the hormones also activate emotional change. Until these changes have levelled out and the adolescent has learnt to control his or her emotions, there will be peaks of feeling when he or she may be depressed, excited, happy, bored, etc. These extremes of feeling are bewildering to adolescents and to their families, and can be difficult to cope with. It is a time when great patience and understanding are needed, always remembering that it is a stage that will pass eventually.

Menstruation

This is the complete process that begins when an egg ripens in the ovaries and is then released (**ovulation**) to be fertilised. The lining of the uterus (endometrium) thickens and fills with blood, ready to receive the fertilised egg. If the egg is not fertilised the lining breaks down, producing the **menstrual flow** (period) from the vagina. This lasts for about 5–7 days, and then the **menstrual cycle** starts again.

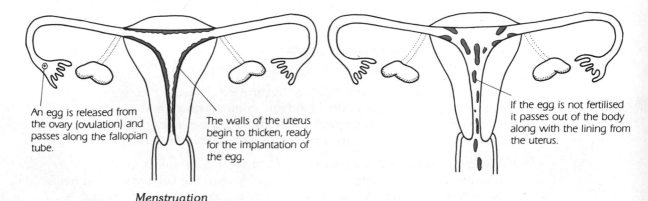

An egg is released from the ovary (ovulation) and passes along the fallopian tube.

The walls of the uterus begin to thicken, ready for the implantation of the egg.

If the egg is not fertilised it passes out of the body along with the lining from the uterus.

Menstruation

The cycle lasts about one month, but may take longer or be irregular in some women. Physical or mental stress can cause a period to be late; poor diet or insufficient food can cause periods to stop altogether.

Ovulation (the release of the egg from the ovary) takes place 14 days before a period is due.

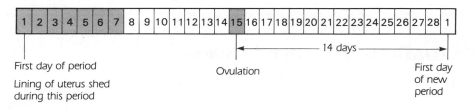

A 28-day cycle

Menstruation often starts when a girl is about 12 or 13 years old. Once menstruation has started a girl is fertile, and able to become pregnant. It will cease at the **menopause** ('change of life'), which is usually between 45 and 55.

Menstrual problems

Some problems are common during menstruation, and very often simple remedies such as a change of diet, more exercise, more rest or better personal hygiene will improve the condition. A doctor should be consulted for severe conditions.

Possible problems include:

- irregular periods. Very often these occur when menstruation starts; they soon settle into a regular pattern.
- period pains (**dysmenorrhoea**). Muscle contractions may cause cramp pains, sickness and dizziness. Pain killers and warmth will relieve the pain.
- very heavy periods or an unusual discharge. This may indicate an abnormal condition, and a doctor should be consulted.
- **premenstrual tension** (PMT). This is a very common condition which results in mental or emotional tension and a bloated feeling for a few days before the start of a period. Headaches, tender breasts and irritability may also occur. PMT may be caused by water retention, and sometimes cutting down on salt intake will help. The condition passes when the period starts.

When the physical changes of puberty have taken place, the male is capable of fertilising a female egg, and the female is able to conceive and produce a baby. However, although the body may be physically capable of these functions, it is still necessary for the emotions to develop. It is during the adolescent period – from puberty to 19 or 20 – that physical and emotional developments link and move towards a mature and adult understanding.

Adolescents may form casual relationships and experiment with sex, but they will also be learning moral values and how to become responsible adults. Many adolescents will be looking for a partner with whom to form a permanent relationship, leading to a home and family. The results of unrestricted sexual encounters can be disastrous, possibly ending in unwanted pregnancies, sexually transmitted diseases or emotional damage.

Sexually transmitted disease

Since the 1960s there has been a steep increase in the number of reported cases of STD (venereal disease), from approximately 175 000 in 1960 to half a million in 1985. These are frightening figures, as the results of STD can be infertility, serious illness or even death, and psychological trauma and acute distress to those infected, their partners and family.

These diseases can be easily passed on from person to person during casual sexual relationships. STDs can be successfully treated when diagnosed early and given professional medical treatment. Special treatment clinics (genito-urinary clinics) have been set up in most hospital departments, and treatment is free. Any person with a STD must not have sexual contact with another person until he or she has been cleared of the infection.

Sexually transmitted diseases

Disease	Symptoms	Results	Treatment
Syphilis	*Painless sores or ulcers on sex organs*	*The infection enters the bloodstream; can lead to disease of the brain or heart, and death*	*Blood test; course of injections*
Gonorrhoea	*Men: burning pain when urinating Women: 70% have no symptoms, some have heavy discharge*	*Infection of sperm tubes and oviduct leading to sterility*	*Antibiotics (course of injections or tablets)*
Non-specific urethritis	*Same symptoms as gonorrhoea, with discharge from penis or vagina*	*Diseases of the joints; eye, skin, and mouth infections*	*Course of antibiotics for both partners*
Tricho-monases vaginalis	*(Women only) Yellow, unpleasant discharge; soreness of vagina and vulva*	*Chronic (persistent) vaginal discharge and pain*	*A course of tablets*
Thrush (candidiasis)	*Men: sore, red tip of penis Women: sore vagina; (Thrush is not always contracted sexually. It is a fungus infection which can also affect the mouth, and can be brought on by taking certain antibiotics.)*	*Chronic condition*	*Tablets or ointment*

(continued)

Disease	Symptoms	Results	Treatment
Warts	*Small growths on penis or vulva*	*Can spread quickly*	*Thorough cleansing; use of prescribed cream*
Herpes	*Looks like a cold sore on the penis or vulva; painful and itching*	*Can cause further infections*	*Prescribed creams or ointment*
Lice and scabies	*Itchiness; parasites can be seen on skin or pubic hairs*	*Can spread*	*Shave area; use DDT lotion*
AIDS (Acquired Immune Deficiency Syndrome)	*Breakdown of the body's natural immune system*	*Increasing weakness and frequently death, often from pneumonia or cancer*	*None yet proven*

Conception

One definition of when life begins is the point when a (female) egg is fertilised by a (male) sperm. This happens naturally when a man and woman have sexual intercourse, and is called conception. The urge to reproduce is very strong in all humans and animals to ensure the continuation of the species. Because human beings are capable of reasoned thinking and have emotions, the act of intercourse (**coitus**) can also be a loving and satisfying experience.

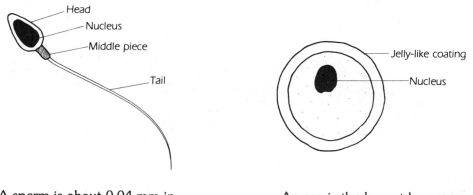

A sperm is about 0.04 mm in length, and has a head which contains the nucleus, a middle piece and a tail. The tail moves about to enable the sperm to swim along, and is lost when it enters the nucleus of the ovum.

An egg is the largest human cell and is about the size of a full stop. It has a jelly-like coating to stop it from sticking to the sides of the fallopian tube.

When the man is sexually aroused his penis will become erect, which enables it to enter the vagina. The penis, like the clitoris, is stimulated by movement until a climax is reached. An ejaculation then takes place from the penis, and the semen, which contains millions of tiny sperm, is released into the vagina. A large number of sperm leak out of the vagina and many are killed by the acid vaginal secretion.

The remaining sperm swim through the opening of the cervix, through the uterus and into the fallopian tube, and press against any newly released egg. One sperm may pierce the egg, and the outer wall of the egg cell will then harden to keep out other sperm. The nucleus of the sperm and the nucleus of the egg fuse together to form a zygote (see p. 38).

Conception does not occur every time intercourse takes place. If it is the right time during the menstrual cycle, and an egg has been released from the ovary, it may well be fertilised, but very often it can take many months before a couple are able to conceive a baby. Perhaps one in five women who are trying to conceive does so straight away, and one in ten takes more than a year to do so.

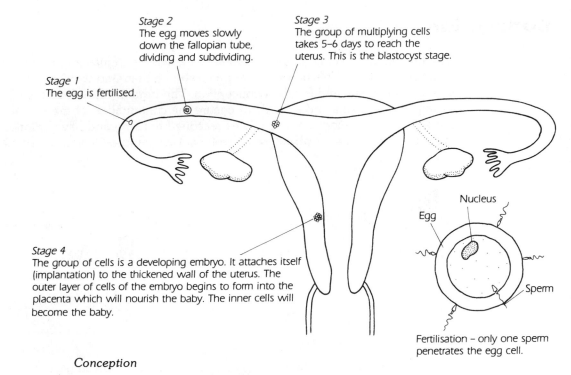

Stage 2
The egg moves slowly down the fallopian tube, dividing and subdividing.

Stage 3
The group of multiplying cells takes 5–6 days to reach the uterus. This is the blastocyst stage.

Stage 1
The egg is fertilised.

Nucleus

Egg

Sperm

Fertilisation – only one sperm penetrates the egg cell.

Stage 4
The group of cells is a developing embryo. It attaches itself (implantation) to the thickened wall of the uterus. The outer layer of cells of the embryo begins to form into the placenta which will nourish the baby. The inner cells will become the baby.

Conception

Infertility

Most doctors will want to wait for a year before sending a couple for special tests if they are worried about their inability to conceive. The family doctor or the Family Planning Clinic will at first advise the couple to try to be more relaxed; being tense, over anxious, tired or in poor general health can all help to prevent a pregnancy. They will also advise them that the best time to conceive is just before ovulation, i.e., about 14 days before the expected start of the woman's next period. The body temperature drops at the time of ovulation and rises just after, so this can be a useful guide; some women who wish to conceive keep a temperature chart as a guide to the best time for trying to conceive. It is also possible to tell from the condition of the **cervical mucus** (a thick fluid in the cervix) when ovulation is due, as the mucus becomes thinner and more plentiful just before ovulation.

Infertility can, however, be much more complex than this, and may require treatment from a specialist. Both partners need to be examined; the man should see a male fertility specialist, and the woman should go to a gynaecologist.

Male causes of infertility

- A low sperm count, i.e., when the semen contains only a small proportion of sperm (less than 30 million sperm per ml). This can be caused by inflammation of the testes owing to mumps or gonorrhoea.
- Being unable to have or maintain an erection (impotence), which may occur if the man is afraid of sexual intercourse or finds it unpleasant, or as a result of illness.
- No sperm being produced because the testes are not working correctly.
- Poor sperm because of general poor health.

Female causes of infertility

- Failure to ovulate. The woman may be unable to produce an egg in the ovary owing to hormonal problems, thyroid disease, or as a side effect of taking the pill over some time.
- Blockage or damage of the fallopian tubes because of infection after disease, miscarriage or termination (abortion).
- Abnormalities of the cervical mucus, which may prevent entry of the sperm to the uterus.
- **Vaginismus** (a spasm of the vagina), which may occur if the woman is afraid of sexual intercourse or finds it painful or unpleasant.

To investigate whether any of these conditions is preventing conception, the first step is usually an examination of the seminal fluid. If there is a low sperm count or the sperm are defective, simple treatment such as cold water splashes daily and wearing looser underwear may be sufficient. Drugs or hormone treatment may also be used. If there is no sperm at all due to a blockage of the sperm tubes, surgery can sometimes correct the problem. If the cause arises from faulty testes there is usually no treatment.

Tests to the female may involve examining the cervical mucus, X-raying the fallopian tubes or using a **laparascope** (small optical device), which is passed into the abdomen to enable the gynaecologist to examine the tubes and ovaries.

Failure to ovulate can be treated with drugs and hormone injections. These fertility drugs bring quite a high risk of multiple births. Abnormalities of the cervical mucus can be treated with the hormone oestrogen quite successfully. Blockage of the fallopian tubes is a more serious condition, needing surgical treatment that does not currently have a high rate of success, although treatment is improving all the time.

Artificial insemination

Many couples anxious to have a family go through these tests and treatments and still find they are unable to conceive. They may then consider **artificial insemination**, which is a method of fertilising the egg by injecting semen into the vagina at the stage of ovulation.

AIH (artificial insemination by husband) is the term used when the semen injected is taken from the husband or partner. This is done in cases where the husband is unable because of physical or psychological problems to eject the semen himself.

AID (artificial insemination by donor) is used in cases where a husband is unable to produce sperm of his own. If the couple are willing, semen from a fertile male can be used.

Semen can be frozen and used at a later stage. Such scientific advances are being made in these directions that the use of artificial insemination is becoming very successful and popular with infertile couples.

Test tube conception is now quite common. In this procedure, known as *in vitro* fertilisation (IVF), eggs are removed from the ovary, mixed with the sperm, and fertilisation takes place. One or more of the resulting embryos is placed at the entrance of the uterus. Implantation is only successful in about 30 per cent of cases. A method of freezing the embryo has now been developed, so that the embryo can be transferred when the chances of pregnancy occurring are high.

Surrogate motherhood is another method by which those couples unable to conceive normally can have a child. A woman who can produce eggs, but cannot carry a child, can donate an egg to be fertilised by her partner's sperm and implanted in another woman's womb, (a surrogate womb); or the surrogate mother can be artificially inseminated with the sperm of the prospective father. In the UK, an official enquiry into the moral dilemmas posed by surrogate motherhood has concluded (in the Warnock report, 1984) that the practice should be made illegal.

There is a lot of controversy about these methods, but many couples who desperately want a baby are willing to try them.

Chromosomes and genes

What are chromosomes and genes and what have they got to do with conception and birth? Why does a boy perhaps have blue eyes like his father and fair hair like his mother? Why do some particular diseases or abnormalities seem to run in families?

The answers to all these questions are linked with the subject of **heredity**. The study of heredity is called **genetics**, and the specialist who deals with genetic problems is a **geneticist**.

Everyone is like their parents to some degree because everyone inherits their parents' characteristics from the egg and the sperm which have fused together.

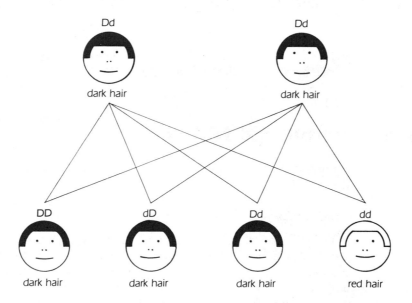

Genetic inheritance ('D' shows the gene for dark hair, 'd' for red hair.)

The female egg and the male sperm each contains 23 thread-like structures called **chromosomes**. When the egg is fertilised it has 46 chromosomes, an equal number from each partner. Each of these chromosomes carries about 2000 **genes**, and it is these that determine the characteristics that are inherited.

Some genes are stronger than others; these are the **dominant genes** and the less dominant are the **recessive genes**. An example of a dominant gene is the one for dark hair, which is stronger than the one for red hair. A dark-haired person may carry a gene for red hair which is overruled by the gene for dark hair.

If the male and female both have the gene for dark hair, then it is likely that their baby will have dark hair. If both dark-haired partners carry a gene for red hair, however, then their child could inherit the gene for red hair from both parents, and would have red hair.

Of the 46 chromosomes in the fertilised egg, 44 will determine the physical structure and function of the child and the other two will determine the sex. The sex chromosome from the female is always the same and is known as X. Some of the male sperm cells will contain the X sex chromosome but others will contain a Y chromosome. When the egg and sperm unite, if the sex chromosome from the male sperm is X then the baby will be a girl (XX); if it is a Y chromosome, the baby will be a boy (XY). It seems to be purely a matter of chance which occurs. For approximately every 105 male babies born in the United Kingdom in 1985, there were 100 female babies.

X Y

- In this drawing, the 23rd pair are the sex chromosomes. Will this combination produce a boy or a girl?

Twins and multiple births

A multiple birth is when two or more **foetuses** (the name given to babies in the uterus) are conceived. The highest number reliably recorded is eight (octuplets). The use of fertility drugs has made the incidence of multiple births more common.

In the UK, one in 90 births produces twins (a higher percentage to West Indian parents), one in 6000 births produces triplets, and one in 500 000 births produces quadruplets. A family history of multiple births means that a multiple birth will be more likely. A woman who has already given birth to twins and conceives again will have a one-in-ten chance of having more.

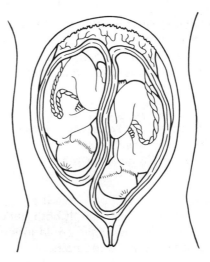

Twins in the womb

Twins can usually be diagnosed by the end of the second month of pregnancy, usually with an ultrasound scan. During the pregnancy the position of each baby can be felt and two heartbeats can be heard.

There are two sorts of twin, **identical** and **non-identical**.

- Identical (**uniovular**) twins develop from one egg, which, after it has been fertilised, divides into two cells which grow into two babies. Each baby looks alike and has the same genes, and they are of the same sex. They share the same placenta and are enclosed by the same outer membrane (see p. 41). If the cell division is incomplete, the result may be Siamese twins, whose bodies are joined at various places.

Identical twins

- Non-identical (**binovular**) twins develop from two fertilised eggs. If more than two eggs are released and fertilised, more foetuses will result. Non-identical or **fraternal** twins are not necessarily of the same sex, and are no more alike than brother and sister. As foetuses, they have different placentas and separate outer membranes.

Blood groups and rhesus incompatibility

Human blood consists of **red cells**, **white cells** and **platelets**, which are contained in a fluid called **plasma**. The red cells contain **haemoglobin**, which is very important as it carries oxygen from the lungs to the tissues and cells that need it. If the haemoglobin level falls or the number of red cells is reduced then the body will suffer from **anaemia**, which results in lack of energy, shortness of breath and pallor. Iron is essential for the formation of haemoglobin, and during pregnancy the foetus draws on the prospective mother's supply, sometimes causing her to have a deficiency which results in an anaemic condition.

Loss of blood during delivery may mean that the mother will need a blood transfusion. She will have had a blood test during her early months of pregnancy to determine her blood group. There are several blood groups, but the most common are **A**, **B**, **AB** and **O** (the letters refer to differences in the red blood cells). We inherit these blood groups through the chromosomes of our parents. Some of these blood groups will not mix, and if the wrong blood is given during a transfusion, the body rejects it. That is why all blood which is stored in blood banks must be carefully labelled. Whole blood can only be stored for about 21 days, but blood plasma and platelets can be frozen and keeps longer.

The second important grouping of blood types depends on possession of the rhesus factor. Everyone's blood is either **rhesus positive (Rh+)** or **rhesus negative (Rh−)**. Only 15 per cent of European women are Rh−, and it is only if the pregnant woman's blood is Rh− that any complications may arise. If the father is Rh+ then the foetus may be Rh+, and during the pregnancy and birth some of the Rh+ blood from the baby may mix with the mother's Rh− blood. The mother then builds up antibodies, which will not affect that child but may affect subsequent babies. The antibodies remain in the mother's blood and if she conceives another Rh+ foetus they will attack the red cells of the foetal blood, causing anaemia and **jaundice** (excess bile in the blood, which turns the skin yellow). This process continues after birth, causing a very severe condition which may result in the need for a transfusion. This dilutes the baby's blood with donor blood compatible with the mother's.

This condition is rarely allowed to get to this extreme now, as the blood test given in early pregnancy will show whether a woman is Rh−. If she is, further tests will be made to see if she is producing antibodies in her blood. The amniotic fluid (which surrounds the foetus in the uterus – see p. 40) can then be tested and if the foetus is having jaundice problems it can either be delivered prematurely or (in early pregnancy) have a transfusion of Rh− blood (an **intra-uterine transfusion**).

The Rh− mother, immediately after the birth of her baby, is given a test to see if any Rh+ cells have entered her bloodstream. If they have, she is given an injection of **Anti-D-Gamma-globulin**, which will destroy these cells before they cause her to start producing antibodies. She is therefore protected for any subsequent pregnancies.

Congenital handicap (handicap from birth)

Fortunately 97 per cent of the babies born in the United Kingdom are perfectly normal.

The handicaps found in the other 3 per cent may be caused by:

- hereditary factors
- mutations
- environmental factors
- disease or deficiency while in the womb
- damage at birth
- metabolic disorders.

Heredity

Some abnormalities are carried from generation to generation, often by healthy people (**carriers**). The difficulties arise when two carriers have children, as they then have a one-in-four chance of having an abnormal child. If two carriers have normal children, they in turn may be carriers.

The most common diseases that are hereditary or have some hereditary factors are **spina bifida** and **Down's syndrome**. (The old name for Down's syndrome was mongolism, but this is now outdated.) Other conditions that may be partly hereditary include hare lip, cleft palate and hip joint dislocations. These conditions result from chromosomal abnormalities. Down's syndrome, for example, is caused by the presence of 47 chromosomes, instead of 46, in every cell. The risk of having a Down's syndrome child increases as the mother gets older.

Some inherited conditions are known as **sex-linked recessive** because they only affect one sex. These conditions are shown in men much more often than in women; the mother can carry the disease without suffering from it. One example is **haemophilia** (a condition in which the blood fails to clot), which is caused by a sex-linked gene transmitted by the female. Although it can, extremely rarely, affect women, there is a one-in-two chance of a woman who carries it passing it on to her sons. **Muscular dystrophy** (a wasting of the muscles) is another example of a serious condition caused by abnormal recessive genes carried by the female and passed on mainly to males. Less serious sex-linked conditions include colour-blindness – about eight per cent of males are colour-blind, which is twenty times the figure for females.

Couples who are planning to have a family, but know that they run the risk of producing a child with an inherited disease or malformation, may seek the advice of a genetic counsellor at a genetic counselling clinic. The counsellor will study their family histories and with the help of tests may be able to assess how likely it is that they will have an affected child. The couple will then have to decide whether they want to take the risk of having a baby that might be handicapped. Genetic counselling can also be given to parents who have had one abnormal child, to give them some idea of the chances of this happening again.

Early tests such as ultrasound (see p. 50) done during the first few weeks of pregnancy, either as a routine measure or to women known to be at risk of producing a handicapped child, can detect two to three per cent of abnormalities.

An expectant mother at risk of having a baby with spina bifida or Down's syndrome will be given an **amniocentesis**, a test in which a small amount of the amniotic fluid is drawn off and examined. This will show whether the abnormal condition is there. If it is, the parents will be offered genetic counselling to help them to decide whether to continue with the pregnancy or to have an abortion.

The Abortion Act (1967) allows for the termination of a pregnancy if there is a risk that the child will be born seriously handicapped. Abnormal foetuses are also more likely to be naturally or spontaneously aborted (when the woman is said to suffer a **miscarriage**) in the early weeks of pregnancy. Six out of ten aborted foetuses are found to have defective chromosomes.

Mutations

Where a gene has been altered or suddenly changed in some way, the resulting gene abnormality may be passed on to the child. These abnormalities are known as mutations, and are, fortunately, rare. Some mutations may be caused by exposure to radiation, X-rays or chemicals, but many are spontaneous, and once the change has taken place there is no cure (although some of the diseases caused can be cured). If a man or woman has a condition caused by a mutation, such as congenital dwarfism (stunted growth), it may be passed on through the sperm or the egg cells to any children.

Environmental factors

Some congenital disorders may be caused by environmental factors, or environmental and hereditary factors linked together. Environmental factors are circumstances outside the body that affect the physical and mental development of the foetus and the child.

Examples of these factors are:

- geographical location. (For example, Scotland has a higher percentage of heart disease than the rest of the United Kingdom.)
- social environment. Poor health care, inferior housing and diet can produce a higher risk of congenital disorders.
- education. Poor general or health education can result in people being unaware of what causes congenital handicap, and of the advice and treatment available.

We can provide a good or a bad environment for children. A good environment will include sound antenatal and postnatal care, healthy living conditions, clean air and water, and opportunities for intellectual and emotional development. A poor environment can produce stunted physical growth, retardation in learning and intellectual development, and emotional problems.

Disease or deficiency while in the womb

Some congenital diseases can be contracted during the nine months of pregnancy by the infection being passed from the mother to the foetus. A typical example is rubella (German measles), which, if it does not result in a miscarriage for the mother, may cause deafness, cataracts or deformity in the child. Other virus infections can also be dangerous. Diseases as different as syphilis (an STD, now rare) and diabetes in the pregnant woman can cause severe problems for the unborn child. A poor or inadequate diet during pregnancy can make the foetus suffer a shortage of vitamins and minerals, resulting in a deficiency disease, and some drugs during pregnancy can have harmful effects. One of the most tragic cases occurred when pregnant women in the early 1960s were prescribed Thalidomide (a sedative), and a number of their babies were born with extremely serious limb deformities; but some antibiotics, steroids and hormones can be harmful to the unborn child too. Pregnant women should take only medicines that have been carefully selected to avoid harming the foetus.

Damage at birth

Lack of oxygen (**anoxia**) at birth can cause some forms of brain damage to the baby. The results may be very slight, or it may be severe, depending upon the amount of damage to the brain cells. It may also result in **cerebral palsy** (spasticity), which is an inability to control some of the muscles.

This lack of oxygen may be caused by insufficient blood reaching the foetus during the birth or by a complication such as the baby being in the wrong position for the birth. Whatever the complication, it requires swift action, as the longer the brain is deprived of blood, the more damaging will be the results. Some of these potential difficulties can be detected during pregnancy and the damage can then be avoided by giving special treatment before or during the birth. This is one of the reasons why good antenatal care is so important.

Metabolic disorders

These occur when there are defects in the metabolic working of the body, that is, the chemical process by which food is absorbed and built up into the cells of the body. These defects, again, may be passed on from parent to child.

A common metabolic disease is **phenylketonuria (PKU)** which is an enzyme deficiency that makes the baby unable to metabolise (use) the phenylalanine (an acid) which is present in milk and other foods.

Fortunately a standard test has been developed which detects the disease, and it is treated with a special diet. There is also a standard test for **hypothyroidism** (thyroid deficiency) which affects growth.

Other examples of metabolic diseases are **cystic fibrosis** (a disease caused by a recessive gene, which causes persistent chest and breathing problems that can eventually be fatal, and affects one in 2500 babies) and **coeliac disease** (which causes inability to digest certain foods).

Although it seems there are a lot of congenital abnormalities that can occur, many can be avoided by early diagnosis and genetic research. It is essential for the expectant mother to discuss any problems or worries she may have early in pregnancy with her doctor or midwife.

Confirmation of pregnancy

There are several signs that will indicate that conception has occurred. However, most of these signs can also be symptoms of other conditions, so diagnosing a pregnancy is not as simple as it may seem.

Signs of pregnancy	Remarks
1 Missing a period	*A reliable sign only if the woman has a regular menstrual cycle. Some women have slight bleeding during the first months of pregnancy.*
2 Changes to the breasts	*May become bigger and more tender. Veins may show up more. These symptoms may just be due to pre-menstrual changes.*
3 Feeling or being sick	*Could be due to other causes.*
4 Needing to pass water more frequently, or being constipated	*Could be a bladder infection or stomach upset.*
5 Increased vaginal discharge	*Could be a vaginal infection or pre-menstrual sign.*
6 Feeling more tired than usual	*Not just a sign of pregnancy!*
7 Going off the taste of certain foods; odd taste in the mouth	*May be other causes.*

A combination of signs 1 and 2 with other symptoms will indicate that the woman is probably pregnant. She may visit her doctor two or three weeks after she has missed a period. It is better for the pregnancy to be confirmed early, especially if the woman suffers from diabetes, or has other conditions which may complicate the pregnancy.

Pregnancy tests

There are several options for the woman who needs an early diagnosis of pregnancy for social or medical reasons, but reliable results are only obtainable about four weeks after conception. For an early diagnosis she may go to:

- the family doctor, who may test if there is a medical reason for the early confirmation (e.g. medical treatment being given for an existing condition, the woman being over 40 years old and therefore at some risk, or when an abortion may be needed).
- the Family Planning Clinic, if she has been receiving contraceptive or other advice from there.
- the British Pregnancy Advisory Service (BPAS), which charges a small fee.
- the Brooks Advisory Service, which charges a small fee.
- a chemist's, where the pharmacist may do the test or send the urine specimen to a commercial testing service.

She can also obtain a do-it-yourself pregnancy testing kit from a chemist's, but these are only reliable if the instructions are very carefully carried out.

The pregnancy test is carried out on a small sample of the woman's urine. Approximately four weeks after conception (six weeks from the first day of the last period) the 'pregnancy hormone' (**gonadotrophin**) is found in the early morning in sufficient quantities to be detectable. The urine sample is mixed with chemicals and will give a positive reaction if the woman is pregnant. A negative result, especially in the very early weeks, is not always correct, as there may not be a sufficiently high level of the hormone to show up in the test.

Most women go to their family doctor when their period is several weeks late and they suspect they may be pregnant. The doctor will probably carry out an internal examination to see if the uterus is enlarged, and will be able to make a positive diagnosis about eight weeks from the last period. A pregnancy lasts approximately nine months, or 40 weeks or 282 days, from the first day of the last period. The doctor will have an **obstetric table** and will be able to give the pregnant woman an expected date of delivery (EDD) although this is only a rough guide, as the actual date of conception is not usually known.

The confirmation of a pregnancy is usually received with mixed feelings. Even the couple who have planned their family and are looking forward to the event will feel apprehensive, especially if it is the first child. Both of them, and especially the expectant mother, will need support and comfort from the other as well as from family and friends, to overcome their first doubts.

Follow-up exercises

Category 1

1   Copy and complete the following description:

The male has _____ testes; these are contained in the
_____ . They produce _____ which are necessary to
_____ the female egg. These _____ travel along the
sperm tube or _____ _____ . It is the job of the
_____ _____ to _____ the semen. The semen
carries the sperm down to the _____ which is made of
_____ _____ .

2   Copy the chart below and use it to list the physical changes that occur
during puberty.

Girls	Boys

3   Which of these statements are true, and which are false?

a)   Women must not engage in physical activities such as cycling,
swimming or jogging during a period.

b)   Poor diet can cause periods to stop or become irregular.

c)   Women must not bathe or wash their hair during a period.

d)   Personal hygiene is very important at this time to prevent soreness
and unpleasant odour.

e)   Nothing can be done to help relieve PMT.

f)   Period pains are caused by muscular contractions which give cramp.

g)   A late period may be caused by tiredness, anxiety and stress.

h)   Having a period is a 'poorly' time and is usually unpleasant.

4 Copy the sentences below, and choose a word from this list to fill in the spaces. (You will not need to use all the words given. Some words may be used more than once.)

complete   identical   heredity   dominant

recessive   genes   incomplete   genetics

non-identical   geneticist

a) The passing on of characteristics from one generation to the next is known as _____ .

b) The study of this subject is called _____ .

c) The specialist who deals with the problems of _____ is called a _____ .

d) It is the _____ which we inherit which make us what we are.

e) Strong _____ are known as _____ .

f) The less strong _____ are known as _____ .

g) Dark hair is an example of the effects of _____ _____ .

h) Uniovular twins are _____ twins.

i) Fraternal is another name for _____ twins.

5 Copy the sentences below, and choose a number from this list to fill in the spaces. (You will not need to use all the numbers given. Some numbers may be used more than once.)

15   22   90   7   94   10   2   80   24   12   97   8   1   23

a) Of the _____ pairs of chromosomes, _____ determine the physical make up of a child and _____ determines the sex.

b) One in _____ births are twins.

c) _____ babies at one birth are known as octuplets.

d) A woman who has already had twins has a one in _____ chance of having more.

e) Binovular twins develop from _____ eggs.

f) _____ per cent of European women are rhesus negative.

g) _____ per cent of babies born in the United Kingdom are normal.

6 Which of the following statements are true and which are false?

a) The frequency of multiple births has increased because of the use of fertility drugs.

b) Twins can be diagnosed by the second week of pregnancy.

c) Fraternal twins are always of the same sex.

d) Identical twins share the same placenta.

e) An incomplete cell division will result in Siamese twins.

f) Non-identical twins have different placentas but share the same outer membrane.

7 Write out the following list and underline the symptoms which indicate early pregnancy:

early morning sickness, feeling depressed, feeling faint, increased size of abdomen, aching feet, missing a period, breasts feeling tender, toothache, hair becoming greasy, desire to pass water more often, indigestion, stomach pains

Category 2

8 What are hormones and how are they produced?

Name the male and female sex hormones.

Write a paragraph about emotional changes during puberty and how children can be helped by their family, their school and themselves.

9 Show, with the use of diagrams, what is meant by the 'menstrual cycle'.

10 For each of the following congenital diseases, give the possible causes, the characteristics and possible treatment:

Down's syndrome, spina bifida, cerebral palsy, phenylketonuria, dwarfism

11 Name three circumstances in which it may be desirable for a pregnancy to be diagnosed within the first few weeks.
Name three methods of obtaining an early pregnancy diagnosis.

12 Write a sentence about each of the following:

a) the composition of blood

b) the work of the red cells

c) the results of the lack of iron in the diet of the pregnant woman

d) testing the blood of the expectant woman during pregnancy

e) the most common blood group

f) blood transfusions in relation to pregnancy.

13 What is the cause of rhesus incompatibility?
How can it be prevented?
What is the treatment if a newborn baby is found to have this condition?

Category 3

14 Physically, boys and girls are maturing earlier and it is possible for girls to become pregnant at the age of 11 (or younger) and for boys to father a child at the age of 14 (or younger). Give as many reasons as you can why it is better for couples to be many years older than this before starting a family.

15 What social factors have contributed to the increase in reported cases of sexually transmitted disease over the past twenty years?

How can these diseases be adequately contained and treated?

16 Write a paragraph each about two of the following statements. These are controversial issues and you should be forming your own ideas on these subjects.

a) When it is known that a couple will almost certainly pass on a hereditary disease to their children, they should be advised not to have a family.

b) Abortion (the termination of a pregnancy) is the taking of human life and should not be allowed.

c) The government should provide more money, through taxation, to improve the poor environmental conditions which can cause congenital diseases.

d) Children with gross mental or physical handicaps are better looked after by state-run hospitals rather than by their parents at home.

Activity

Blood group	Can receive blood from:	Can give blood to:
A	A and O	
B	B and O	
AB	All groups	
O	O	

Fill in the last column on a copy of this chart.
Which is the most common blood group?

4 Development of the Foetus

The three trimesters

The nine months of pregnancy are divided into three equal parts, known as **trimesters**. During the first trimester (13 to 14 weeks) all the different parts of the foetus' body are formed. During the second and third trimesters, all these parts grow and develop. By the end of the second trimester (26 to 28 weeks) the foetus is sufficiently well-formed to stand a chance of survival outside the womb.

The umbilical cord and the placenta

The fertilised egg (or **zygote**) which is the start of the human baby divides itself over and over again, and by the seventh day after fertilisation implants itself in the lining of the uterus. For the first six to eight weeks it is known as an **embryo**. During this time the cells develop rapidly, taking on their individual jobs of forming bone, blood, organs, etc., and by the end of the eighth week the embryo begins to resemble a human.

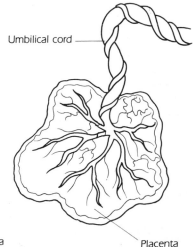

Umbilical cord

Blood vessels carry blood
from the foetus to the placenta

Placenta

The placenta and umbilical cord

The developing embryo must be fed and protected. This is done by means of the **umbilical cord** which attaches it to the **placenta**. Seven days after implantation the outer cells of the embryo have burrowed into the lining of the uterus and started to form into the placenta. Some of the pregnant woman's cells are broken down to form pools of blood which supply oxygen and food for the baby.

The placenta is a red, spongy disc of tissue. As the foetus enlarges so does the placenta; at birth it weighs about 500 g (1 lb) and is about 20 cm (8 in.) across.

The umbilical cord develops from the placenta to link it with the embryo. During pregnancy the cord gets longer; at birth it is about 50 cm (20 in.) long.

The work of the placenta and umbilical cord is vital, and it is important that nothing interferes with their function. These two organs only grow during pregnancy, and immediately after the baby is born they are expelled (the **afterbirth**).

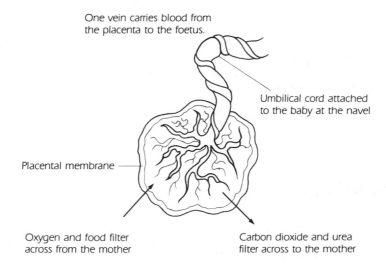

One vein carries blood from the placenta to the foetus.

Umbilical cord attached to the baby at the navel

Placental membrane

Oxygen and food filter across from the mother

Carbon dioxide and urea filter across to the mother

The mother's and foetus' bloodstreams

Jobs done by the placenta

Providing nourishment	The developing embryo or foetus is of course unable to eat or digest food. Nutrients from the pregnant woman are therefore broken down and passed in her blood into the placenta to be used by the embryo or foetus.
Providing oxygen and carrying away carbon dioxide (CO_2)	The human body needs oxygen to live. We breathe in air and use oxygen, exhaling the waste product as carbon dioxide. The pregnant woman supplies the embryo or foetus with oxygen through her blood supply. The oxygen crosses the placenta and the waste carbon dioxide is carried back in the same way.

(*continued*)

Removing other waste products	Other waste such as **urea** is passed across the placenta to be got rid of in the woman's urine.
Acting as a barrier and protecting the foetus against harmful substances	The placenta can filter out many of the germs, infections and drugs which the pregnant woman may have in her body. Unfortunately it cannot filter all of them, and some harmful drugs do get through. Viruses, such as the rubella virus, and the harmful effects of smoking can also get past the placenta and damage the foetus, especially during the early weeks when the embryo is still forming various parts of the body. However, some of the antibodies cross the placenta and help to protect the embryo or foetus and the baby from diseases.
Producing hormones	Large amounts of hormones such as oestrogen and progesterone are produced, and the pregnancy hormones that maintain the placenta and regulate the pregnancy.

A layer of cells forming a fine membrane divides the foetal blood from the mother's blood. In this way the blood of the foetus and of the mother are completely separate. |

The amniotic sac

This is a bag full of fluid in which the foetus develops. It is made of two thin, colourless membrane sheets, the outer one being the **chorion** and the inner layer the **amnion**. After a few weeks this sac fills the **uterine cavity** (space inside the uterus). The amniotic fluid (sometimes known as 'the waters') surrounds the foetus and acts as a protective environment. There are 150 ml (5 fl. oz) of liquid in the sac by the time the foetus is ten weeks. By the end of pregnancy there are 1.5–2 litres (about 2½–3½ pints). The amniotic fluid is made up of water, salts, fats and small amounts of foetal urine. It carries out the following functions:

- providing a liquid environment at a constant temperature suitable for growth
- protecting against knocks and bumps
- allowing the foetus to begin its swallowing and breathing movements in preparation for breathing after birth
- helping to guard the foetus against infection.

As the foetus develops it sheds live cells from its skin into the amniotic fluid. At 14 to 16 weeks some of the fluid can be drawn off and these cells tested to check for abnormalities. This is called amniocentesis.

The stages of development

- **At 4 weeks**   The embryo has a head and a tail end, a back and a front. Tiny swellings indicate the beginnings of arms and legs. The heart begins to beat. The embryo is 5 mm (0.2 in.) long.

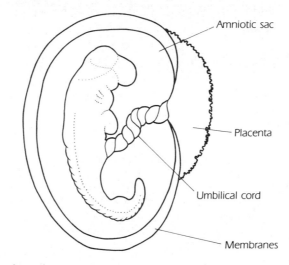

The embryo at 4 weeks

- **At 8 weeks**   The major organs of the body are formed, the limbs, hands and feet have formed. The head is large and facial features are clear. The embryo will have started to grow all it needs to be a human baby. It will be 3 or 4 cm (1–1.5 in.) long and weigh about 10 g (0.35 oz).

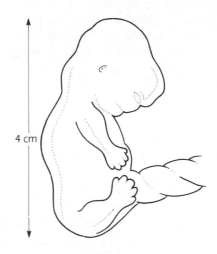

The embryo at 8 weeks

● **Between 8 and 12 weeks**   The embryo is now called a foetus. During this stage it is developing rapidly. It has a heart, a brain, a digestive system, bones and muscles, and the brain can now give instructions to the bones and organs enabling the foetus to kick, swallow, and move its arms and head. The tooth buds appear. The kidneys function, allowing some urine to be passed into the amniotic fluid. The distance from the top of the foetus' head to the base of the spine (**crown–rump length**) is about 7½ cm (3 in.) and it weighs about 28 g (1 oz). It is now possible to tell the sex of the foetus.

Umbilical cord

Placenta

Amniotic sac

The foetus at 12 weeks

● **At 16 weeks**   At four months the foetus is still floating freely in the amniotic sac. The growth of the skull is rapid, and an ultrasound examination at this stage can detect abnormalities such as spina bifida. The expectant mother can be offered an abortion if an ultrasound-scan (see p. 50) reveals that the foetus is abnormal. The foetus' skin is getting thicker and the bones are hardening. It weighs about 135 g (4.8 oz).

● **Between 16 and 24 weeks**   Very fine hair (**lanugo**) begins to grow over the skin of the foetus, and the eyelashes and hair on the head grow. The eyelids are still closed. Fat under the skin makes the foetus less wrinkled, and it develops a white greasy covering (**vernix**). The foetus' movements are becoming more energetic and the expectant mother will be able to feel them. It will be lying in the **foetal** position, with back bent and knees drawn up towards the chin. Up to this stage the foetus is **pre-viable** – that is, it would stand no chance of survival if born, because the vital organs are incapable of working properly. The foetus weighs about 400–500 g (14–17.5 oz) at 20 weeks and about 600 g (21 oz) at 24 weeks.

By the end of this stage the foetus' heartbeat can be heard through a special stethoscope.

- **At 28 weeks**   The foetus is about 24 cm (9.4 in.) long, weighs about 800–1000 g (1 lb 12 oz–2 lb 3 oz), and is considered viable. From this time, a foetus' death must be registered. It has been recommended that this should be brought down to 24 weeks, as some foetuses are viable at this stage. In a good special care baby unit a 28-week foetus has a 70 per cent chance of survival.

  This is the end of the second trimester, or gestation period.

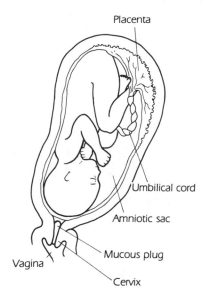

The foetus at 28 weeks

- **Up to 32 weeks**   The foetus has a very good chance of survival if born prematurely at this stage. It will be able to withstand almost all outside influences including X-ray, ultrasound (both may be dangerous in the early months of pregnancy), shock, knocks and drugs, but it is suspected that the expectant mother's smoking can harm the still-developing cells of the foetus' brain. Any infection will have less severe effects than at earlier stages. The head and body are in the same proportions as in a newborn baby and the lungs are maturing, although the foetus is not yet breathing. It weighs about 1600 g (3 lb 8 oz), and is getting too big to float about freely.

- **At 36 weeks**   All the vital organs have matured, a lot of fat has been laid down and early wrinkling of the skin has disappeared. The lanugo has nearly disappeared and the foetus is making normal physical movements (e.g., clutching its fingers, kicking, etc.). It should have moved into the correct position for birth, with the head down towards the cervix so that the crown of the baby's head (**vertex**) will appear in the vagina first. The foetus now weighs about 2.5 kg (5 lb 8 oz) and the crown-rump length is about 31 cm (12 in.).

● **The 9th month (Up to 40 weeks)**   During the last few weeks of pregnancy the hair on the foetus' head is thicker and the bones of the skull become harder, although they remain soft enough to be squeezed through the cervix at birth. By the 40th week the foetus is fully developed. It may still have a slippery greasy covering but this may disappear if the foetus is in the uterus for over 40 weeks. The head will move lower down the uterus with the spine parallel to the mother's. In two to three per cent of pregnancies the **presentation** (position) of the foetus is with the bottom down towards the cervix, which can cause complications at birth. This is known as the **breech position**.

A full-term foetus (40 weeks) weighs from 2.8 kg–4 kg (6 lb 2 oz–8 lb 12 oz). Although it is not fully understood what triggers off the birth, it is thought that this moment occurs when the foetus is mature enough to survive the outside world.

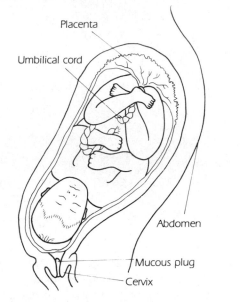

The foetus at 40 weeks

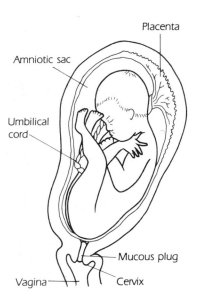

The foetus in breech position

Changes to the expectant mother during pregnancy

Weight

Probably the most noticeable change is an increase in weight. Obviously the expectant mother is going to put on some weight, and this will be carefully checked when she goes to the antenatal clinic. The increase is due to enlargement of the uterus and breasts, weight of the foetus, afterbirth and waters, and general changes in the mother's body. The total weight gain should not exceed 12 kg (26 lb 8 oz); not more than 4 kg (8 lb 12 oz) of this total should be put on during the first 20 weeks. If the expectant mother is gaining weight too rapidly she must not try to slim, but should take medical advice about diet.

The effects of being overweight during pregnancy include:

- increased pressure on heart and other organs.
- tiredness and breathlessness.
- varicose veins and swollen feet and ankles.
- stretch marks on the abdomen.
- depression because of unsightly areas of fat.
- difficulty in getting rid of excess weight after the birth.

Unusually high weight gain may be a sign of **toxaemia** (see p. 49).

Weight gain of mother during pregnancy

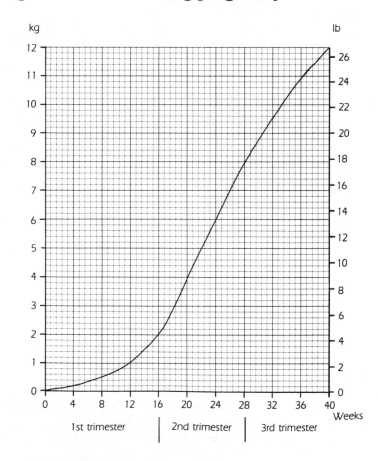

Posture during pregnancy

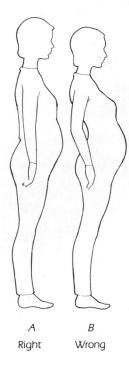

Standing   Stand with a straight back as in A, not arched as in B. Spread weight evenly on both legs. Sit down on a high stool to do jobs such as washing up, ironing, cooking, etc.

A
Right

B
Wrong

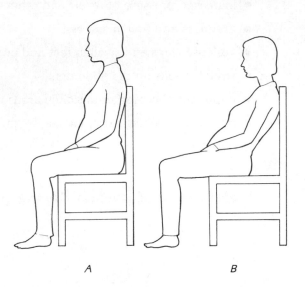

A

B

Sitting   Press the back into the back of the chair. The upper part of the body should not slump. Rest feet on a stool, or support the whole of both legs. Does A or B show correct sitting posture?

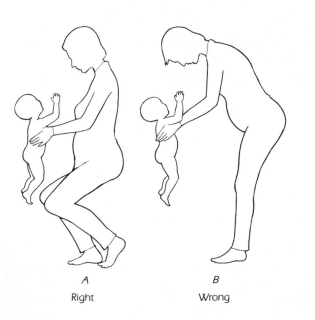

A
Right

B
Wrong

Lifting   Bend the knees, not the back, when lifting a heavy object. Keep the legs apart for balance.

Other changes during pregnancy

Blood changes	The volume of blood increases by 40 per cent during pregnancy so that the foetus can be provided with the necessary oxygen and nourishment. The foetus draws upon the mother's store of iron to make essential haemoglobin, and this dilutes her blood and may cause anaemia. The increased blood flow may result in flushing and sweating.
Kidneys and urinary system	During pregnancy more fluid is needed for the extra blood supply, production of the amniotic fluid, and foetal development. As a side-effect, the kidneys produce more urine and the bladder needs to be emptied more often. Pressure on the bladder from the enlarging uterus will also create a desire to pass urine more often. This is quite normal, but if the passing of urine is accompanied by a smarting, burning sensation, it indicates a urine infection. This type of infection is common during pregnancy and should be reported to the doctor or midwife. Towards the end of the pregnancy some women experience **stress incontinence**, when coughing will cause the loss of small amounts of urine. This condition clears up after the birth.
Organs that increase in size	The heart, uterus, vagina, fallopian tubes and veins in the legs increase in size during pregnancy, because of the extra work they have to do. The enlarging uterus presses on the lungs and may cause breathlessness or fainting. There may also be periods of rapid heart-beat.
Food and digestive changes	The expectant mother may crave certain foods and go off other foods that are fatty or highly flavoured and difficult to digest. Cravings are usually for fruit and chocolate but may be for unexpected things such as coal or toothpaste. These food fads may upset the bowel routine and the pregnant woman can become constipated, or suffer from nausea.
Teeth and gums	The gums may become soft and spongy and more likely to bleed. This condition can encourage tooth decay, so careful dental hygiene and treatment are essential.
Hair and nails	These both tend to grow more quickly during pregnancy, and hair may become greasy sooner than normal.
The skin	Some expectant mothers find they develop spots and blemishes more easily. As the pregnancy becomes more advanced and the size of the abdomen increases, stretch marks may appear on the abdomen if the skin is fine and not very elastic. These wavy irregular marks will fade after the

(continued)

birth. Oils or creams may be rubbed on to help the marks fade, but are not very effective.

Enlargement of the breasts	This begins early in pregnancy and is due to an increase in the fat surrounding the breasts, and to development of the milk secreting glands. At about the fifth month of pregnancy the breasts may begin to secrete a small amount of **colostrum**, a thin milky fluid. If this is gently expressed during pregnancy by pressing the nipple between fingers and thumb, it will help clear the milk ducts. The nipples should become quite prominent; if they are flat or inverted the expectant mother may be advised to wear nipple shields or shells to draw out the nipple gently. A good strong bra will help to support the breasts as they grow heavier and make them more comfortable. Some expectant mothers also wear a night bra for this purpose.
Hormone effects	Progesterone, an important pregnancy hormone, is responsible for softening ligaments around the joints and pelvis and for relaxing muscles. This can result in the ligaments of the foot arch stretching, which can cause fallen arches. The softening of the pelvic ligaments can cause backache, especially as the expectant mother gets bigger and there is a shift in her centre of gravity. Poor posture during pregnancy, when sitting, standing and lifting, is likely to increase the backache and can cause permanent damage.

Complications during pregnancy

There are a lot of conditions which can cause the mother discomfort and some pain during pregnancy (and these are discussed later in this section, on p. 54), but they are minor ailments which only require simple treatment. There are, however, some conditions which can be very serious for both the mother and the baby, and these complications must be carefully watched for throughout the pregnancy. If antenatal care is started early enough and continued regularly, many of these dangers can be treated.

Complication	Symptoms	Cause and result	Treatment
Ectopic pregnancy ('Tubal' pregnancy)	*Severe pain on one side low down in the abdomen, one or two weeks after a missed period. Affects about 1 in 350 pregnancies.*	*A fertilised egg gets stuck in the fallopian tube and begins to grow there. Very often due to a damaged tube.*	*Removal or repair of the damaged fallopian tube.*

(continued)

Complication	Symptoms	Cause and result	Treatment
Anaemia	*The expectant mother will feel tired and listless. The baby may suffer. May be mild or severe.*	*Lack of iron. Very common during pregnancy, especially after several pregnancies and when the expectant mother is undernourished.*	*Taking iron and folic acid tablets.*
Antepartum haemorrhage *There are two main types:*	*Vaginal bleeding in late pregnancy. Pain.*	*This is a severe condition involving complications with the placenta.*	
• **Placenta praevia**	• *Heavy bleeding.*	• *The placenta lies in the path of the foetus, close to or covering the cervix. Causes heavy bleeding.*	• *The placenta can become partly or totally separated from the uterus. Immediate medical and hospital care is needed.*
• **Abruptio placentae**	• *Bleeding from the vagina and constant pain.*	• *Separation of some of a normally positioned placenta from the wall of the uterus.*	• *Can interrupt the oxygen supply to the baby. A serious though rare complication, needing immediate medical treatment.*
Kidney and bladder disorders	*Pain in the small of the back. Pain when passing water. Headaches.*	*May be a simple infection or may be linked to diabetes or eclampsia.*	*Regular urine checks will detect the condition. Treatment may be bed rest, antibiotics, and/or reducing salt intake.*
Toxaemia or pre-eclampsia	*High blood pressure (**hypertension**), swelling of legs, hands and face. Protein in urine. High weight gain. Develops in late pregnancy.*	*Cause of toxaemia is unknown. May result in damage to the expectant mother and the baby. The expectant mother may have fits (convulsions).*	*A serious condition – may be mild or severe. Treatment may be bed rest, sedatives, antihypertension drugs, low salt diet and/or diuretic tablets.*
Fibroids and ovarian cysts	*Swellings on the wall of the uterus or the ovaries. May cause pain and bleeding.*	*Both of these are growths – fibroids arise in the uterus, cysts in the ovaries. Usually **benign** (not dangerous). May get bigger during pregnancy and cause discomfort.*	*Fibroids are usually left, but ovarian cysts may be removed in early pregnancy. Can hinder the development and delivery of the baby. The condition may lead to the need for a Caesarean delivery.*

These conditions are very rare and can nearly always be diagnosed and treated before they become serious. The chart below shows some of the routine special tests which are carried out during pregnancy if any complications are suspected.

Pregnancy test	How it is done	Why it is done
Ultrasound scans	High frequency sound waves are directed at the pregnant woman's abdomen and reflected back to give a picture on a TV screen. The operator can pick out important developments of the foetus. A simple, painless test usually done after 16 or 17 weeks of pregnancy.	To check the stages of development of the foetus. To check whether a miscarriage is threatened. To help to detect any abnormalities of the head or spine.
Amniocentesis	A fine needle is placed in the pregnant woman's abdomen under ultrasound control, and a sample of the amniotic fluid which surrounds the foetus is drawn out for testing.	To test for spina bifida, Down's syndrome and other abnormalities, in women where there is high risk of an abnormality occurring.
Blood sample tests at 16 weeks	A measured amount of blood is withdrawn from the pregnant woman's arm.	To detect defects in the nervous system of the foetus.
The fetoscope (a fine optical device)	The fetoscope is mounted on a needle which is passed into the pregnant woman's abdomen. The doctor can see through the fetoscope.	To look for external abnormalities. To take samples of foetal blood to check for blood disorders.

Follow-up exercises

Category 1

1   a)   Is this an embryo or a foetus?

      b)   At what stage of development is it? (in weeks).

      c)   Name the parts A, B, C and D.

      d)   Describe the baby at this stage of development.

      e)   Is it possible to tell the sex of the baby at this stage?

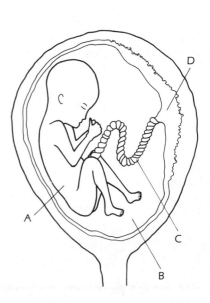

2   Copy and complete the following sentences:

a)   The amniotic sac is _____ .

b)   The amniotic fluid guards the foetus against _____ .

c)   The chorion and the amnion are _____ .

d)   The foetus is viable when it is at the _____ stage. This means _____ .

e)   Pregnancy is divided into three _____ which are _____ weeks long.

f)   The top of the baby's head is known as the _____ , and is the _____ .

g)   The length of the foetus is known as the _____ – _____ _____ and is measured from _____ to _____ .

h)   The bones of the baby's skull are soft so that _____ .

i)   When a baby is born bottom first it is known as a _____ _____ . This type of birth happens in _____ per cent of births.

3   **Anagrams**   Unscramble these words and then describe the changes which take place during pregnancy to *five* of them.

LOBOD   INYKDES   ENIVS

RAHTE   SMUG   LASNI

SNIK   STESABR   CSSEMUL

Category 2

4   The placenta and the umbilical cord only develop during pregnancy. How does the body get rid of them when they have finished their work?

Describe the work done by both these organs and some of the complications relating to them which may occur during pregnancy.

5   Study the graph on p. 45 showing the weight gain during pregnancy. Use it to fill in the weight gains in a copy of the chart at the top of p. 52.

Time in weeks	Weight gain
0–12	1 kg (2 lb 4 oz)
13–16	?
17–20	?
21–24	?
25–28	?
29–32	?
33–36	?
36–40	12 kg (26 lb 8 oz)

6 Make a list on a copy of the chart below of some symptoms which may occur during pregnancy and the possible serious complications which they could indicate.

	Symptoms	Complication
Example 1	*Vaginal bleeding*	*Complications with the placenta, or miscarriage.*
2		
3		
4		
5		
6		
7		

Activity

Look at the graph on p. 45 showing the mother's weight gain during pregnancy. Make a similar graph (scale 2 cm to 1 kg) to show the weight gain of the foetus from 8 weeks to full term using the information given on pp. 41–4. (Use an average value where a range is given.)

5 Care of the Expectant Mother

Perinatal mortality rate

Pregnancy and childbirth are often surrounded by many 'hi-tech' procedures in the West. We sometimes forget that childbirth is a normal and natural occurrence, and women in many Third World countries give birth without such procedures. However, the perinatal mortality rate (babies born dead – **stillbirths** – plus deaths of infants under one week) and the number of children who die in the first year of life is much higher in Third World countries than in the richer Western World, as can be seen in the chart below.

Perinatal mortality rates

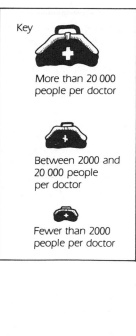

Key

More than 20 000 people per doctor

Between 2000 and 20 000 people per doctor

Fewer than 2000 people per doctor

Country	% of children who die in first year	Number of people per doctor
Afghanistan	26.9	
Australia	1.7	
France	1.4	
UK	1.6	
India	12.2	
Jamaica	2.0	
Japan	1.0	
Kenya	5.1	
Nigeria	16.3	

(continued)

Pakistan	11.3	
Sweden	0.8	
USA	1.6	
West Germany	2.0	

Basic medical care

Being pregnant is not an illness and most expectant mothers go through the nine months with only minor ailments. These can often be cured or relieved by simple remedies such as dietary changes, more rest, exercise or a different mental attitude. No medicines and drugs should be taken during pregnancy, especially during the early stages, unless prescribed by the doctor.

Minor ailments during pregnancy

Minor ailment	Causes	Simple remedy
Pregnancy sickness	Possibly hormone imbalance (if sickness is very severe). This usually occurs in the morning, and generally disappears after the 12th week of pregnancy.	Get up in the morning slowly. Have a cup of tea and a plain biscuit or fresh sweetened fruit juice with soda water. Follow a low-fat diet, with no spicy foods and small, frequent meals. Very severe cases need medical treatment.
Constipation	Incorrect diet. Increase in iron in the diet. Higher levels of progesterone in the body.	Take extra fluids (a total of at least four pints a day), and roughage (from raw fresh fruit and vegetables). Do not take laxatives. If necessary the doctor will prescribe a mild non-purging type.
Haemorrhoids (piles)	Swelling of veins of the anus, caused by pressure and/or constipation.	Prevent and correct the condition by correcting the diet and getting more rest.
Heartburn	Pressure on the stomach may cause the acid content there to press up into the gullet, giving a burning sensation.	Eat only small meals, and more often. Avoid indigestible foods such as fried foods, or foods with a lot of spices or strong flavours. Do not lie down when you have just eaten. Take drinks after, not during, a meal. Sleep with several pillows if attacks occur at night.
Backache and aching feet	Increased pressure. Use of different muscles used in different ways.	Wear support garments such as support tights and pantie girdle. Choose sensible shoes that support the feet well. Rest when necessary. Keep posture correct and lift heavy objects carefully. (continued)

Minor ailment	Causes	Simple remedy
Frequent passing of water	Enlarging uterus pressing on the bladder.	Unavoidable during pregnancy, and little can be done. Pain when passing urine should be reported to doctor.
Dry skin and hair	Poor diet. The baby will be taking the nutrients it needs and may deprive the expectant mother.	Use a good cream or oil on the skin, and a good quality shampoo on the hair. Increase vitamin B intake by eating wholemeal bread and yeast extract. Increase all vitamin-rich foods, especially fresh fruit and vegetables.
Varicose veins	Overweight. Pressure on the legs. Family history of the condition.	Exercise the legs. Put the feet up often, and don't stand for long periods. Wear support tights. Do not cross the legs when sitting.
Tiredness	Weight gain. Body changes.	Take an extra nap in the afternoon. Fresh air will aid healthy sleep. Get help with the housework, and sit down to do it if possible. Put the feet up whenever possible.

Things to avoid during pregnancy

There are several things which can be hazardous for the expectant mother and which she should avoid during her pregnancy.

- **Smoking**   There is no doubt that smoking can harm the unborn baby. It increases the possibility of miscarriage during pregnancy. Tests have shown that when the child of a cigarette smoker is born, he will have cyanide compound in his urine. Babies born to smokers are usually 150–250 g (5–9 oz) smaller than average and they may be premature. The child may have a poor start to life because the development of his brain may be affected and his resistance to disease reduced.

- **Drugs**   Addictive drugs can be especially dangerous to the expectant mother. They can enter the baby's bloodstream and make him addicted; he will then need to be weaned off them when he is born. The baby of an addicted mother may have a low birth weight and/or serious malformations. Any woman who is hooked on heroin, cannabis, glue sniffing or any similar habit should get help before a pregnancy is started, and should consult her doctor as soon as she knows she is pregnant.

- **Alcohol**   In large quantities alcohol will damage the foetus, causing congenital abnormalities, and an alcoholic mother's baby will (as with drugs) be born addicted. Even small quantities might damage the foetus. There are also the obvious physical dangers which can threaten a woman in a drunken state.

- **X-rays**   The rapidly developing cells of the foetus are especially at risk from X-rays and all forms of radiation. Doctors will not take X-rays during pregnancy unless absolutely necessary, as it may be after an accident or illness, and then the pelvic region will be protected.

- **Vaccinations and immunisation**   The foetus' most vulnerable time during pregnancy is the first 14 weeks, so no risks should be taken at this stage by the pregnant woman having vaccinations or immunisation. If it is urgent that the expectant mother travel abroad and she therefore needs typhoid or cholera protection she must get advice from her doctor. Polio protection should have been obtained before pregnancy as the disease can be very severe if caught during pregnancy.

- **Lead**   Research is being carried out into the possibility of lead damaging the developing foetus, and especially into the risk during the formation of the baby's brain cells. Lead from petrol fumes pollutes the atmosphere and can be inhaled; it can also be absorbed into the body from paints which contain lead, and drinking water which has passed through lead pipes.

  The expectant mother should therefore avoid dense traffic as far as possible and get plenty of fresh air, and if her home has any paint containing lead, it should be stripped off by someone else and replaced. If her home has lead water pipes, she must draw off several pints before she actually drinks any, because the lead dissolves into the water when it has been standing overnight or for long periods. She should also eat plenty of calcium rich foods, because the calcium helps to reduce the amount of lead absorbed into the body.

- **Caffeine**   This is a stimulant found in tea, coffee, cola (such as Coca-Cola) and some medicines. Too much caffeine is not good for the expectant mother and she should therefore drink her tea and coffee fairly weak and reduce the quantity of cola-type soft drinks she takes. Plenty of water and fruit drinks are best.

There are still a lot of old wives' tales which the expectant mother may hear from a well-meaning friend or relation. Some may be frightening and silly, such as 'Don't eat strawberries during pregnancy, the baby will be born with a strawberry mark.' They should all be ignored.

How many old wives' tales do you know? Write them down in your note book and discuss them in class.

Miscarriage and those at risk

Correct care and medical attention are essential during the early stages of pregnancy. It is during the first 12–14 weeks that a **miscarriage** is most likely to occur. A miscarriage is the accidental ending of a pregnancy; an abortion is the deliberate ending of a pregnancy. (Doctors may use the term 'abortion' to cover the end of any pregnancy before the 28th week.)

One in six fertilised eggs fails to develop properly and a miscarriage results. Three out of every four miscarriages happen before the twelfth week.

Women especially at risk of miscarriage are those who:

- are over 35.
- have had difficulty conceiving.
- have a history of miscarriage (two or more previous miscarriages).

A miscarriage may be caused by:

- placenta failure. There may not be enough of the hormone progesterone (see p. 18) to keep the placenta in place.
- a badly deformed foetus. The foetus is naturally rejected and a miscarriage occurs, usually within the first twelve weeks.
- an inefficient cervix. The muscles in the neck of the womb are weak and the neck opens early, usually around the 20th week.
- general illness and/or infectious illness with high fever during the early months.

Having a miscarriage for any of the above reasons does not mean it will happen a second time. Miscarriages can often be avoided when the cause of a first one is known, and can be guarded against.

Sometimes the expectant mother may be misinformed about causes. Causes that will *not* bring about a miscarriage include thunderstorms; having the bath too hot; sexual intercourse; stretching; getting bad news; swimming; a fall; and bending. Nevertheless common sense should always be used by the expectant mother especially if she may be prone to miscarriage.

A miscarriage in the early weeks may appear to be a normal period. There may be a few contractions or cramps and a passage of blood clots from the vagina. A late miscarriage is like a mini-labour. The cervix opens and all the contents of the womb are shed.

After a miscarriage the parents will feel mixed emotions – relief perhaps if the baby was unwanted or deformed, but more usually sorrow, frustration and fear that it may happen again. Expert counselling may be needed.

Caring for herself

The expectant mother can do a great deal to help herself to have a healthy pregnancy. The medical care and checks which she receives from her GP and antenatal clinic will make sure that any of the more serious problems are detected and dealt with, but with a positive attitude to her health and by using her own common sense, she can avoid the minor problems as well.

If the expectant mother has developed some good basic health rules in preparation for her pregnancy, she will have a sound base to work from.

Food

If she follows a good eating plan based upon a balanced diet, many of the minor problems of pregnancy will not occur. Such things as constipation, indigestion, heartburn and nausea can be helped by adjustments to her diet. Every expectant mother should have a good idea of basic nutrition, both for her own sake and for the sake of her family.

There are five main food groups:

A	**B**	**C**	**D**	**E**
Meat	Milk	Cereals	Fresh fruit	Fats
Fish	Cheese	Nuts	Salads	Oils
Eggs	Yoghurt	Pulses	Vegetables	
		(e.g., beans, lentils)		

To achieve a balanced diet and avoid dietary problems:

- Have at least two items from each group every day. For example, have meals containing meat, fish or eggs with some dairy products, cereals for fibre, at least two lots of fresh fruit and vegetables, and small amounts of fat.

- Groups A, B and C are protein foods, which are essential for the expectant mother. Choosing foods from group A or B with group C foods will ensure a complete amino acid balance, and a well-planned vegetarian diet will give all the necessary nutrients during pregnancy. Vegans (vegetarians who eat no animal produce), however, may not have enough Vitamin B12. They may need to supplement their diet with Vitamin B12 tablets.

- The foods in groups C and D will give the roughage which is required for expulsion of waste, and will help to prevent constipation.

- Group D will give many of the necessary vitamins. Fruit and vegetables should be eaten raw or only lightly cooked, as overcooking destroys much of the food value. Have some Vitamin C every day, such as an orange or a blackcurrant drink.

- Fats and oils (group E) are obtained from animals (saturated fats) or vegetables (polyunsaturated fats). Too much animal fat may be unhealthy, so use vegetable oils for cooking. Do not eat too much fat, or oil of any sort; it is indigestible and can cause nausea and heartburn as well as excess weight.

- Iron is essential during pregnancy to prevent anaemia, which can cause tiredness, dizziness and headaches. Red meat, offal, cocoa and watercress are all good sources of iron. The doctor will prescribe iron tablets if necessary.

- The expectant mother should not be 'eating for two'. Overweight can cause severe problems such as swollen feet and ankles, strain to the heart, breathlessness and fatigue. The expectant mother will be weighed every time she goes to the clinic, and her diet regulated if she is becoming overweight. Too much weight put on during pregnancy is difficult to take off afterwards; total weight gain should not be more than 12 kg (26 lb) (see p. 45). Carbohydrates provide energy but eating too much carbohydrate produces fat, so avoid too many potatoes, cream cakes, fried foods, sweets and puddings.

- Strongly flavoured foods such as curries, chutneys and pickles may cause indigestion and heartburn and should therefore be avoided.

Women on special diets because of medical conditions, e.g., diabetes, should consult their doctor when they become pregnant.

Right

Right

Wrong

Nutrition during pregnancy

It is suspected that dietary deficiencies just before conception and during pregnancy can cause physical handicaps to babies: for example, severe lack of calcium or Vitamin D can contribute to bone deformities and rickets. One source of Vitamin D is sunlight, so immigrants to the UK who are used to sunnier climates may need to increase the amount of Vitamin D in their diets. If the diet of the expectant mother is sensible, balanced, and varied, she should not need to take vitamin or iron tablets – unless advised to do so by her doctor.

Nutrition during pregnancy

Nutrients	Needed for	Found in	Results of deficiency
Proteins	Growth and repair	Animal sources: meat, fish, milk, cheese, eggs Vegetable sources: cereals, nuts, pulses	Stunted growth; rickets; slow healing of wounds; slow repair of fractures
Carbohydrates	Warmth and energy	Bread, sugar, jam, honey, potatoes, syrup, corn	Listlessness; tiredness; irritability; susceptibility to cold
Fats		Lard, butter, suet, oily fish, margarine, vegetable oils	Tiredness; loss of energy; inability to concentrate; dry skin
Vitamins	Healthy working of the body	Fresh fruit and vegetables, fish liver oils, dairy produce, yeast, nuts, margarine	Diseases such as scurvy and beri-beri; bone and teeth formation retarded or weakened, poor skin; less resistance to disease
Minerals		Salt, red meats, offal, vegetables, milk, cheese	Anaemia; cramp; glandular troubles; poor bones and teeth; poor muscular power
Water		Drinks, fruit, vegetables	Dehydration

Clothing and footwear

The expectant mother is obviously going to change shape gradually throughout the months of her pregnancy. Some women are so excited about the event that they jump into maternity wear in the first few weeks! Most women, however, will find that their normal clothing, if loose fitting, will do for the first five to six months.

Clothing is important to the expectant mother. It can make her feel happy, confident and comfortable, or depressed, ungainly and huge. She should bear the following points in mind:

● Maternity wear should be fun, not just a shapeless cover-up tent. Go for strong colour and patterns or something pretty. Highlight the face with a white collar or frill, a good shoulder line, or fullness from the yoke or shoulders. Exciting and different styles, patterns, fabrics and colour combinations will distract attention from the bump!

- Comfort is essential. Don't constrict the waist, bust or abdomen. Clothes should be loose and easy fitting, in warm, light fabrics for winter and cool, absorbent fabrics for summer. Natural fibres such as cotton and wool absorb moisture best and avoid a cold, clammy feeling.

  Shoes and other footwear must be comfortable. The feet may swell at times, and during pregnancy a woman may need a size larger shoe.

- Safety is another essential. Skirts that are long or full or too tight at the hem, belts, fastenings – all these can be a hazard to the woman who is not quite as stable on her feet as normal because her balance is affected by her enlarged abdomen. Shoes can be especially dangerous. They should be well fitting, and preferably attached to the foot with laces or a strap. Sandals and slippers that are loose, floppy, or backless, can cause an expectant mother to trip, or fall down stairs.

- Hygiene must be a factor. During pregnancy the extra exertion may cause excess perspiration, especially in warm weather, so all maternity wear should be easily washed and need little ironing. The expectant mother is not going to want the extra work involved in laundering complicated clothing. Natural fibres with a special non-iron finish or stain-resistant treatment, or fabrics that mix synthetic and natural fibres, are all suitable.

- Cost must also be taken into consideration. Starting a family is an expensive time and the expectant mother will not want to spend a lot of money on special clothing for herself, especially as she may not want to wear it after the baby is born. She can save money by making some clothing herself – the styles can be very simple. She may be able to buy maternity clothes from a friend who has finished with hers, or she may know someone who is a couple of sizes bigger than she is with some clothes to spare. Jumble sales and sales of work can also be a useful source.

  It is nice, though, if she can splash out on one or two special garments during pregnancy. They will boost her morale and make her feel and look good.

- As the pregnant woman's figure changes she is going to need garments that give support. Her breasts will enlarge and she will need some larger, firmer bras. As the size of the abdomen increases she will usually need stretch pantie girdles, possibly with a support strap. These will all make for comfort, and relieve backache and strain. The muscles are being stretched during pregnancy and without support they may lose some of their elasticity, so that a good figure will be difficult to regain after the birth.

  Maternity tights should have a stretch panel. Petticoats should hang from the shoulders or bust; waist petticoats should stretch or have an adjustable waist.

Exercise and rest

This is very much a matter of common sense. Exercise is important for health during pregnancy. Walking is especially good, and any other sport or physical activity the expectant mother generally does can be continued. Swimming is a good general exercise, and cycling, tennis and dancing can continue until she feels uncomfortable due to her increasing shape or unsteady balance.

It is important, however, that she does not tire herself or overdo any of these activities. Rest and relaxation are essential for a healthy pregnancy. If the expectant mother has an active job she should plan her day so that she can put her feet up and have a rest during the day. If she has other children to look after she should rest with them after lunch. An hour's rest morning and afternoon is beneficial.

During the first three months the pregnant woman may feel tired and sleepy, and during the last three months she will feel fatigue from the extra demands made upon her body. High hormone levels may mean that the expectant mother has very vivid dreams. This is quite normal.

It is important to learn how to relax and this will be taught at the special relaxation classes (see p. 72). To relax totally she should lie in one of the positions shown below, supported by cushions.

Excessive tiredness should be reported to the doctor as it may be a sign of anaemia or other abnormality.

A

B

C

Relaxation positions
A *Lying on the back, with cushions under head and legs*
B *Lying on the side, with cushions under head and between knees*
C *Lying partly on front, with cushions under head, abdomen and knee*

Hygiene

Personal hygiene during pregnancy is especially important. During pregnancy it is normal to have a simple vaginal discharge; frequent washing and changes of undergarments are essential to prevent odour and infection.

The skin produces more sebum (fatty secretion) during pregnancy. This, with the extra physical effort involved and higher body temperature caused by the effects of increased progesterone, means that the body perspires more. It is therefore important to wash and dry well, specially under the arms, under the breasts and the vaginal area. Skin, hair, teeth and nails will all suffer if they are not given regular attention with the use of mild soaps, shampoos and conditioners. The expectant mother will also feel better and more relaxed if she knows she looks and smells clean.

Emotional state

The emotions play an important part during pregnancy. The changing balance of the hormones upsets the emotional balance, and the expectant mother may find that she swings from feeling excited and happy to being miserable and depressed. Even if she is pleased at the news of her pregnancy she will feel anxious and worried about the prospect of becoming a mother. These fears will soon pass, especially if she receives the support, advice and comfort she requires from her partner, family and doctor. Persistent depression and anxiety may affect her sleep and appetite, which will in turn affect her baby. She must therefore discuss any problems with her doctor or health visitor and try to change her attitude of mind. The old saying that a happy mother will produce a happy baby has got an element of truth in it. Doctors will only supply tranquillisers for extreme cases of depression, because of the need to avoid unnecessary drug-taking during pregnancy.

This is a list of alternatives to drugs, which can help to change the emotional state. Can you add to the list?

- A few days away on holiday or visiting relations.
- Going out for the evening to the cinema or a pub, or for a meal.
- Buying a new outfit, or, if the prospective mother enjoys making things, getting some fabric to make a garment.
- Joining an evening or day class and learning a new skill.
- Going along to a local Mother and Baby Group, Young Wives Group, or a branch of the group MAMA (Meet A Mum Association). It is easy to talk over problems with other prospective or new mothers, and encouraging to find that they suffer depression also.

Many new expectant mothers feel guilty because they are depressed; they feel inadequate at the thought of so much responsibility, and they feel insecure at the thought that their husbands may not love them so much as they advance into pregnancy. This is when it is important that the prospective mother realises that these mixed and complicated emotions are all part of her condition and the problems exist only in her own mind.

63

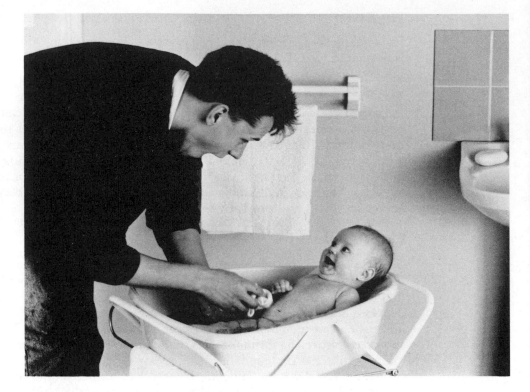

Father and baby

The prospective father

The part played by the prospective father is going to be very important during pregnancy, and in the bringing up of the child. If he is excluded and made to feel unwanted by his partner when she is pregnant he may well lose interest and decide that child-rearing is all part of a woman's world. He may have been brought up in an atmosphere like this, where father went out to work and was the disciplinarian, and mother looked after the house and brought up the children. We are now, luckily, in an age where parents share the work and responsibilities of bringing up children; both father and mother have important contributions to make to their children's future. It has been recognised for a long time that marital stress and constant quarrels between parents can damage children's characters during the vital formative years, giving them severe psychological problems, and making them incapable of sustaining a happy relationship themselves. This is why it is essential for a couple to discuss and plan their attitudes towards their prospective children, before they are even conceived.

The woman who faces her pregnancy without the company of the father is much more likely to suffer depression and physical upsets. She does not have anyone to talk over her problems with or to give her any active help, or to check that she is taking proper care of herself. These are all part of the responsibilities of the prospective father.

The expectant mother should be able to depend upon her partner to give her emotional support and encouragement; help her with the household jobs, especially the heavier work and tiring jobs like shopping; look after her if she is not too well; cheer her up when needed; and take an active interest in the development of the baby and the forthcoming birth. He should be as interested as she is in making preparations, and should be involved in the choice of clothing and equipment and preparing the baby's room. This is a lot of extra work and responsibility for him, and his partner should remember that he needs encouragement and love at this time. Unless there are complications during pregnancy there is no reason why the physical side of lovemaking cannot continue, and the couple should get both physical and emotional enjoyment from each other's company during the period of waiting.

Don't forget – it is easier to give up smoking and alcohol and to keep to a sensible diet if someone else is doing it with you!

People who look after the expectant mother

One of the reasons that there is quite a low perinatal mortality rate in the UK is the care given to the expectant mother, and the specialist help supplied, by the following people:

- **Family doctor** (GP)   The family doctor is usually the first person to be consulted if a woman thinks she is pregnant. It is quite possible that the doctor will be part of a group practice at a health centre. He or she may be a GPO (general practitioner obstetrician), i.e., a family doctor who specialises in care of pregnant women and children. Some GPs run their own antenatal clinics; otherwise they may refer the expectant mother to a hospital or local antenatal clinic. In any case the doctor will give general care and advice during the pregnancy.

- **Health visitor**   The health visitor is a RGN (registered general nurse) with at least three months' midwifery experience who has attended a one-year technical college course. She or he does in fact look after the whole community, and is usually attached to a health centre, a general practice or a local welfare clinic. She or he may also work as a district nurse, providing nursing at home for people who need it. The health visitor may run the antenatal clinic and the child welfare clinic, and usually gets to know families very well.

- **Community midwife**   The midwife is a RGN who has taken the added qualification of SCM (state certified midwife). She or he is qualified to look after the expectant mother, to deliver the baby either at home or in hospital, to give drugs if needed, and to care for mother and baby when they leave hospital. If the midwife is at all anxious, or any problems arise, she or he will always call in a specialist. The midwife is in charge of the care of mother and child until ten days after the delivery, when the responsibility becomes that of the health visitor.

- **Obstetrician**   The obstetrician is a doctor who specialises in looking after women during pregnancy and birth. The expectant mother will receive a check-up from the obstetrician when her pregnancy is confirmed, and she will be examined at intervals throughout and at the end of her pregnancy to make sure there are no complications. The obstetrician will make the necessary decisions if any difficulties arise, such as the need for a Caesarean section (see p. 104). A midwife or doctor carrying out a home delivery can call upon emergency services if there is any difficulty.

- **Gynaecologist**   The same doctor may be both a consultant obstetrician and a gynaecologist. The gynaecologist co-operates closely with the obstetrician, as he or she is qualified and specialises in the treatment of women's diseases and reproductive disorders.

- **Paediatrician**   The paediatrician specialises in the treatment of children up to their early teens. He or she may be attached to a maternity unit and will examine the newborn babies for defects. The paediatrician also acts in a consultant capacity in child health centres, hospitals, schools, etc.

- **Neonatologist**   The neonatologist is a doctor who specialises in the care of the newborn baby, and is usually a paediatrician.

- **Social worker**   The expectant mother may have problems which are not simply medical, such as finance, housing, a broken marriage, or psychological problems. In this case she can discuss her problems with a social worker; sometimes there is one attached to the health centre.

Further help is available at the antenatal clinic.

The antenatal clinic

The first visit to the antenatal clinic will usually be made a few weeks after the pregnancy has been confirmed. An appointment will be made by the doctor or health visitor for the expectant mother to visit the clinic, which may be at the health centre, or part of the maternity unit of a hospital. The clinics are usually very busy places with lots of people, and lots of things going on. Many expectant mothers find them bewildering and impersonal at first, but after a few visits they will appreciate the care and knowledge with which they are treated.

First the expectant mother will go to the *reception desk* to give her name, and be given an appointment card.

Then she will see the *midwife* who will fill in an antenatal record sheet. She will be asked about:

- the date of the first day of her last period.
- details of previous pregnancies, including any history of miscarriage, abortions or twins.
- any illnesses or complications she may have had, such as diabetes.
- any smoking habits or addiction to drugs or alcohol.
- her social circumstances, such as housing conditions, her job and her partner's job

At this stage the expectant mother may wish to ask some questions herself, such as:

- What are my chances of having twins?
- What state benefits can I claim?
- When is the baby due? Shall I give up work?

What other questions do you think the expectant mother may wish to ask at this stage?

Tests

The next stage involves various routine tests, which will be done frequently throughout pregnancy:

- The *urine* is tested for protein (albumen) which could indicate toxaemia; for glucose (sugar) which could indicate diabetes; and for germs and infections.
- The *blood* is tested. A small amount is taken and tested to find the expectant mother's blood group, to detect any signs of anaemia or syphilis, and to test her immunity to rubella.
- The *blood pressure* is measured so that future comparisons can be made, and so that if the level is high further tests for toxaemia can be made.
- The *weight* is checked. This will be done regularly to make sure that the expectant mother is not putting on too much weight, or losing weight.
- The *height* is also recorded.

Medical examination

This will be carried out by the doctor and will involve a general examination and an internal one. The doctor will examine the breasts and nipples, heart and lungs, and ask about the pregnant woman's general health. The internal examination will involve:

- a cervical smear test (to check for cancer of the cervix).
- checking the size and position of the enlarging uterus.
- checking the pelvis to see it is large enough to allow the passage of a baby.
- making sure there are no ovarian cysts.

All these tests and examinations are essential to see that the expectant mother is strong and healthy and to detect any abnormalities at a very early stage, when something can be done about it.

Information

The prospective mother then has a *final interview* with the antenatal sister, who will give information about free prescriptions, dental treatment, free milk, iron and vitamin tablets and supplementary benefits. She may also give information about booking a bed for the delivery, and she will make the next appointment for the expectant mother. She will give her information about the antenatal classes that can be attended later in the pregnancy.

Many clinics issue the expectant mother with a co-operation card. This is a record of the pregnancy from the very first visit and contains details of the tests which have been carried out and their results, her height, weight and blood pressure. Any abnormalities or problems are noted down. The expectant mother keeps this card and takes it with her whenever she visits the antenatal clinic, so that, even if she does not see the same medical team every time, there is still a continuous check on her progress.

Visits to the antenatal clinic should take place every four weeks up to the 28th week of pregnancy, then every two weeks up to the 36th week of pregnancy, and then every week until the birth. Obviously the visits will be more frequent if there are any complications.

Diary of a pregnancy

Up to 12 weeks

- The pregnancy will have been confirmed by the family doctor.
- The first visit to the antenatal clinic will have taken place; health check, medical examination, blood and urine tests will have been done.
- The expectant mother will be thinking about the options open for the birth of the baby and will seek guidance before making a choice.
- She will try to give up smoking and alcohol and not take any drugs unless prescribed.
- She may suffer from sickness, tender breasts, and more frequent visits to the toilet.
- She will try to get more rest and exercise and have a sensible diet.

The period from the 8th to 12th week is the commonest time for miscarriage; after this the foetus is well established.

Up to 16 weeks

- The expectant mother has settled down to the idea of pregnancy and is now feeling content. Sickness and tiredness are decreasing.
- Iron and vitamin supplements may be needed from this stage to ward off anaemia.
- She should be eating plenty of fresh fruit and vegetables and two tablespoons of bran a day.

The mother may have an **ultrasound examination** or **scan** at this stage. High frequency sound waves are used to produce a picture on a screen of the developing foetus. In this way some abnormalities can be detected at an early stage. The abdomen is rubbed with oil and then a probe is rubbed gently over the skin. This probe gives off and then picks up high frequency sound waves which are fed into a system that transforms them into pictures. The ultrasound examination is used to:

- work out the age of the foetus (accurate to within eight days).
- diagnose multiple births.
- show the position of the foetus and diagnose a breech birth.
- show up abnormalities such as spina bifida.
- show the foetal heart beat (from seven and a half weeks on).
- show where the placenta is situated and whether there will be any complications with it.
- locate the amniotic fluid in the womb so that some may be drawn off for an amniocentesis if necessary.

A scan is not used too early in pregnancy unless there is a serious condition such as a threatened abortion. The sight of the tiny embryo on the TV screen is a great thrill to a mother and gives her the first visual confirmation that a baby is there.

Up to 24 weeks

- The expectant mother will have a definite lump above the pubic bone and may need to start wearing looser clothing. She will have put on about 4 kg (8.8 lb) and noticed a definite enlargement of the breasts.
- If spina bifida or Down's syndrome is suspected an amniocentesis may be given, but doctors usually leave well alone at this stage if possible.
- Sickness and nausea symptoms should have stopped.
- Breasts may begin to produce a small amount of colostrum.

Up to 28 weeks

- The expectant mother will have seen the hospital in which her baby will be delivered, and be starting to get to know the doctors and midwives.

- She will have felt the first foetal movements; the foetal heart-beats can be clearly heard.
- She will make arrangements to attend antenatal and relaxation classes.
- She will give some thought to how she is going to feed the baby – breast or bottle.

At the end of this period the foetus is legally classed as a baby and is viable – that is, it may survive if born prematurely.

Up to 36 weeks

- The baby is kicking and changing position constantly. If it is in the wrong position the doctor may try to change it. This can be risky, and many babies turn themselves later in any case.
- The prospective mother may be feeling breathless and tired more often. She should be planning to give up work shortly, especially if there are any problems.
- She should now be going to the antenatal clinic once a fortnight.
- Hormone tests may be carried out to see that the placenta is functioning as it should.

The expectant mother has another blood test at 30 weeks to check the haemoglobin count.

Up to 40 weeks

- The baby should be in the correct position for birth with the head descended into the lower part of the uterus.
- Vigorous foetal movements may disturb the expectant mother's sleep at night as well as during the day.
- The expectant mother is usually getting anxious about the birth. She should have everything prepared (see the information in Section D).
- She may suffer minor complaints such as heartburn, swollen and aching feet and legs, varicose veins, and haemorrhoids, and she is likely to feel clumsy and ungainly.
- She needs lots of rest, help and physical and emotional support.

By the 36th or 37th week the baby's head will have passed into the cavity of the pelvis. The pelvis is the bony 'cage' at the base of the spine, which has an inlet, a cavity and an outlet. The baby's head passing through the inlet and into the cavity is called **engagement**.

By the 40th week everything should be ready for the birth, including the baby!

Antenatal classes

The antenatal clinic will look after the physical needs of the expectant mother and detect any problems that may arise during the development of the foetus, but antenatal education is also very important in giving the expectant mother the knowledge about pregnancy, labour and birth that will give her the confidence to go through these stages much more easily. Any experience is much less frightening if you clearly understand what is happening, how and why. It is at antenatal classes that the expectant mother will be taught all she needs to know about the pregnancy and birth. The prospective father will also be encouraged to attend so that he knows how he will be able to help, and so that he feels an important part of the birth process.

Antenatal education should include:

- advice on preparation for parenthood.
- the physiological and psychological details of pregnancy and birth.
- information on methods of pain relief during birth – drugs, relaxation, neuro-muscular control, and breathing.
- information on the development of the foetus.
- advice on care during pregnancy – diet, rest, exercise, and avoiding non-prescribed drugs.
- preparation for feeding – breast and bottle.
- handling and caring for the newborn baby.
- a visit to the unit where the birth will take place, with a tour of the labour ward, a demonstration of equipment that may be used, and an introduction to nursing staff.
- exercise classes to practise breathing and relaxation.
- discussion groups and question-and-answer sessions so that both parents can ask about things they do not understand.

These types of classes are available free under the National Health Service and are held at health centres, hospitals or special units. Some are better organised than others, and there are some classes organised privately by special groups such as the National Childbirth Trust, which charge a small fee. The NCT is very keen on childbirth being a shared experience between both parents and believes in a comprehensive preparation and full understanding of the natural process of child bearing.

Classes usually have a programme of about seven to nine units and are held in weekly sessions a few weeks before the baby is expected. They may be run as mainly information, mainly exercises, mainly discussion or, best of all, a mixture of all three. They will be taken by a health visitor or midwife. The course content should include:

- **Information** Conception, development of foetus, physical problems and health during pregnancy, pregnancy tests, preparations for the birth, labour and childbirth, looking after the newborn baby, postnatal care; films, slides and videos showing development and birth; visit to the labour ward.

● **Exercises**   Relaxation exercises – how to recognise tension, relaxing each part of the body, sleep and relaxation, posture, massage, breath control, calm and regular breathing, the levels of breathing for each stage of labour; mock labour using the breathing and exercise techniques that have been taught.

If fathers attend these sessions they will understand all the stages the expectant mother goes through and will be able to give invaluable help, especially at the birth.

● **Discussion**   Every session should have a few minutes for discussion and summing up so that any problems, however trivial, may be solved.

The antenatal class is also a good place to meet other expectant mothers and possibly form new friends. It is quite likely the expectant mother will see some of her classmates at the hospital when she goes into labour, and this will make her feel less apprehensive.

Exercises at an antenatal class

Follow-up exercises

Category 1

1 Plan a three day menu guide for an expectant mother who is:

   a) a housewife on a very limited budget.

   b) going out to work each day and taking a packed lunch.

   c) a vegetarian.

2 *a)* Trace this outline figure of an expectant mother into your book.

   b) Select suitable styles and fabrics, from the examples shown here and listed below, to give your expectant mother a variety of clothes to see her through her pregnancy. Colour your drawings

     Fabrics: Corduroy   Fine knitted wool
                Cotton lawn   Heavy wool rib
                Cotton jersey Polyester cotton
                Printed cotton Brushed cotton check

   c) Try to design a few outfits yourself, and make a list of the important points you would consider.

   d) How would you launder a garment made from each of the fabrics listed above?

3 Study the illustrations of footwear shown. Which styles would not be suitable for an expectant mother to wear and why?

Draw and describe some shoe styles which would be ideal for wearing during pregnancy. What would they be made from and how much would they cost?

4 At what stages of pregnancy may the expectant mother have a scan and for what reasons?

Is this an internal examination and is it likely to be painful?

5 Give two features of pregnancy at each of the following stages:

12 weeks   24 weeks   36 weeks

Category 2

6 Look at the chart on p. 53.

a) In which countries would a child be most likely to die before the age of one year?

b) Which countries in the West have a high percentage of doctors in relation to the number of people?

c) If there is a high percentage of doctors to look after the population, would you expect a high or a low perinatal mortality rate?

d) Why is medical care so important during pregnancy and why should *every* expectant mother take advantage of all the medical care offered?

7 What is the difference between the work done by:

a) the health visitor and the midwife?

b) the obstretrician and the paediatrician?

8 Put yourself in the place of an expectant mother who has just visited an antenatal clinic for the first time. Describe what happened and what your feelings were.

Begin 'Today I went to the antenatal clinic for the first time', and finish off by saying 'I will go again next month because . . .'

9 What is meant by 'antenatal education'?

How do antenatal classes help to make the processes of pregnancy and birth less frightening?

10 Why should prospective fathers be encouraged to attend antenatal classes along with expectant mothers?

11 List the ways in which the husband can help and support his partner during pregnancy using the following headings:

Household tasks – Emotional support – Preparations for the baby – His partner's health.

Category 3

12 The infant mortality rate (deaths of infants under one year of age per 1000 births) in 1939 was 46 per 1000; in 1974 it was 16 per 1000; in 1980 it was 11 per 1000. The perinatal mortality rate (stillbirths and deaths of infants under one week per 1000 births) in 1977 was 16.9 per 1000; in 1980 it was 13.3 per 1000; and in 1983 it was 10.3 per 1000.

What factors do you think have contributed to this steady decrease in the deaths of babies and young children?

Activity

Think of a sensible sum of money to spend on maternity wear. With this money you must buy or make underwear, tights, one pair of shoes, a nightie and some outer garments.

Describe, price, and illustrate each item you choose. You could use some catalogues to help you.

6 Preparations before the Birth

Getting things ready for the baby

There are so many things to be done before a new baby arrives, and if the expectant mother is continuing with her job to within a few weeks of the birth it is sensible to start buying clothing and equipment, and preparing the nursery, as soon as possible after the pregnancy is confirmed. She will also not feel like tackling heavy jobs or long bouts of shopping in the later months of pregnancy, and it will give both parents a lot of pleasure to start preparing early.

The baby's room

The baby will probably be in the same bedroom as his parents for a short time, or he may have to share a room with another child. If it is possible to convert a small room for his use as a nursery this is ideal.

These points should be considered before starting:
- Hygiene
- Safety
- Adaptability
- Cost
- Attractiveness and suitability
- Good planning and design.

- **Hygiene**   If the room has been used as a storage room it must be thoroughly cleaned out, floor scrubbed and walls redecorated. All decorations and equipment bought should be cleanable, with no areas where bacteria can form.

- **Safety**   This is the room where the child will sleep, play and be fed. Surfaces and equipment as far as possible should be non-toxic, non-slip, and non-flammable. Heating, lighting and electric points should be safe.

- **Adaptability**   The baby will not be a baby for long, so his room should be planned with the possibility of adapting it for a toddler and later for the needs of a schoolchild.

- **Cost**   It is expensive to equip a room for a baby. Money can be saved if the parents are do-it-yourself enthusiasts, but specialised jobs such as electrical work must be left to experts. Savings can also be made by buying from jumble sales, markets or shop sales, or by borrowing or buying from friends.

- **Attractiveness and suitability**   Remember – a child will learn from and react to his surroundings. Bright primary colours are exciting and stimulating, soft pastels are more restful and relaxing. Decide what the main function of the nursery is to be.

- **Good planning and design**   Positioning of furniture and equipment is important, especially if the room is small, to give maximum free floor space and ease of use. Equipment and furnishing should be simple, functional and well designed (see p. 78).

Use washable wallpaper or emulsion, and check that all paint is lead-free nursery paint. Windows should have safety catches, with a small top window for ventilation. Lined or thick curtains will help to keep out draughts and darken the room. Floors should not be slippy, hard or cold. Haircord carpeting or carpet tiles or cork tiling are ideal as they are warm, hard-wearing and easily cleaned.

The best type of heating is central heating that will give a constant temperature of 24 °C (75 °F). Otherwise use a radiant wall-heater fitted high up or a convector heater with a guard, fixed to the wall. Lighting is best controlled with a dimmer switch. Attractive wall lights, night-lights and central lampshades can be bought or made. It is important that parents can hear the child when he is put to bed. If the nursery is some way from the other rooms a baby alarm intercom system should be used.

Once these points have been taken care of, the baby's room will need to be equipped and furnished.

Plenty of *storage space* is essential. This can be provided by having cupboards with hanging space and shelves, a chest of drawers, built-in shelves, or a specially designed changing fitment with storage compartments. These will also provide a flat working surface for changing and dressing the baby. A thick towel or foam changing-mat on top of the chest of drawers is useful.

A tiny baby needs to feel warm, comfortable and secure in *bed,* and therefore a large cot is not really suitable until he is about six months old. Until then he should sleep in a crib, Moses basket, pram or carrycot. The high sides will protect him from draughts and make him feel secure. A carrycot with transporter wheels is useful as it doubles as a pram, and a small pram with detachable wheels serves the same purpose. All of these should be lined with a blanket for warmth and safety. The baby will need a thin mattress, waterproof sheet, sheets and blankets – *but no pillow.* When the baby is able to sit up and is moving about energetically, he will need a full-size cot. There are lots of different designs and special features, making the choice of cot difficult.

- Essential features include: lead-free paint; stability; a mattress that fits the size of the base; bars correctly spaced (75–100 mm or 3–4 in. apart); childproof catches; and smooth surfaces.

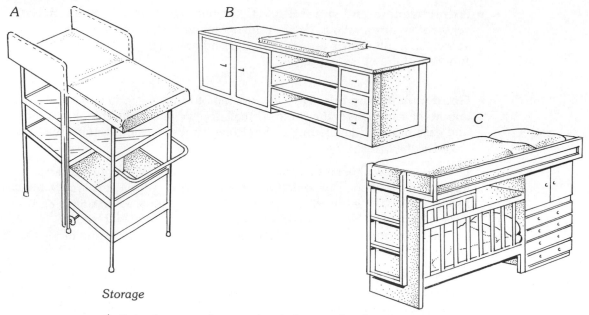

Storage

A *Baby dresser with space for clothing and a changing mat on top*

B *Built-in unit with cupboards, drawers, open shelves and a flat top for a changing mat*

C *Bunk bed fitment, for use when two children share the room*

- *Other useful features include: a cot drawer to fit underneath; a moveable mattress base to adjust to lower positions as the baby becomes active; a foam-padded cot bumper to protect the baby from draughts and banging his head; a padded, removable end panel; and the ability to convert to a divan bed as the child gets older. All these special features add to the basic cost of the cot.*

The following items of bedding will be required:

- waterproof sheets that cover the mattress and can be boiled.

- sheets that are comfortable, soft, easy to wash and need minimum ironing. Cotton is cool for summer, and flannelette warm for winter. Fitted sheets make bed making easier. For economy the best parts of old normal size sheets can be made into cot sheets.

- blankets that are light and warm and machine washable. Cellular blankets made from wool, cotton or mixed fibres are ideal. The blankets should not have fringes and should have satin-bound edges to protect the child's face. Plastic thread should not be used to bind the edges because it is thick and resilient and can choke a tiny baby. Blankets should be large enough to tuck in securely.

- pillows. (They are *not* used for the first twelve months.) They should be the correct size for the cot, and are best filled with synthetic filling which is soft, washable and non-allergic, with a soft cotton cover.

Crib   Moses basket   Basic cot

Cot with drawer storage   Cot that adapts to a bed   Travel cot

Carrycots and cots

Duvets or continental quilts make bed making easier, and are light, warm and cosy, but should only be used for the older child as there may be a danger of suffocation for a young baby. They should be made from washable terylene to British Standards specification, be the correct size, non-toxic and flame-resistant.

It may be possible to *bath* the baby in his own room, at least for the first few months until he is big enough to go into the proper bath. There are several designs to choose from including plastic baths (oval or with a moulded back) that may be purchased with a special adjustable stand. There are baby baths which fit across the normal bath, made from rigid plastic or plastic sheeting. Some baths adapt to a changing unit and others are collapsible for travelling. Metal baths should not be used as they may overheat and burn the baby. As a temporary measure the baby can be bathed in a large bowl or in the sink, if the taps are covered over.

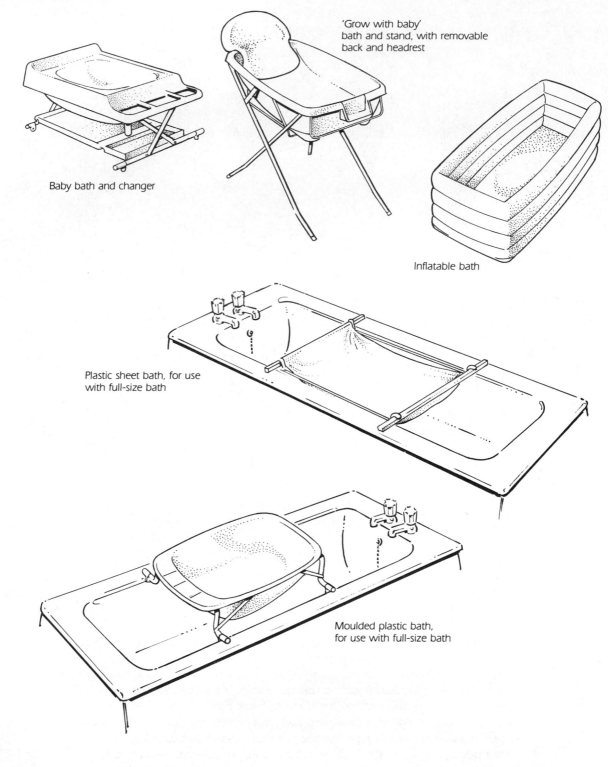

'Grow with baby'
bath and stand, with removable
back and headrest

Baby bath and changer

Inflatable bath

Plastic sheet bath, for use
with full-size bath

Moulded plastic bath,
for use with full-size bath

Baby baths

A comfortable, low chair without arms is useful for when the baby's parents are feeding him or sitting with him when he sleeps or plays.

There are lots of things that can be bought or made to brighten up the room and make it more attractive. They will also help to stimulate and educate the child. A baby is influenced by his surroundings from a very early age and his physical and intellectual progress will be developed by the things around. These could include mobiles above the cot; cut-out pictures on the windows; wall friezes and collages of numbers, letters, or animals; a growth chart; fluorescent shapes on the ceiling; and pictures of nursery rhyme and TV characters.

There is a *Nursery activity* on p. 271.

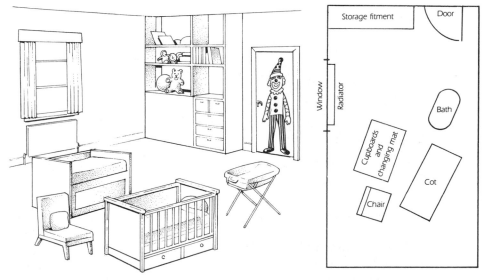

A possible layout for a baby's nursery

Choice of other items of large and small equipment

The buying of a *pram* can be an expensive and bewildering experience, as there is such a wide choice. It is best to leave buying this item until late in pregnancy or after the birth. Very often grandparents are pleased to buy this, or money can be saved by buying second-hand or from a discount warehouse. The usual points of hygiene, safety, cost and design apply, as a pram is not a bargain if it causes an accident or does not suit the mother or child. Designs available include large coach-built, with solid body and fabric hood and cover; solid body with detachable wheels; fabric body with detachable base; carrycot/traveller body with collapsible chassis. Some designs allow for the pram to convert to a carrycot, pushchair and baby seat.

It is important that the pram should be weather-resistant, well-balanced, the correct height for the mother, and comfortable, and have very safe brakes, padded upholstery, an easily cleaned padded mattress and an anti-glare hood. Carrying types should have strong handles and a detachable hood, with safe

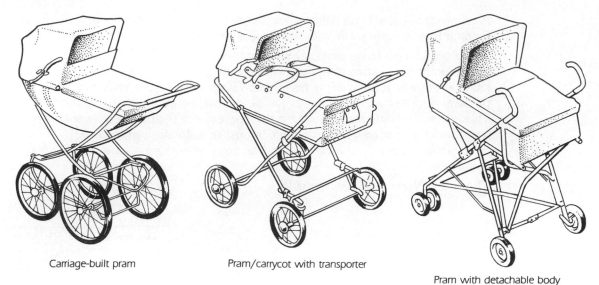

Carriage-built pram

Pram/carrycot with transporter

Pram with detachable body

A range of prams

chassis attachment points. There should be two harness attachment rings and points for attaching a canopy.

Accessories include sun canopies, cat nets, shopping bags and baskets, backrests and pram harness and reins sets.

Pushchairs and buggy/strollers again provide a difficult choice as there are so many to choose from. Pushchairs tend to be heavier and less compact, but more comfortable and stable. Buggies are ideal for travelling as they are very light, compact and manageable. Many of them allow the baby to face either forwards or towards the pusher, and have adjustable seats. It is important that the wheels run smoothly and that there is a reliable brake. There should be points for attaching a safety harness and a footrest. The automatic locking catch should always be checked so that the pushchair cannot fold up when the baby is in it.

Pushchair and buggy accessories include see-through waterproof hoods and aprons; all-in-one waterproof covers to put in front of the child; cosy-toes that protect the child's legs and keep him warm; parasols and sun canopies; hooks to fit onto the handles to take shopping bags; and pushchair baskets.

High/low chairs become necessary when the child is taking solid food and beginning to feed himself. They may be made of wood or tubular steel, usually with a padded seat. They should be comfortable and easily wiped down. They will have a tray of wood or plastic and many of them are designed to convert to a small chair and table. Some models have a canvas seat and back on a tubular frame, and fold to take up very little space.

Other models are designed to fit on to a normal dining chair; a small moulded plastic or canvas seat hooks over the chair back or slips over the chair seat. One type can be secured to the table with tubular arms. These all have the advantage of being portable. However, a small upturned stool put on the seat of the dining chair, with a cushion in and secured with a scarf to the back of the chair, serves the purpose just as well.

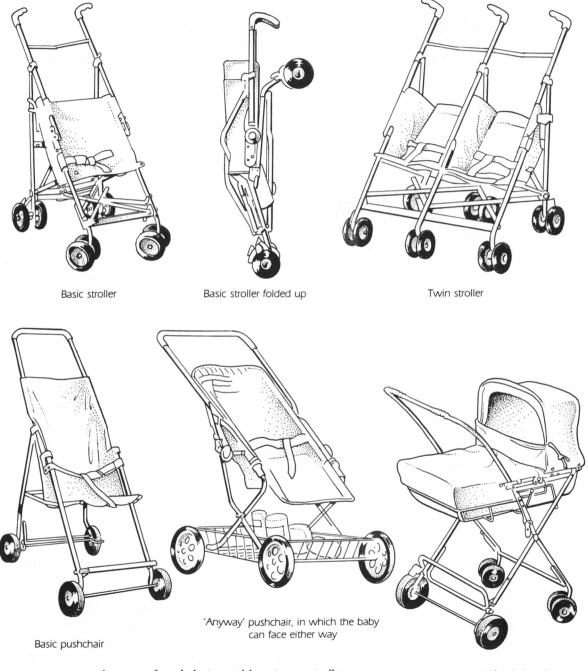

Basic stroller

Basic stroller folded up

Twin stroller

Basic pushchair

'Anyway' pushchair, in which the baby can face either way

Three-in-one pram/pushchair/carrycot

A range of pushchairs and buggies or strollers

A **baby sling or carrier** can be most useful for small babies and can be very inexpensive. Babies enjoy the close contact with the parent, and slings make shopping trips much easier as the baby does not have to be left outside shops in his pram. Some slings are of a very simple design and only suitable for tiny babies. The type of sling which goes diagonally across the back and chest provides some support but means that the parent only has one free arm. Most carriers are designed to be worn back or front, with strong webbing, and adjustable straps. Some have a head rest, and some have a lightweight detachable frame that gives greater comfort. An all-in-one carry cape is available, and helps to protect the child from the weather. Baby carriers are cheap and useful, but they can be dangerous for bigger or very active babies who may topple out; or the straps or fabric may wear out and break suddenly.

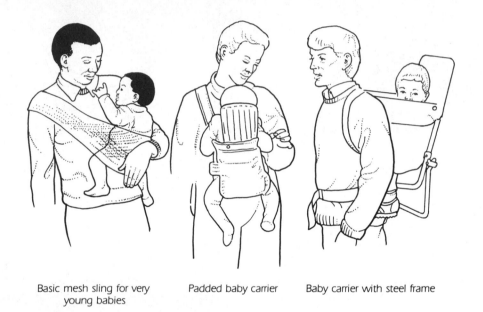

Basic mesh sling for very young babies   Padded baby carrier   Baby carrier with steel frame

Three types of baby carrier

A **safety harness** is an essential piece of equipment when the baby is sitting up and active. It is usually made of strong webbing, with adjustable straps and back safety fastening with side clips for attaching to a pram, pushchair, high chair, or a walking rein.

A **potty** is another piece of essential equipment. It should be made of easily cleaned, boilable plastic, and should be stable with a firm base. It should have a rounded or flattened rim for comfort, rounded corners, and an attractive pattern or colour. It should be of a suitable size and have a splash guard and an integral handgrip. Potties can be bought with a lid if required.

Choice of baby clothes and textiles

The collection of first-size baby clothing is called a **layette**. These first items of clothing are very attractive and expectant mothers tend to buy far too many and waste money on non-essentials. Many of the garments can be hand-knitted or sewn; they take very little fabric or yarn and making them is a pleasant, relaxing occupation during pregnancy. Often expectant mothers are overwhelmed with gifts of baby wear or have them passed on from friends with babies. It is best to buy only the essentials and then wait to see what extras appear. All clothing and textiles for a baby should be easily washed, safe, comfortable and easily put on and off. They should be made in suitable fabric that will withstand frequent washing, and should be good value for money and of simple style and design.

Basic necessities are:

3 or 4 envelope neck vests (cotton or mixture)

3 stretch all-in-one suits (for day)

3 nightdresses (cotton, polyester or flannelette)

2 or 3 matinée jackets or cardigans

2 hats

2 pairs mittens

1 shawl or blanket

3 pairs bootees

6 small towelling bibs

2 dozen terry towelling nappies and 6 nappy pins (see p. 128 for choice of nappies)

6 muslin nappies or 4 Ever-dri nappies or box of nappy-liners

2 swaddling sheets

1 sleeping bag or pram set

4 pairs plastic pants.

Extras that may be needed include scratch mittens, and for a summer baby a summer hat, cotton socks, stretch cotton top and knickers.

Natural fibres are the best choice as they absorb moisture, are soft and comfortable, and have a natural feel. Cotton is good for summer wear especially if given non-iron, non-flammable, crease-resistant properties. Wool is warm and soft for winter but it may irritate a child's skin. Fibres that are a mixture of synthetic and natural make for easy-care, crease-resistant, strong fabrics.

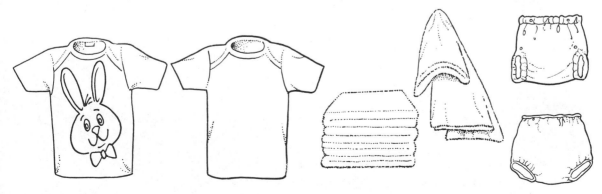

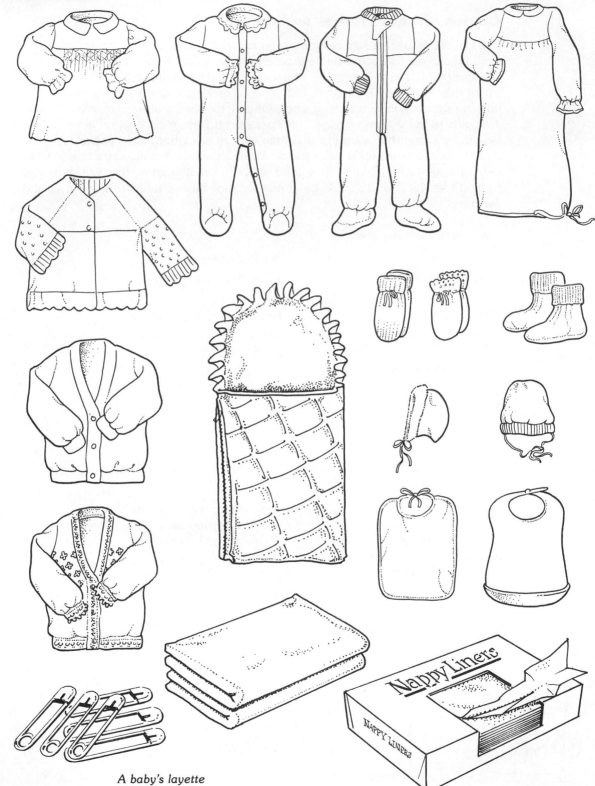

A baby's layette

The baby will also need a *basket* containing his own toiletries. The container may be a specially divided box with a lid, suitable for carrying, or it can be a simple plastic container or a basket which can be lined and made attractive. It should contain:

cotton wool

baby wipes

small round-ended nail scissors

flannel or sponge

safety nappy pins

a soft hair brush

baby shampoo

antiseptic cream

baby soap or bath liquid

baby cream, oil or lotion

baby powder

zinc and castor oil cream.

The baby will also need two soft bath towels for his use only, and the parents will need a plastic backed towelling apron to wear while bathing him.

A baby's basket and box

Consumer advice

When buying equipment and clothing for the baby, money can be wasted on articles which later prove to be unsatisfactory. It is worth spending some time and effort seeking advice before the purchases are made.

The following are possible sources of advice.

- Reputable shops will have assistants willing and able to advise, not just anxious to make a quick sale.

- Child care magazines, women's magazines and television advertisements all give consumer information.

- Manufacturers publish leaflets and booklets about their products which may be collected and compared.

- Health visitors and assistants at the antenatal clinic will be able to advise.

- Other mothers, family and friends can be asked about their experience of the products and the shops that sell them.

- Citizens Advice Bureaux and local Consumer Advice Centres should be able to help.

- Many good quality articles carry a label which has been issued by private or government organisations, which guarantee a certain standard. Examples are:

    the Kitemark, issued by the British Standards Institution. The BSI only awards the Kitemark to products that have been examined for safety and quality, and carries out regular inspections to see that goods are up to standard.

    the London Design Centre label, awarded to products that it considers are well designed and functional.

Preparing for the birth

One of the important decisions the expectant parents will have to make is whether to have the baby at home or in hospital.

This decision will be influenced by:

- the facilities available in the area in which the expectant mother lives.
- the expectant mother's medical record and the danger of any complications at birth.
- the advice given by her doctor and midwife.
- her own inclinations.
- her living conditions.
- the availability of help before, during and after the birth.

The choices open to her for delivery are:

- in hospital – a maternity unit or a GP unit.
- the 'domiciliary-in-out' (domino) system.
- at home.

Most women choose to have their baby in a hospital. The pregnant woman's own doctor or health visitor is the best person to advise her, but she can also get advice from the National Childbirth Trust or the Community Health Council. The main reasons she may have for a home delivery may include a desire to be with her own family in her own home for a natural event; a fear of hospitals due to previous unpleasant experiences; and the lack of privacy in most general hospitals. She may feel happier and more relaxed in her own surroundings, and therefore have an easier and more rewarding birth experience.

The expectant mother will be encouraged to have a hospital delivery if any of the following circumstances apply to her. Her doctor will always consider her safety and the safety of the baby as the most important thing, and delivery in hospital, where special equipment and expertise are available if anything should go wrong, is the safest procedure. However, after discussion with the doctor and midwife, the final decision is hers.

Special circumstances:

- Having a first baby – unexpected complications may arise.
- Having a fifth or subsequent baby – the mother's muscles may be weaker and the uterus could rupture.
- Having a history of miscarriage or pregnancy complications.
- Having a multiple pregnancy – twins, triplets, etc.
- Being 35 and over – there are greater risks involved, especially in a first pregnancy at this age.
- Being very young (under 16).
- Having had a previous Caesarean section or other obstetric surgery.

- Having a small pelvic area – the baby may get stuck. Women shorter than 1 m 55 cm (5 ft 2 in.) and with feet smaller than size 4 may come into this category.
- Having an abnormally large or very small baby – best delivered in hospital.
- Having a medical condition such as diabetes, heart conditions or physical malformation.
- Being very much overweight.

The advantages to the expectant mother of a hospital confinement are that she will receive expert care and attention, and will be able to rest and have none of the responsibilities of home. The babies may be taken to the nursery at night so that the mothers can sleep; more pain-relief drugs and equipment are available; and she will get training and help in looking after her baby from trained nurses.

There is usually only one hospital that any one GP uses, but if there is a choice the mother should check up on the hospital conditions and policies and choose the one that suits her best. Her doctor will book a bed for her and this is best done as early in pregnancy as possible.

The **maternity unit** attached to a hospital will usually consist of the antenatal clinic, the antenatal ward, the labour wards, the operating theatre, the postnatal wards, the special care baby unit, and the nursery. The expectant mother will be encouraged to visit the unit well before the baby is born and to attend antenatal classes.

The **GP unit** only exists in some areas. It may be attached to the hospital maternity unit or it may be separate. The expectant mother is looked after during pregnancy by her own doctor and the community midwife, who then deliver her baby in the GP unit. This gives continued personal care and removes some of the impersonality from childbirth.

The **domino system** is only available in some areas. This is a system which combines home and hospital care. The expectant mother is cared for throughout pregnancy by the community midwife (domiciliary care). When she starts labour she goes into hospital, accompanied by the midwife, who delivers the baby. A few hours after the birth, if the mother and baby are fit, they return home and the midwife looks after them there. In this way the expectant mother has the advantages of a hospital delivery and those of domiciliary care from familiar people.

Home confinement

If the expectant mother decides on home confinement she must first consult her own doctor. Her doctor may not be an obstetrician, in which case he or she will recommend someone else. The GP or obstetrician will only agree to a home confinement if the expectant mother is in very good health with no indications of complications, has had two or three previous healthy confinements, and has a reasonably large home with adequate help. The prospective mother must also book for a midwife to attend the home delivery and look after her after the birth.

The room for delivery at home must be hygienic and germ free. It must be large enough to hold two tables (for equipment), the cot and a firm, fairly high bed for the delivery. The floor will need to be covered and equipment such as a plastic sheet, kettles, hot water bottles, a bed pan and wash basins must be provided. Good heating and lighting facilities are also needed. The clothing for the mother and baby must also be ready well in advance. All these preparations must be done well before the **EDD** (estimated delivery date) in case the baby is early.

Hospital confinement

For a hospital confinement the expectant mother should have a suitcase packed at least six weeks before she is due. The suitcase should contain:

three front-opening nightgowns

slippers and dressing-gown

one bath towel and one hand towel

two flannels

soap, talcum powder, shampoo, toothbrush and toothpaste

paper tissues

brush and comb

make-up

sanitary belt and sanitary towels

books, writing paper, envelopes, stamps and magazines

things to do, such as knitting

small amount of money (no valuables)

three front-opening nursing bras.

Clothing for the mother and baby to go home in usually has to be brought in when needed as there is very little storage space in hospital.

Other preparations

There are several other things to be done in preparation for the birth:

- Make arrangements for any other children to be looked after, preferably by relatives, otherwise by friends, neighbours or the social services.
- Plan out the food to be left, and if possible stock up the freezer with cooked and uncooked dishes.
- The prospective father may be able to arrange to have paternity leave so that he can be with his partner during and after the birth.
- If the family do not have a telephone, they must know where the nearest one is which they can use (perhaps belonging to a neighbour). They should also keep a list of phone numbers handy which may be needed, e.g., for the doctor, the maternity unit, the taxi, grandparents and other relations.

● Transport to hospital must be considered. If the family have a car this must be available; otherwise a neighbour or relative might help. Taxis, or in an emergency an ambulance, may be called.

● If the prospective father is going to stay for the birth, he should plan to take comfortable clothing, drinks and some food, and be prepared to sit about for long periods!

Having these preparations made will help to avoid panic and confusion when labour starts. Many babies decide to make their entrance in the middle of the night, which is not always very convenient!

Breast or bottle feeding

Another decision to be made well before the baby arrives is whether the mother is going to breast or bottle feed the baby. There is no doubt that breast feeding, which is the natural way, is the best thing to do.

Breast milk and cow's milk differ greatly in composition. Breast milk is richer in unsaturated fats, soluble protein and lactose than cow's milk, which has a

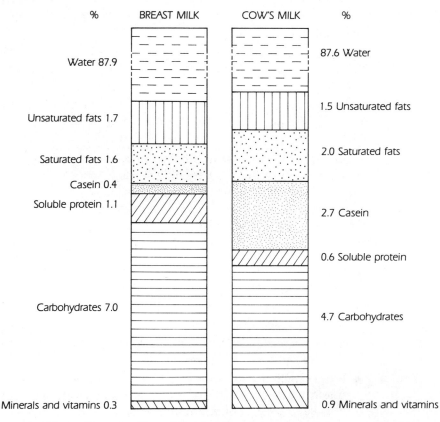

The composition of breast milk and cow's milk

substantial excess of casein and minerals. Breast milk is perfectly suited to the baby throughout the various stages of the baby's progress.

During pregnancy the expectant mother will be able to discuss the matter with her doctor, her midwife or the National Childbirth Trust. She will be advised how to look after her breasts during pregnancy, to avoid any problems later. She should:

- wash her breasts daily and apply a little body lotion (not alcohol to harden the nipples as this can cause cracking later).
- wear nipple shields if her nipples become inverted (turned inward).
- from the 22nd week onwards, express any colostrum from her breasts daily to keep the milk ducts clear.
- wear a good support bra. The breasts usually increase 8–10 cm (3–4 in.), and therefore a larger size bra is needed. A sleep bra will help to give support and comfort at night.

Advantages of breast and bottle feeding

Breast	Bottle
It gives the baby all the nutrients required, in balanced amounts.	*The person giving the feed can see how much the baby is taking.*
The milk is easily digested, and not likely to cause tummy upsets or constipation.	*A bottle can be given by other people and therefore the mother is not tied down.*
It helps to prevent allergies and infections. The mother's immunities are passed on through the milk for the first three months.	*The mother can return to work if necessary.*
The milk is the correct temperature.	*The father can help with feeding, so feeling involved.*
It is convenient, with no bottles to be made up and sterilised.	*It is tiring and draining for the mother to breast feed for a long period.*
It is much cheaper than packet milk.	*Some mothers do not enjoy the feelings of breast feeding, especially if it becomes painful or they are worried that the baby is not getting enough milk.*
*It assists the uterus in getting back to normal, by stimulating production of the hormone **oxytocin**.*	*The mother does not have the possibility of milk leaking from the breasts.*
It uses 1300 calories a day and therefore helps the mother reduce her weight.	*Breast feeding can cause embarrassment to some mothers, especially if it has to be done in public places.*
It helps build up close contact between mother and baby – psychological bonding.	
It is a satisfying experience for mother and baby. The mother's natural instinct to feed her baby is being satisfied.	

There is always the danger that a milk feed can be made up incorrectly by ignorant or careless people. Brain damage can result if the milk is too concentrated. Bottles and other equipment that is not sterilised properly can cause severe stomach upsets and gastroenteritis.

The new mother must make it quite clear to the hospital staff or the midwife that she wishes to breast feed her baby, even if she has some difficulties to start with.

You can see from the chart on the previous page that the advantages of breast feeding far outweigh those of bottle feeding, and any mother who can give her baby the advantages of the breast, even if only for a few weeks, should do so. There are physical and psychological advantages for both baby and the mother, which can continue well after the breast feeding has stopped. However, if a mother has tried to breast feed and finds she is unable to do so, she should not feel guilty; many babies are reared very successfully on a bottle.

Follow-up exercises

Category 1

1   Imagine the following situations:

   a)   Your mother-in-law has offered to buy the pram for the new baby. She is willing to pay a good price.

   b)   You have very little money to buy equipment and you are looking for a second-hand cot.

   c)   You notice that your local shop has a sale and they have a child carrier at half the normal price because it is faded.

   d)   You live in a very small flat and have not got room for a baby bath and stand.

   e)   Your friend has offered to give you her baby's potty which she has finished with.

   Think about these situations and in each case explain the points you would consider, and the advice you would take, before purchasing or accepting the stated pieces of equipment.

2   Why would you *not* buy or make baby clothes with these design features?

   a nightdress with buttons down the back

   a dress with openwork lace trim at the edge of the sleeves

   a very fluffy wool matinee jacket

   a shawl with a mainly openwork pattern

   a vest with a tight-fitting neck

3   Put the correct fastening with the correct garment.

garment	fastening
baby's bib	buttons and buttonholes
baby's cardigan	Velcro
baby's sleeping/carrying bag	ribbon or tape to tie in a bow
back opening of nightdress	zip fastener
all-in-one baby stretch	press studs or poppers

4   Put a suitable fibre or fabric with each article. Look at a catalogue such as
    Mothercare's to help you.

article	*fabric/fibre*
pram suit	winceyette
baby hat for summer	polyester cotton
matinée jacket	100% cotton fabric
baby gown	velour
shawl	100% acrylic fibre
vest	stretch towelling
summer day dress	all wool knitting yarn

5   In your notebook, draw the care label which you would expect to find
    inside these garments:

pure wool wrap-over vest

stretch body-suit (80% cotton, 20% nylon)

fleecy carrying cape (70% acrylic, 30% polyester)

cotton lawn dress.

How would you hand wash all these garments?

Category 2

6   What advice would you give to women in the following situations about
    where to have their baby?

   a)   An expectant mother with a comfortable home and two small
        children, who did not like the impersonal hospital system of her two
        previous births.

   b)   A woman in her late thirties expecting her first child.

   c)   A healthy expectant mother who would like a home confinement but
        is worried about what would happen if any unexpected complications
        arose.

7   Describe what the prospective father can do to help his partner with the
    final preparations to be made before the birth.

Category 3

8   Since artificial feeding (bottle feeding) was introduced into Third-World
    countries, there has been a much higher death rate in babies due to
    feeding problems. Try to give some reasons for this.

Activities

1 Design, sketch and colour a motif which could be embroidered or appliquéd on a baby's nightdress or a baby's day dress.

2 As a class project make a cot quilt of patchwork. Every member of the group could embroider one square. Have a theme for your quilt such as numbers and letters, animals, or TV characters. Use simple shapes and keep it colourful, and line your quilt with wadding.

You could donate your quilt to one of the children's charities to be used, or sold to raise funds.

3 Do a consumer survey chart on all the makes of baby toiletries you can find. Put the chart in your notebook like this:

Example

Baby soaps

Manufacturer's name	Cost	Weight	Packaging	Design	Perfume	Comments
Smith's	50p	120 g	Unwrapped	Rounded for easy handling	Pleasant, not too overpowering	Quite expensive. Lathers well. Mild and soft.

If you work in pairs or groups you could survey different things such as talcum powder, baby lotion, or baby shampoos. Your conclusions should indicate which manufacturer's product is the best value for money.

SECTION C Birth and Postnatal Care

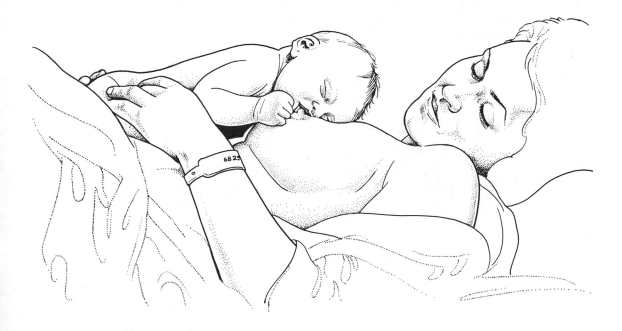

7 Birth

The start of labour

The birth of the baby will be triggered off by hormonal changes, probably started by the foetus. This is known as 'going into labour', because giving birth is indeed very hard labour, usually accompanied by discomfort and some pain. If the expectant mother has been well prepared for the birth she will understand what is happening and will be able to use the relaxation techniques which she has practised during pregnancy. This will make the birth easier, as it is fear and tension that tighten the muscles and create more pain.

The baby will be lying in a head down position (vertex presentation), ready for birth (Figure A).

Any abnormal presentation should have been corrected by this stage, but some babies do manage to get into awkward positions such as breech presentations (Figures B and C) or transverse presentation (Figure D), and a Caesarean section may be necessary.

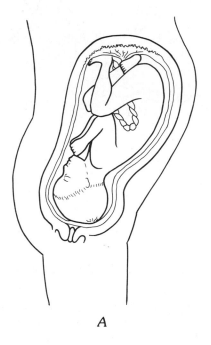

A

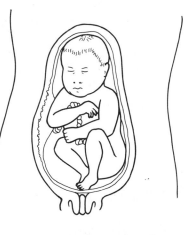

B

Positions of the baby just before birth

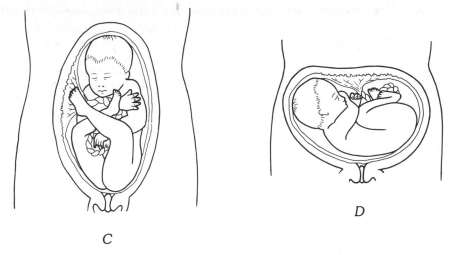

C

D

The onset of labour is usually quite slow and gives the expectant mother time to make final preparations and get herself to hospital. Labour usually starts in one of the following ways:

- The expectant mother may have a 'show'. This means that the plug of blood-stained mucus that fills the neck of the cervix is passed through the vagina.
- The 'waters may break'. The bag of fluid in which the baby is floating may rupture as labour begins and the pregnant woman will get a rush of 'water' from the vagina.
- The expectant mother will start getting regular contractions. They may be mild at first, like a little backache, but these 'pains' will increase and become more regular.

If any of these symptoms occur the expectant mother should contact her doctor and the hospital, or the midwife if it is to be a home confinement. If the confinement is to be in hospital, she will be admitted in preparation for the birth.

Sometimes the expectant mother will find she has had false labour pains and she will have to return home for a bit longer. Throughout pregnancy the uterine muscles contract in readiness for labour. These are false contractions (**Braxton Hicks' contractions**) and can be mistaken for the real thing towards the end of pregnancy.

When the expectant mother who is having a hospital confinement is admitted for the birth she will:

- report to the admission desk where she will give her name and hospital number, so that her pregnancy and medical record can be found.
- be taken to the obstetric department to be seen by the midwife. She will change into a hospital gown, her temperature and blood pressure will be taken, her abdomen felt and the foetal heart-beat listened to, and she will perhaps be given a suppository to empty the bowels ready for the delivery.

- possibly have a bath (or a shower if the waters have broken).
- have a vaginal examination to see how advanced the birth is, and then go to the first stage labour ward.

For a home confinement the attending midwife will carry out these preliminary procedures in preparation for the first stage of labour.

The stages of labour

Labour is divided into three stages.

The first stage

This first stage of labour is the time when the regular contractions open up the neck of the cervix. Before labour begins the cervix is usually closed. The muscle fibres of the uterus tighten rhythmically (**contractions**). This has the effect of drawing up the cervix and gradually opening it up until it is fully dilated to a width of 8–10 cm (3–4 in., or five fingers' breadth). The baby's head will have engaged in the mother's pelvis and the membranes of the amniotic sac will probably have burst.

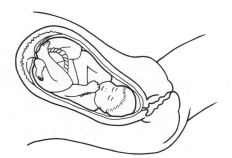

Cervix being taken up

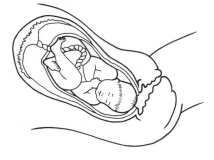

Cervix almost fully dilated

This first stage of labour can last from one to 24 hours, as the baby's head descends slowly and the cervix dilates. During this time the mother is best kept occupied, doing small jobs, walking about, chatting to visitors. Her partner can give comfort and reassurance at this stage.

Towards the end of the first stage the contractions will be getting stronger and more regular, and the expectant mother will want to push.

The second stage

When the cervix is completely dilated and the baby's head is showing (crowned), the mother will be encouraged to push hard with each contraction so that the baby's head will emerge. This is the hardest work and usually takes 15–30 minutes. It is best if the head is born slowly and eased out of the birth canal, to avoid damage. The baby's head is a tight fit in the mother's pelvis, and the skull bones are soft enough to mould together, giving an elongated shape, to allow the head to pass through. The head regains its normal shape within 24 hours of birth.

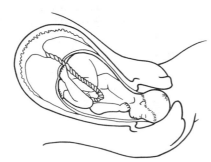

Baby's head in birth canal

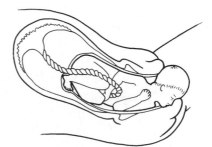

Head being born

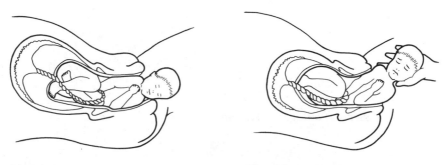

Head born

Shoulders emerging

Once the head is born the baby is twisted half round by the midwife to arch its back and allow the passage of first one shoulder and then the other. The rest of the body slips through very easily. This marks the end of the second stage of labour.

Throughout this stage the midwife, and doctor if needed, will encourage and help the mother, telling her when to push, when to relax, when to take long breaths and when to pant. Her previous relaxation and breathing exercises will stand her in good stead. If her partner is with her he too will be able to give her encouragement and instructions. He can wipe her face, massage her back, help with the gas and air mask and talk to her, and eventually he and the mother will be able to welcome their baby into the world together.

101

As the baby's head is born her nose and mouth will be cleared of mucus, and the midwife will check that the umbilical cord is clear of her neck. As the rest of the body emerges the baby will begin to breathe, cry and move about. With the oxygen from the air she breathes she will quickly become pink, and the cord can be clamped and cut. Oxygen may be needed to help with the baby's first breathing. She will be placed on the mother's body for body contact, and may be put to the breast to establish a good foundation for feeding. Suckling also helps the uterus to contract, by stimulating the production of oxytocin (see p. 93).

The third stage

After the baby has been born the placenta separates from the wall of the uterus and is pushed out by one more strong contraction. The mother may have been given an injection to help to shrink the uterus and the midwife will ease out the placenta and the cord. They will be examined to see that they are complete, as any part left in the uterus can set up an infection. A relaxing blanket bath and a rest after all her hard work will complete the birth.

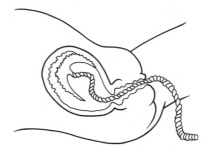

Separation of the placenta

Pain relief during labour

Many women in labour find that they require some pain relief as the contractions become stronger towards the end of the first stage. There are several choices.

- **Drugs that act on the central nervous system** The most commonly used one for childbirth is **pethidine**. It is very safe and an injection given during the first stage of labour will dull the pain to a more acceptable level, whilst still leaving the woman conscious. If large doses are given, late in labour, the drug can cross the placenta and affect the baby's ability to breathe. A mixture of pethidine and inhalation of gas and oxygen may be used for stronger relief.

- **Gas and oxygen**   A mixture of 50 per cent nitrous oxide (laughing gas) and 50 per cent oxygen breathed in through a hand-held mask (inhalation) is the simplest form of analgesic. The mother can control the flow of gas, only using it when the pain is intense. It can cause the mother to feel drowsy and nauseated, but it does not harm the baby, and the extra oxygen may benefit him.

- **The epidural block**   This blocks the nerves that carry the pain messages and can give complete pain relief. It is administered as an anaesthetic drug injected into the lower part of the back during the first and second stages of labour. The pain relief lasts for one and a half hours, and then the drug can be topped up. It is useful in cases of very painful or prolonged labour and can be used for Caesarean sections, breech births and multiple births. It needs a skilled anaesthetist to administer it and is therefore not always available.

  The epidural block does have some disadvantages, and tends not to be used if other pain relief methods are sufficient. It can prolong labour, and it can dull the normal pushing sensations so that forceps may be needed. The mother is also deprived of some of the feelings of giving birth, which she may regret later.

- **Natural childbirth**   Many women who prepare for childbirth with relaxation techniques, breathing exercises, and a thorough knowledge of how to control their bodies, are able to get through childbirth without any analgesics at all. Some new methods such as hypnosis, acupuncture and electrical impulses are being tried out. Most sensible women will seek advice during pregnancy and rely on the method that suits their own circumstances and personality.

Special treatments and conditions

Induction

Usually labour starts quite naturally, but sometimes it needs to be triggered off artificially. This is called **induction**. The birth may be induced for the following reasons:

- The baby is late, i.e., 10–14 days overdue.
- The mother's health is at risk, e.g., she may develop pre-eclampsia or severe bleeding.
- There may be expected complications such as a breech or multiple birth.
- The foetus may be showing distress signs such as uneven heart-beat or changes in movement, so that there is anxiety about the foetus' health.
- The expectant mother may have had problems previously, such as a Caesarean section or stillbirths.
- Sometimes it may be performed for social reasons.

Induction may be done in the following ways:

- **Surgical induction** – the waters are artificially ruptured to allow some of the fluid to escape.
- Giving a **hormone drip** into a vein in the arm. This has the effect of starting the birth, or hurrying it up if labour is very slow.
- The use of prostaglandin pessaries. These are natural drugs which help to soften and ripen the cervix, causing it to open.

An induced birth is a perfectly normal one, although it may be rather slow.

Forceps delivery

Forceps consist of two curved metal instruments which are used to form a protective cage around the head of the unborn baby. The baby can then be gently pulled, in time with the contractions, and helped along the birth canal. The forceps may make red marks and slight bruising to the baby's head, but these quickly disappear.

A forceps delivery may be needed if:

- the mother is too exhausted or frightened to push and needs assistance.
- the baby is distressed and delivery needs to be speeded up.
- the baby is in an awkward position – breech or transverse.

Ventouse extraction

As an alternative to a forceps delivery the doctor may decide to use a special cap attached to a suction pump, which is applied to the baby's head. This is then used to encourage the head out. It can be used even when the cervix is not fully dilated, but cannot be used for a breech or a premature baby. It is known as a **ventouse** or **suction delivery** and may leave a little bump on the baby's head, which disappears in one or two days.

Episiotomy

The **perineum** (skin and muscles between the vagina and rectum) is stretched considerably at the time of birth to allow the passage of the baby's head. Sometimes it won't stretch enough and is in danger of tearing. If this is the case, the doctor or midwife will make a small straight cut (an **episiotomy**) after giving a local anaesthetic, and the cut can then be stitched up later. An episiotomy is usually needed with a forceps delivery, a breech delivery, and when it is necessary to speed up the birth.

Caesarean section

This is an operation carried out to deliver the baby by cutting through the abdomen into the uterus just below the bikini line, and lifting the baby out. This is usually done under general anaesthetic, or sometimes, if the mother wishes to be conscious for the birth, using a local anaesthetic such as an epidural. It is a safe operation and may be a life-saving measure, for both mother and child.

A Caesarean section may be done because of **elective** (pre-planned) or **emergency** reasons.

Elective reasons include: having a very large baby, too big to come in the normal way; having had several previous Caesareans; a multiple birth; a breech or transverse presentation; the mother having a heart problem or not being able to cope with a normal birth; or the mother having large fibroids or an ovarian cyst.

An emergency operation may be needed if: the baby shows distress symptoms; the mother's blood pressure becomes very high; she has placenta problems; or the cord falls down ahead of the baby.

A Caesarean section will cause some discomfort after the birth and usually requires an eight to ten day hospital stay.

Foetal monitoring

It is useful to be able to track the heart-beat of the baby during birth to ensure that all is going well. It is especially useful if the child is in danger. The monitoring can be done with a foetal stethoscope, which is a hollow metal tube placed on the mother's abdomen, through which the midwife can hear the heart-beats. The more modern technique uses an ultrasound detector placed on the mother's abdomen, or an electrode attached to the baby's head. The print-out on a sheet of paper will indicate any foetal distress.

The use of the monitoring equipment does restrict the movement of the mother.

Drips

If the mother is becoming exhausted during labour she may be given a drip of glucose into a vein in her arm. This will give her a quick release of energy to cope with the birth.

Premature babies

A **premature** or **pre-term baby** is one born before 36 weeks. A baby born weighing under 2.5 kg (5½ lb) is called a **low birth-weight baby**.

Doctors will try to delay the birth of a pre-term baby if possible by prescribing bed rest and sedation for the mother. It is possible for a baby to live if born after only 24, or more usually 28, weeks of pregnancy, but the complications can be serious and special care is needed. A premature birth may be caused by a multiple birth, pre-eclampsia, placenta problems, or illness in the mother.

Being a few weeks pre-term is not serious, but very early babies may have problems with temperature control, feeding, breathing, and possibly jaundice. They have only a thin layer of fat under the skin and therefore cannot keep themselves warm, and may suffer from hypothermia; they may not be able to suck for several weeks and will need feeding through a tube with expressed breast milk; or their breathing may be affected because the lungs are immature, resulting in **respiratory distress syndrome**. The baby may be given extra oxygen.

Low birth-weight babies (or **small-for-dates**) do not grow and feed properly in the womb. They look very small, skinny, old and wrinkled. Like pre-term babies they need special care to combat infection and special feeding to build up their weight. Babies weighing as little as 1 kg (2 lb) at birth can now survive.

Babies needing special care when born will be taken immediately to the special care unit, where they will be placed in a warm **incubator**. The incubator is a cot with a perspex cover, in which the heat and humidity can be carefully controlled. The atmosphere is clean and sterile to prevent infection, and there is a special mattress that monitors the baby's breathing, and bleeps a warning when necessary. The incubator has portholes to allow the baby to be fed, cleaned and changed with as little exposure to the outside air as possible. The parents are encouraged to be involved with the care of the baby as much as possible, to establish a close physical and emotional bond.

A pre-term or low birth-weight baby leaves hospital when she is able to feed and maintain temperature, and the mother knows how to care for her. She usually catches up with a normal baby during his first year, though this takes longer in the very pre-term, particularly those below 32 weeks.

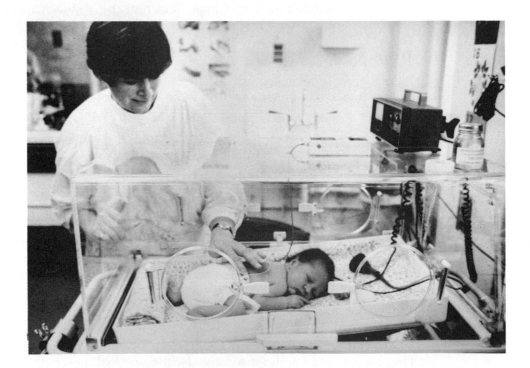

Incubator care

Care of the mother after birth

Immediately after the birth, when the placenta has been delivered and checked to make sure that it is complete, the mother will be cleaned, made comfortable, given a drink and allowed to rest. She will want to see and hold her baby and to make sure that the baby is all right. During the following few days and weeks:

- her uterus will shrink and get back to normal, usually within six weeks. Breast feeding will encourage this shrinkage.
- her breasts will enlarge, and produce first colostrum for two or three days, and then milk.
- the perineum may be sore for a while due to bruising, but will soon heal.
- any stitches which have been needed will be removed a few days after the birth. (Dissolving stitches are often used for an episiotomy.)
- she will be encouraged to get onto her feet and be mobile very soon after the birth, to get the circulation and body functions working normally.
- she may experience minor problems after the birth, such as constipation, backache, piles, soreness where the stitches were and some bleeding. These conditions usually clear up within a few weeks.
- postnatal exercises are encouraged to help the mother to get the pelvic and abdominal muscles back to normal, regain her figure, and help with any stress incontinence problems experienced during pregnancy (see p. 55).

Postnatal exercises

Postnatal depression

This is a very common experience for new mothers, usually caused by varying hormone levels. After the first joy and excitement over the birth, almost all mothers have feelings of depression, resulting in weepiness, feeling inadequate and unable to cope. This mild form is known as **baby blues** and soon wears off.

One in ten women suffers from PND more severely, beginning from three weeks to six months after the birth. They become moody, easily distressed, reject their partner and child, cannot sleep, have a poor appetite and feel anxious and guilty. This condition needs medical counselling. Drugs may be prescribed but simpler treatment, such as kindness and understanding from friends and relations, going out, taking up hobbies and discussing the problem, will often be valuable.

One in 500 new mothers suffers a much more severe depression known as **puerperal psychosis**, which needs emergency remedies involving psychiatric care. The Infanticide Act (1938) states that a woman cannot be found guilty of the murder of her child within twelve months of its birth if she is suffering from severe postnatal depression.

Organisations that can help include the Association for Postnatal Illness, Parents Anonymous, the Samaritans, and the Meet A Mum Association.

Postnatal check-up

This should take place about six weeks after the birth. This six-week period is known as the **puerperium**, and by the end of the six weeks the reproductive organs should have returned to their proper size. The check-up can be carried out by the woman's own GP, or at the hospital where the baby was delivered.

At the check-up the doctor will:

- check the mother's weight, blood pressure and urine.

- if an episiotomy was needed, check that this is healing.

- give a routine smear test.

- offer contraceptive advice.

- check on the mother's emotional condition.

It is an opportunity for the mother to discuss any problems she may have, physical or mental. It is an important check-up and mothers should insist that it is thorough.

Care of the baby after birth

The newly born baby may have certain odd characteristics that disappear very quickly.

- She may look blue, because she has been deprived of oxygen during the birth. As soon as she starts to cry she draws in oxygen and the blueness disappears.
- She may be covered in slippery vernix (the waxy substance that protects the skin). This washes off easily.
- She may be covered in lanugo (fine hair). This soon comes off.
- She may have a short stump where the midwife has cut the umbilical cord close to the baby's navel. This stump shrivels and drops off within about a week.
- Her head may be flattened by having been squeezed through the birth canal; it may have a small swelling if she was a suction delivery; and there may be bruises and red marks caused by forceps. These should clear up within a few weeks, and the head will become the correct shape. There will be a **soft spot** (**fontanelle**), a diamond-shaped area at the top of the baby's head where the bones of the scalp have not fused together. They will do so within 12–18 months.
- Her eyes may be sticky and bloodshot. This soon clears up. Babies cannot focus their eyes properly and they may look as if they squint, but they soon begin to control their eye movements.
- She may have a birthmark or strawberry mark. Birthmarks are often just red patches which quickly disappear; strawberry marks are raised red patches which sometimes get bigger, but usually disappear after a year or two. Birthmarks are due to the enlargement of tiny blood vessels just below the surface of the skin and usually disappear by the time the child is six months old. Some birthmarks, however, are permanent, such as **port wine stains** (red or purple patches). The GP will give advice on these. They can be camouflaged cosmetically, if they distress the child.
- She may have spots or rashes; most newborn babies develop these. They can be milk rashes or heat rashes or an allergic reaction to certain conditions. Usually they clear up without any treatment, but the doctor at the clinic will give advice.
- She may develop jaundice a few days after birth, and look yellow. This usually clears up very quickly, but a more severe condition will need treatment.

Even with all these conditions the baby will still look beautiful to her parents!

Treatments for the newborn baby

The newborn baby will be weighed and measured, have the diameter of her skull measured, and be examined to see that all physical parts – eyes, ears, nose, fingers, toes, etc. – are normal. This examination will be done immediately after the birth by the midwife or doctor who has delivered the baby. The paediatrician will examine inside the baby's mouth, check her heart and lungs, and feel the abdomen to see there is no swelling and everything is in the correct place. The baby's hips will be checked to see that there is no dislocation, as it is important that treatment is started very early if there is any abnormality. Her bowel movements will be noted – she should have a bowel movement by the end of the first day.

The baby's **reflexes** will also be tested at this stage. A baby will have a spontaneous reaction to certain stimuli. These reactions are called **automatic reflexes**, and they are:

- the **rooting** reflex. If the baby's cheek is touched, she will turn her head to that side and try to locate with her mouth the thing that touched her.

- the **grasp** reflex. The baby will strongly grasp anything put into her hand. Her feet also show the same curling movement.

- the **stepping** reflex. If the baby is held up so that her foot is in contact with a surface, she will bring her other foot up as though stepping or walking.

- the **sucking** reflex. The baby will suck on anything placed in her mouth.

- the **Moro** reflex. When the baby is startled she will fling out her arms, spread out her hands and then clench them.

- the **placing** reflex. When the baby's foot is brought up under the edge of a surface, she will lift her foot and place it on top of the surface.

- the **startle** reflex. When the baby is startled by a loud noise or bright light, she will draw in her arms and clench her fists, and may cry.

These reflexes help to test the baby's nervous system. The reflexes disappear as the baby grows older and more co-ordinated.

After the sixth day of life, a sample of blood may be taken from the baby to be checked by the **Guthrie test** for **phenylketonuria**, which is a rare but treatable cause of mental handicap, and to be tested for thyroid deficiency, which affects growth. A test for cystic fibrosis is being studied and may become a routine screening.

All these tests are important, and must be carried out to make sure that the baby is normal and healthy.

The baby's birth has to be registered within six weeks (three weeks in Scotland) from the day she was born. This must be done at the local Register Office. The Registrar will record the birth and give the parents a birth certificate and a National Health Service number for the baby, with the form to register the baby with a doctor.

Follow-up exercises

Category 1

1 Place these phrases in the correct order to show the process of birth. Arrange them under the headings 'Onset of labour', 'First stage', 'Second stage' and 'Third stage'.

Umbilical cord cut

Baby's head is born

Cervix fully dilated

Baby put to mother's breast

Contractions every 10–15 minutes

Placenta separates from wall of uterus

Baby's nose and mouth are cleared

One shoulder passed through neck of cervix

Plug of blood-stained mucus released from neck of cervix

2 Explain the meaning of the following terms:
- Braxton Hicks' contractions
- the baby's head being engaged
- the transverse position
- Caesarean section
- the waters breaking.

3 *a)* Which of these twin babies would you
expect to be born first?

b) Why?

c) What might happen to the second baby?

d) What type of birth might be necessary for
the second baby's safety?

4 What is a premature birth and what can cause it?

Category 2

5 Describe the ways in which the prospective father can help his partner
during labour. What are the advantages of his being present at the actual
birth?

6 In what circumstances might the following treatments be needed?

- induction
- forceps delivery
- episiotomy
- foetal monitoring

7 How can the new mother regain good physical health and emotional
stability after the birth of her child?

8 . Make a list of the treatments and tests given to the newborn baby.

Category 3

9 Carry out some research into the subject of pain relief during labour. Who
was the first woman in this country to have an analgesic during childbirth
and what was it? Compare it with present-day methods of relieving pain
during childbirth.

8 Looking after the Newborn Baby

Establishing a routine

After the birth of her baby, the mother will stay in hospital for several days. The length of time varies, depending upon how she is, how the baby is, and if there were any complications at birth, but usually five to six days is sufficient. This is a valuable time for the mother to rest and regain her strength, and to become emotionally adjusted. She gets rest from the chores and problems of her home and family. A good maternity unit will see that she has a close contact with her baby and is taught how to feed him, bath him and change his nappy. She will also be able to ask about anything which is worrying her about her own health or that of the baby.

But however well they have been instructed in the hospital, most mothers are nervous and lack confidence when they first get home and the responsibility of a tiny baby is entirely theirs and their partners'. There will be a lot of work to do and it is essential that the mother has:

- plenty of rest
- good, plentiful food and fluids
- sleep
- fresh air and exercise.

These things will help her to regain her normal health, and to get over the hard work of giving birth. She will be dependent upon the willing help of her partner, relations and friends. If her partner can get paternity leave, or if her parents or parents-in-law can take over some of the housework for a week or two, this is a great help.

Within a few weeks she should have developed a daily routine, fitting round the baby's feeds and bathtime, and the needs of the rest of the family. A typical daily routine may be like this:

6.00 a.m.	Baby's first feed of the day.
6.30–7.30 a.m.	Another hour in bed.
7.30 a.m.	Get up, prepare and eat breakfast with the family.
8.30 a.m.	Partner and children go to work and school; clear breakfast things.
9.00 a.m.	Prepare baby's bath and bath baby. *(continued)*

113

10.00 a.m.	Feed.
10.30 a.m.	Wash nappies and do other washing.
11.00–11.30 a.m.	Mid-morning break and rest.
11.30 a.m.	Go shopping or do housework.
12.30 p.m.	Prepare and have lunch.
1.30–2.00 p.m.	Clean and feed baby
2.00–3.30 p.m.	Rest and play with baby; go for walk.
3.30–5.00 p.m.	Housework; prepare evening meal.
5.00 p.m.	Evening meal.
6.00 p.m.	'Top and tail' baby; give bedtime feed.
6.30 p.m. onwards	Hopefully the evening is her own to relax, spend time with her partner and rest of the family.
10.00 p.m.	Feed baby.

This is only an example of the sort of routine a mother can establish, and will vary according to how often the baby needs feeding, whether or not he is a fretful baby, and what the needs of the rest of the family are, but if she tries to organise her time she will get through much better. She should always be able to break her routine if she wishes, so that if it is a lovely day and she feels like going for a walk she should do so and leave the chores for later.

It is important that she has plenty of time for her baby, to establish close maternal bonding and rapport with the child. During the first few weeks she and the baby will be very close, and she will be very preoccupied with his welfare. This closeness is very natural and is sometimes known as **primary maternal preoccupation**. Fathers can become very jealous at this stage and they must be made aware that it is a normal condition, resulting from the mother–baby contact in the womb. After a few weeks these feelings are not so intense.

Whilst the mother is still regaining her strength, there are several ways in which she can save time and energy:

- Cut down on routine cleaning. As long as floors are kept clean and furniture dusted, the polishing, window cleaning, cleaning metals, etc., can be left for a few weeks; or perhaps a kind relative would help occasionally.

- There will be a lot of washing to do, and a washing machine is invaluable. Energy can be saved by not ironing things such as sheets, pyjamas, handkerchiefs, and by letting things drip dry.

- Shopping is very wearing, and concentrating it into one big food shopping expedition weekly or even monthly will cut down on the time and energy it takes. The mother can usually find someone to look after the baby occasionally, and she will be able to buy a few necessities when she takes the baby out in the pram.

- Food preparation is a demanding job, but careful planning will give nourishing meals that are quick and simple. This is a time when packeted, tinned, and frozen foods can be used to advantage. If they are combined with eggs, bread, fresh fruit and vegetables, salads, fresh fruit juice and plenty of milk, the nursing mother will get a balanced diet.
- Friends and relations will all want to see the new baby, but they should not expect to stay, as this causes extra work and stress for the new mother.

This is the time when *labour-saving electrical appliances* are essential. Equipment such as a washing machine, tumble dryer, vacuum cleaner, fridge and deep freeze, food processor or electric blender are all invaluable, and it is much more sensible for grandparents to spend money on one of these as a gift rather than a large, expensive pram or giant soft toy.

Many mothers find it necessary, or may wish, to return to work fairly quickly after the birth. If possible she should remain at home looking after the baby for the first six months. This will allow her time to regain her own strength, breast feed the baby, and establish a close bond and a satisfactory routine. It is hard work running a home, having a job and caring for a new baby, and if she returns to work too soon her physical and emotional state may suffer.

If she does return to work she must make sure that the baby will be well cared for, by the father, a willing relation or friend, or a registered child minder.

Relationships

The mother and father

It is easy at this stage for fathers to feel left out. If they have been involved during pregnancy and the birth they will probably have deep paternal feelings. They should be just as involved after birth, and not only with washing up and doing the shopping! Father and mother can share dressing and bathing the baby, changing nappies, and taking the baby out in the pram. If the baby is bottle fed the father can make up bottles and feed the baby sometimes, and this will give the mother a break and a rest.

One of the important occupations for the father will be to play with the baby, so that there will be a strong bonding between them from the start. Even if the father is out at work and not home until late, opportunities should be made for him to be with his child at some stage every day. Bringing up a child is a shared relationship, not just a job for the mother with the father brought in only when the child is naughty.

Parents do not always agree about how their children should be brought up and cared for, and this can lead to friction and arguments. Some parents are noisy and aggressive when they argue, but the fight is usually soon over. It is not always possible to talk things out rationally and quietly, especially when strong emotions are involved. Children live through these situations and are

115

not unduly harmed by them, as long as they still feel loved and secure afterwards. Sometimes a noisy, quick flare-up is better than long-drawn-out silences in a fraught atmosphere that children do not understand and therefore fear.

The birth of a child should strengthen the relationship between the mother and father, as long as they can both be aware of each other's need to adjust physically and mentally after the birth of the baby. It will take several weeks for the mother to regain her strength, and the demands of the baby will exhaust her. It may be some time before she desires sexual activity, and her partner must be patient.

The extended family

Many grandparents will have been almost as excited by the birth as the parents, especially if it is a first grandchild. It is important that they are encouraged to feel involved, not only in providing presents for the baby, but in looking after him as well and giving the parents a much needed break. Grandparents obviously have experience of looking after children and like to be consulted when problems arise. Some mothers feel jealous and possessive with their babies and resent what they feel is interference from their in-laws, but this is a pity, as babies can benefit greatly from a close, loving relationship with grandparents.

Other members of the **extended family**, such as aunts, uncles and cousins, should also be involved. They help to share the responsibilities of rearing a family, and give the child, as he grows up, feelings of security and continuity. The small **nuclear** unit of mother, father and child that makes up the modern Western family norm can be a very isolated and lonely one, and parents should make an effort to keep in contact with the rest of their relations.

Siblings

A new baby may present problems if there are already other children in the family. The mother and father will have spent time preparing their other children for this new arrival, and they will be looking forward to seeing their new baby brother or sister. However, the first excitement will soon wear off as they realise that the new baby takes up a lot of their parents' time and energy and they will not get the attention they used to have. Much will depend upon the character of the older children. If they are fairly placid, able to play by themselves and feel secure, then they will welcome the new baby with few reservations. For an older child who is very sensitive and used to having the whole of his or her mother's attention, the intrusion of a new baby can be very traumatic, and can result in a jealousy which never really disappears.

Signs of jealousy in toddlers or young children can include:

- clinging to their mother all the time, and not wanting to let her out of their sight.
- not wanting to go to bed, or having nightmares.
- bed wetting, and reverting to babyish ways.
- aggressive behaviour towards the baby and other children.

- temper tantrums and attention seeking.
- becoming withdrawn, moody and unresponsive.

Parents can help to combat this jealousy by:

- setting aside special times especially for the other children.
- the father and other relations giving more time to the other children.
- encouraging the other children to help their mother bath the new baby, prepare his pram, get his clothes out, etc., and giving older children the responsibility of taking the baby for walks and playing with him (under supervision).
- constantly telling the other children how much they are loved and needed.
- never comparing the virtues of the new baby with the poor behaviour or achievements of his brothers and sisters; for example, by saying 'the new baby is already trying to sit up; you weren't doing that at his age'.

Sometimes parents over-indulge their other children, in order to try to avoid jealousy arising. A happy balance should be sought, and parents should remember that it is natural for siblings to be competitive. They will not be all the same – some will have stronger personalities and be natural leaders – but they will all contribute to the development of the others, and help to make each other more independent, caring and generous.

Special requirements of the newborn baby

New parents tend to be terrified at the smallness and fragile appearance of the new baby, but babies are tougher than they appear. When they are born there are quite a lot of things that they can do, and one very useful one is crying. This is their method of letting their parents know that they are in distress, and the signal should not be ignored, as tiny babies do not cry for nothing. These are some of the reasons why a baby cries:

- **Hunger**   If a baby is breast-fed it is difficult to estimate how much milk he has taken, and he may be hungry again quite soon after a feed. A mother will soon come to recognise the hunger cry.
- **Thirst**   A baby may be thirsty and just require a drink rather than being fed.
- **Temperature**   The baby may be too hot or too cold, and therefore uncomfortable.
- **Physical pain**   This may be due to something sticking into him, such as an open nappy pin or a lump in the mattress, or it may be due to a condition such as **colic**. This is usually caused by wind and the inability to digest food properly. Many babies have regular colicky periods, often in the evenings. These may last for the first two or three months, but then usually disappear. The pain cry is usually a sharp scream; the baby becomes red in the face and draws up his legs. It is a different cry from the hunger cry.
- **Fear**   Sudden loud noises, bright lights and sudden movements will frighten a baby and make him cry.

Characteristics of the newborn baby

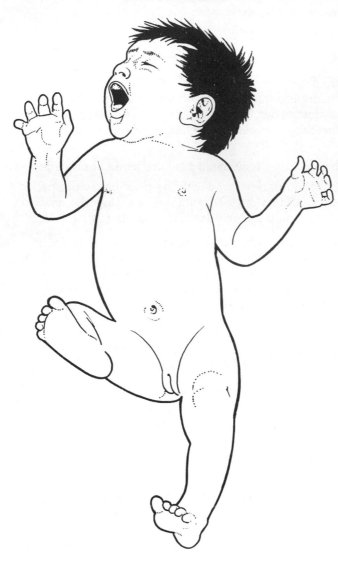

There is a soft spot (fontanelle) at the top of the head.

The head is further developed than the trunk, and a quarter of the trunk's size.

Hair is usually dark, soft and downy, and often rubs off during the first few months after birth.

The eyes do not focus clearly, but the baby can see. Most white babies are normally born with blue eyes, whereas, for example, babies of Afro-Caribbean and Asian origin are normally born with brown eyes.

Fingernails and toenails are complete at birth.

The breasts may be enlarged at birth because of the mother's hormone changes, but will gradually flatten.

The section of umbilical cord protruding from the navel will shrivel and fall off after a few days.

The limbs remain drawn up to the body for some time.

The average weight at birth is 3.2–3.3 kg (7–7½ lb); the average length of a baby is 46–53 cm (18–21 in.).

- **Dressing, undressing and bathing** Many babies do not like these processes at first and will cry, but they will soon get used to them and after a short time will enjoy their bath.
- **Discomfort** This is often caused by a dirty or wet nappy. Some babies cry if they cannot get into their favourite position for sleep. Many babies cry when they are just getting off to sleep.
- **Boredom and loneliness** As the baby gets older and becomes more aware of his surroundings and of other people, he will want to be involved in things. Even small babies can be propped up to look at things going on around them. Often all they want is a cuddle and the close contact of mother.

The remedies for the reasons for crying given on pps 117 and 118 are obvious. Mothers should not leave a baby to 'cry it out' because they are afraid that by picking him up they may be spoiling him.

As well as being able to cry, normal babies are born able to breathe, suck, and eliminate waste, and with their sense receivers (eyes, ears, skin, tongue and nose) in working order. They can relate sounds and sights, and quickly learn the smell and sight of their mother. In the first four weeks of life babies can see different shapes; hear and distinguish noises; recognise different smells; relate sound and sight, and relate sound and touch. They are born with all these basic abilities, and these will grow and develop rapidly with the correct conditions and stimulation.

The following are the essential requirements of a baby. Without them he would either die, or become very ill – physically or emotionally.

- Food
- Hygiene
- Warmth and protection

- Sleep
- Clothing
- Love and security

Food

Breast feeding

We have already discussed the advantages of breast feeding, and how the expectant mother can prepare herself for breast feeding her baby (see p. 92). Any problems that are going to occur usually do so at the beginning. Once mother and baby settle down to a routine, breast feeding is a satisfying and rewarding experience for both.

- The new baby may need help to begin sucking. The midwife will help him to find the nipple and will hold him there until he gets used to the idea of sucking.
- Both mother and baby must be comfortable and well supported. A low arm chair is best, with a cushion to support the mother's arm if needed. The nipple should be well into the baby's mouth and his nose should be clear.

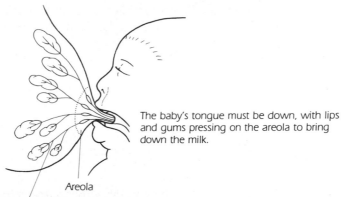

The baby's tongue must be down, with lips and gums pressing on the areola to bring down the milk.

Areola

Tubes bringing milk to the nipple

Breast feeding

- It is normal for the baby to lose a few ounces after the birth (up to 10 per cent of birth-weight), but he will make up his birth-weight within two or three weeks. Some mothers worry that they have not got enough milk, and this can lead them to give up breast feeding. As long as the breasts are stimulated by the baby sucking, there will be sufficient milk produced. If the mother is very anxious, she can **test weigh** the baby to check on his intake. (Test weighing is weighing the baby before the feed and after.) The difference in weight is the amount of milk he has taken.

- To ensure successful breast feeding, the mother should care for herself by having a sensible diet with plenty of calcium-rich foods and lots of fluids. She should wear a good nursing bra, and care for her nipples by applying lanolin cream to keep them soft.

- Cracked and sore nipples can develop if the baby is not feeding in the best position, or if he bites the nipple. Lanolin cream will relieve the cracking, and the baby can just feed from one breast for a while until the other is better.

- At first the baby should be fed when he seems to want it. This is known as **demand feeding**. This may be inconvenient, but he will soon make his own routine. At first he will feed every two or three hours, but later he will fall into the four-hourly pattern of six feeds per 24 hours.

- Breast feeding can only be successful if mother and baby enjoy it. A tense, tired mother will upset the baby. She should try to be calm and relaxed, and use the breast feeding time to establish a close maternal bond.

- A baby can be breast fed up to the age of two or three years, according to the mother's preference. Most mothers in Western countries, however, stop breast feeding when the baby is between nine and twelve months. Even a few weeks of breast milk will give the baby a good start in life. Breast feeds can be topped up with complementary bottle feeds if the mother is unwell and not producing sufficient milk, or if she has to leave him for a short time.

Advice on breast feeding can always be obtained from the midwife or doctor, from the baby clinic, or from the National Childbirth Trust, which prepares information leaflets on the subject.

It may seem that fathers cannot help with breast feeding, but they *can* help by giving the mother encouragement, seeing that she rests and relaxes, and eats the correct diet. Breast feeding should be seen as a natural thing, not as an embarrassing necessity. These days many large shops, public buildings, ladies' toilets and bus, rail and air terminals provide special rooms for nursing mothers, and public opinion is beginning to accept the idea that breast feeding can take place in public.

The nursing mother must remember that some things will be absorbed into her milk and passed on to the baby. She should therefore avoid alcohol, strongly flavoured foods and all drugs unless prescribed by her doctor.

Bottle feeding

There are some mothers who cannot breast feed and some who do not want to do so. Babies can be fed very successfully with dried milk and will thrive just as well, but certain rules must be observed.

- Bottles, teats and equipment used must be absolutely clean and sterile.
- Feeds must be made up exactly as instructed on the dried milk carton, with very careful measuring of powder and water.
- Only boiled water should be used for the food.
- The dried milk should be checked to see that it is not out of date.
- Skimmed dried milk such as Marvel should *not* be used for feeding a baby. Tinned evaporated milk is not recommended. Ordinary liquid cow's milk is only suitable when the baby is over six months old.

Some babies are allergic to cow's milk protein; some of the symptoms are diarrhoea, vomiting, cough, wheezing and eczema. Goat's milk can be used instead of cow's milk, but some infants are allergic to that as well. In any case, it should not be used undiluted before six months old, and extra vitamins and iron may be needed. Soya milks are available for babies who are animal milk intolerant, but a doctor should be consulted first. Dried cow's milk does not contain the immunities that breast milk does and breast fed babies are less likely to suffer from infections, allergic problems or cot deaths.

When being bottle fed, babies should be held very closely. The person giving the feed should talk to and look at the baby to establish love and a sense of security. A baby should *never* be left with a bottle propped up in his mouth, to feed himself.

A knife with a level blade to level off dried milk powder

A scoop from the box of dried milk to measure out the amount needed

A kettle, as water should always be boiled

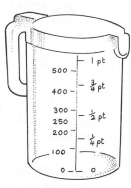

A glass or plastic measuring jug with a clear measuring scale, a good pouring lip and a comfortable handle.

Equipment needed for bottle feeding

Choice of bottles

There are two sizes available, 200 ml (7 fl. oz) and 100 ml (3.5 fl. oz). (There are 20 fl. oz in a pint.) The small size bottle is useful for boiled water and fruit juice.

Bottles may be made from heat-resistant glass or plastic. The plastic ones have the advantage of being unbreakable, lightweight and cheap, but they do tend to get stained and discoloured after much use. Glass bottles remain clear and hygienic looking, but will break if dropped, and can be slippery and heavy to hold. Disposable bottles are available, but are more expensive to use.

All bottles should have a clear measuring guide and be boilable. Those with a wide neck are easiest to fill and to clean.

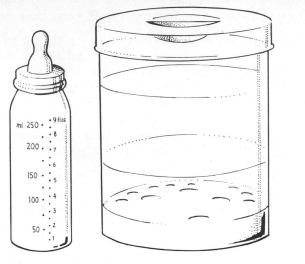

A feeding bottle, teat and sterilising unit

Teats

These are made of rubber and should be shaped to fit the baby's mouth. They should be bought to match the bottle being used, as different bottles have different shapes of teat. The teat can usually be bought with a small, medium or large hole, which will help to regulate the rate at which the baby can suck the milk. A tiny baby will need a larger hole, as he has not got a very strong suck; a hole can be enlarged with a hot, fine needle. Usually a teat has only one hole, but some have three small holes to allow for a faster flow of milk.

Teats will become misshapen quite quickly and will need replacing *every few weeks*. It is sensible to have at least four feeding bottles and teats, so that some can be sterilised whilst others are in use. A complete kit can be bought, which contains a sterilising tank, four bottles, teats and cover cups, a float (to hold bottles down), a measuring jug and a leveller. These are useful as they all fit in together and are convenient when travelling.

Sterilising and cleaning

It is essential to clean and sterilise feeding equipment thoroughly. Babies cannot resist bacteria well and can easily suffer tummy upsets and possibly gastroenteritis, which can be fatal.

After every feed, bottles, teats and equipment must be washed in hot soapy water. A bottle brush must be used to get to the base of the bottle, and the teats should be turned inside out and rubbed with salt to remove particles of milk, then rinsed in cold water before being sterilised.

There are two methods of sterilisation:

- *Boiling* Teats and bottles must be immersed in a large saucepan of water and boiled for ten minutes. They should be left in the same water until needed.

- *Chemical* The chemical may be in the form of a sterilisation tablet which is dropped into the correct quantity of water, or it may be a sterilising liquid which is used with water in the correct proportions. The bottles and teats are immersed in the solution, taking care to see that all the air is out of the bottle, and they are left there until needed (for at least 30 minutes). The solution needs changing daily. Manufacturer's instructions should be carefully read and followed. The bottles and teats may be rinsed before use with *boiled* water, to get rid of the chemical taste.

It is important that bottles and teats are washed and sterilised after every feed.

Making up the feeds

Important points:

- Wash your hands before beginning.
- Read the instructions on the packet and follow the directions carefully.
- Use the scoop provided in the packet. Do not press the milk powder down too closely; this concentrates the food and can eventually cause the baby severe kidney damage. Make sure, however, that the scoop is full, otherwise the milk solution will be too weak.

- Do not add anything, such as sugar, salt or flavourings. The milk has been carefully balanced to give the infant all the nutrients he needs.

- The water used must be boiled and then cooled.

- A full day's food can be made up and the bottles kept in the refrigerator.
- Fold down the top of the bag containing the milk powder and cover with the lid. Store the milk in a cool, dry cupboard.

1 Boil a kettle and allow it to cool

2 Wash hands.

3 Take the bottle and teat out of the sterilising liquid, and rinse with boiled water if you wish.

(*continued*)

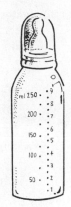

4   Pour the correct amount of boiled water into the graduated bottle. Check against the bottle's measuring scale with the bottle at eye level.

5   Put the required number of scoops of milk powder into the bottle, levelling off each scoop with a straight-bladed knife.

6   Put the teat and cap on to the bottle. Shake well to mix the milk powder and water together.

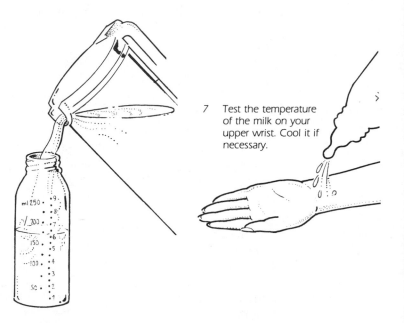

7   Test the temperature of the milk on your upper wrist. Cool it if necessary.

Or Pour the correct number of fluid ounces of water into a measuring jug. Add the required number of scoops of milk powder. Stir well with a sterilised spoon until the powder is mixed in. Pour the milk into the bottle, and put the teat on to it.

When the bottle has been made up, the temperature should be tested by shaking a few drops of milk on to the inside of your wrist. If it is too hot the bottle can be held under running cold water for a few seconds to cool. If the teat is blocked the sides of the teat should be gently rubbed together, but the teat should be held under boiling water afterwards to re-sterilise it. You should never suck the teat yourself to unblock it or test the temperature. If the baby is not quite ready for his bottle it can be kept warm in a jug of boiling water or in an electric bottle warmer. Babies will drink cold milk but seem to prefer it warm.

Giving a bottle feed:

- Sit comfortably and hold the child very close.

- Test the temperature of the feed. Have a cloth ready to wipe up any spills.

- Allow baby to feed, and then gently remove the bottle to allow the air pressure to adjust, otherwise the teat will flatten and the baby will get no milk.

- Always make sure the bottle is tilted sufficiently for the milk to be in the teat, or the baby will be sucking air and will get wind.

- Stop occasionally to burp the baby. This is done by holding the baby over one shoulder and gently rubbing his back, or by sitting him up on your knee and gently patting his back, or lying him face down across your knees and gently rubbing his back. When the baby burps he may bring back a little milk. This is called **posseting** and is quite normal.

Sometimes a baby gets tired and falls asleep during his feed. If gently wiggling his toes or stroking his cheek does not waken him, he has probably had enough. Babies should not be forced to finish up their bottle, just because that is the amount the packet says he should have. He will regulate his own amounts. Any left-over milk should be thrown away, not re-used.

The new baby will need feeding approximately every three hours. He will also require night feeds until he is about 4.5 kg (10 lb) in weight, when he will be on to fairly regular four-hourly feeding. A 4.5 kg (10 lb) baby will be taking 150 ml (5 fl. oz) of food five times a day at about 6.00 a.m., 10.00 a.m., 2.00 p.m., 6.00 p.m. and 10.00 p.m. Breast fed babies will need supplementary vitamins. Vitamin drops are available at the clinic and the health visitor will advise how and when to use them. Babies enjoy a drink of cooled, boiled water, and vitamin C can be introduced into the water by adding orange, blackcurrant or rose-hip juice. The baby should gain weight and show a healthy development on a milk diet for the first four months, at which stage mixed feeding will start.

Hygiene

It is essential that a baby is kept clean and fresh. Bacteria, stale perspiration and dirty nappies can all cause skin rashes and inflammation, which if not treated will cause the baby much distress and could become serious. A baby cannot clean himself, and it is pathetic to see a dirty, smelly baby.

The mother will have been shown the bathing routine in hospital, or by her health visitor, and a baby should be bathed daily if possible before either the 10.00 a.m. or the 6.00 p.m. feed. At first he may be frightened and will scream, but after a few days, and as the person bathing him becomes more confident, the baby will begin to enjoy it. It is an ideal time for parents to talk and sing to their baby and to establish a close contact. It is also an ideal opportunity for the father to be involved, and other children in the family will enjoy the chance to help. If the child cannot be bathed daily, he should be 'topped and tailed' morning and evening. This means cleaning his face and nappy area thoroughly. At every nappy change he will need his bottom and genitals wiped and dusted with baby powder.

General points about bathing

See pp. 80 and 87 for choice of equipment and toiletries.

- Make sure the bath and chair are at a comfortable, safe height. If the bath is resting on a stool, it must be completely stable.

- A baby should *never* be left unattended in his bath, and a small child should not be allowed to bath a baby unattended.

1 Prepare everything first.

- The infant must be supported at all times and held firmly.

- Use good quality soap and toiletries. Cheap ones can cause skin problems.

- The temperature of the water must be tested with your elbow before putting the baby in. It should be just comfortably warm. Have a jug of hot water close by to top up if the water gets cold – but do *not* add it while the baby is in the bath.

- The room must be warm (especially in winter) and free from draughts.

2 Put cold water in the bath, then hot, to a temperature of 85°F/29.4°C.

3 Put on a waterproof towelling apron. Undress the baby on your knee or a changing mat, and wrap him in a warm, soft towel.

- Everything should be ready before bathing begins, including clean clothes and a clean nappy; clean, soft, warm towels (one large and one medium); and a nappy bucket for the baby's dirty clothes.

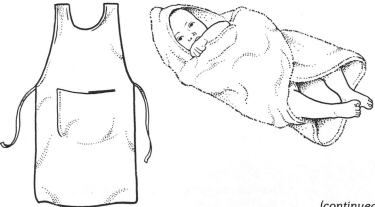

- The baby is usually bathed before his feed, and if he is bottle fed the bottle should be made up ready and kept warm in a jug of water.

- The atmosphere should be calm and relaxed and then the baby will enjoy his bath and feed and will sleep well afterwards.

(continued)

4 Holding the baby firmly on your knee, clean his face with damp cotton wool swabs. Do not use soap.

a Wipe his eyes from inner corner outwards. Use a fresh piece of cotton wool for each eye to prevent transferring any infection.

b Wipe his nose and clean gently. Do not poke cotton wool bud up his nostrils or into his ears.

c Wipe just inside and behind both ears. Use a different swab for each ear.

d Wipe over his face and the folds of his chin.

e Pat his face dry gently with a soft towel or nappy.

5 Tuck the baby under one arm, hold his head over the bath and wash his hair.
Use shampoo only once or twice a week. Rinse well and pat dry.

6 Unwrap the baby from the towel. Keeping him on your knee, soap him all over, especially under his arms, between his legs, and behind his knees. Lower him gently into the warm water and rinse him well.

7 Take the baby out of the bath and put him on a large soft towel on your knee or a changing mat. Pat him dry, especially in the folds of his skin. Apply the talcum powder to his body occasionally. If the nappy area is sore apply zinc and castor cream, and do not powder over it. Dress him in clean clothes and give him his feed.

This bathing routine is suitable for the very young baby, but special care must be taken until the umbilical stump drops off, as it may need special cleansing and a dressing. As the baby gets older and is able to support his head and sit up, he can be put straight into his bath to be washed. It is best to protect the floor at this stage, as babies love to splash!

As the baby's nails lengthen they will need cutting. Only small, round-ended nail scissors should be used. If he will not keep still, you may have to wait until he is asleep to cut them.

Nappies and nappy care

Basically there are two types of nappy, fabric and disposable.

Fabric nappies

- *Muslin squares* are soft and less bulky and therefore very good for tiny babies, but they are not very absorbent. They can also be used as nappy liners inside a terry nappy.
- *Terry nappies* are made from thick, soft, absorbent cotton towelling. The more expensive they are, the better the quality. They are usually 60 cm (24 in.) square, but shaped terry nappies are available, which are finer towelling with a double thickness down the centre panel. They are neater, less bulky and easier to put on, but are more expensive.

Disposables

- *All-in-one* disposables consist of a disposable pad with a one-way lining and a plastic outer cover. Self-adhesive tabs are used to secure them. They may have shaped elasticated legs, and come in five sizes. They are the most expensive of the disposable type.
- *Two-piece* disposables consist of a disposable pad that fits into special plastic pants, which may be tie-on or popper pants. The absorbent pads come in different thicknesses and sizes, and may be bought as separate pads or on a roll to cut off the length needed. These are cheaper than the all-in-one disposables.

Both types have points for and against them, and the parents have to choose which will suit their life style.

Advantages of terry nappies

- They are thick, soft and absorbent.
- If thick, good quality ones are bought and they are carefully washed, they should last through one and possibly two children.
- Used with good plastic pants, they do not leak as easily as disposables.
- They do not need changing quite as often as disposables.
- They can be used for other purposes, as a small towel, for example, or as a bib.
- They are possibly more comfortable than some disposables.

Disadvantages of terry nappies

- They cost a lot of money for the initial outlay of two dozen nappies.
- They have to be washed and sterilised after every use. This is an unpleasant and time-consuming job.
- There must always be a bucket of cleansing solution to soak them in.
- Unless carefully washed they become hard and stained.
- They are bulky, especially for a tiny baby.
- They are difficult for families where the laundry and drying facilities are poor.
- They must be used with waterproof pants.
- The baby can become allergic to the soap powder or fabric softener used.

Advantages of disposables

- They are thrown away after use so no washing is involved.
- The cost of buying is spread out; if bought in bulk they may be cheaper.
- They are very useful if the person caring for the baby is ill, has inadequate washing facilities, is away on holiday or goes out to work, or is travelling with the baby.
- They are much easier to put on and need no nappy pins.
- They are less bulky and are shaped for comfort.
- They are available in different sizes.

Disadvantages of disposables

- They can be expensive.
- They are not as absorbent as terry nappies and tend to leak round the edges.
- They need changing frequently or they go into wet lumps.
- They can block the toilet if not flushed away properly.
- They are bulky to store and to carry home from the shop.

Some manufacturers have a delivery service for disposable nappies, and in some areas there is a nappy washing service for fabric nappies. Many mothers use a combination of both types. They have a good supply of fabric nappies for normal use, and buy disposables for the special occasions described above.

Other necessities are:

nappy liners. These go inside the nappy and help to prevent the nappy staining, make it easier to get rid of the nappy contents, and help to protect the baby's skin. *Ever-dri or one-way liners* are thin, washable liners made from a special material that allows the urine to pass through the liner and be absorbed by the terry nappy. The baby's skin remains dry and there is less risk of nappy rash. *Disposable liners,* made from fine fabric or paper, are designed to be thrown away when dirty. They are sold in packs of 200, and are quite cheap. *nappy pins.* These should have a safety catch, to prevent them springing open while in use. *waterproof pants.* Made from nylon, plastic or PVC, these are used to cover the nappy to protect the baby's clothing. They may be elasticated, or fastened with poppers or side-tie fastenings. Some have frilly nylon covering to make them look prettier. They should be soft and washable and the elastic should not be too tight. Cheap ones go hard and crack after a few washes.

Putting on a nappy

This will depend upon the size and age of the child and the type of nappy. The usual folds are the triangular and the oblong, which are quick and easy, but tend to be bulky and do not have extra thickness where it is needed. Special foldings of nappies take longer to do, but give less bulk round the legs and extra absorbency where it is needed.

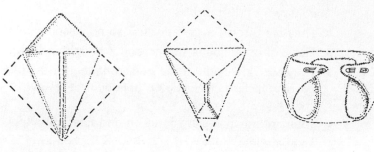

Kite fold

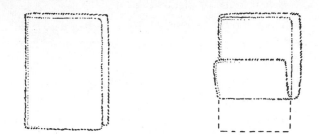

Oblong fold – one third folded up for extra thickness

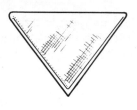 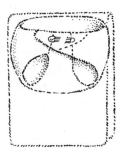

Triangle fold – muslin triangle with terry nappy round waist
like a skirt – useful for a very small baby

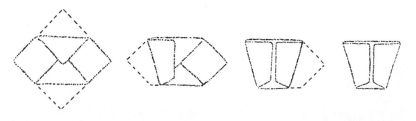

Parallel fold

Special folds for nappies

Care of fabric nappies

All fabric nappies must be sterilised and washed after use. Nappies that are not correctly laundered will cause the baby to develop nappy rash. They can be sterilised by using a special sterilising powder or by being boiled.

Nappy care routine:

- Have two buckets with nappy sanitising solution in them. (Make up the solution exactly as stated in the instructions.) The nappies should be rinsed before being put to soak; then wet nappies can go into one bucket, and soiled nappies into the other. The buckets will need to have lids.
- The nappies should be left for several hours (as instructed on the packet) to clean and sterilise.
- They should then be rinsed several times and dried. They are then ready for use.

The nappies will also need a frequent hot, soapy wash, especially if they become stained. Good quality soap flakes or powder should be used, not a detergent. They can be washed in a washing machine or by hand. Thorough rinsing to remove all the soap is essential, and fabric softener can be added occasionally although some babies may be allergic to it. The nappies should be dried outdoors whenever possible.

Nappy rash

This is very painful for the baby and can develop into a serious condition quickly. The most common kind of nappy rash is **ammonia dermatitis**, when a strong smell of ammonia is present. **Seborrhoeic dermatitis** often starts in the nappy area, making the skin red, shiny and sore.

Causes of nappy rash:

- Dirty nappies may have been left on too long.
- There may be a strong ammonia content in the baby's urine.
- Strong detergents may have been used to wash the nappies, and they may have been insufficiently rinsed.
- The baby may be allergic to fabric softener and to some soaps, powders or creams.
- The baby's skin may be sensitive to waterproof pants, or the elastic round the legs and waist may chafe and cause a rash.

Treatment:

- Cleanse and dry the baby thoroughly after removing the dirty nappy.
- Change the baby's nappies more frequently.
- Leave off plastic pants. Let the baby lie on a towel without his nappy whenever possible.
- Check that nappies are being washed and sterilised properly. Use vinegar in the rinsing water if the rash is ammonia dermatitis.
- Zinc and castor oil cream will relieve minor soreness, but if the condition persists a doctor should be consulted, and will probably prescribe a Nystatin (antibiotic) ointment.

Warmth and protection

The temperature-regulating system of a baby is by no means as efficient as that of an adult, especially in low birth-weight babies and those under 3.6 kg (8 lb). They are best in a room which is at a constant 20–1 °C (68–70 °F). As the baby gets bigger and develops a layer of fat, he is also better able to control his body temperature, and he will be quite happy, if well wrapped up, at temperatures of 16 °C (60 °F).

A baby's body temperature can drop very rapidly and he can quickly develop **hypothermia** (very subnormal body temperature) if he is left outside in his pram or in an unheated room and there is a sudden drop in temperature. The baby's head is large in relation to his body, so it has a relatively large surface area which loses a lot of heat. He should have several layers of lightweight garments or bedding, rather than heavy clothing or blankets that constrict his movements. His extremities, i.e., hands, feet and ears, need extra protection and should always be covered in cold weather. Small babies can be kept warm by being held very close to their mother. Mothers of low birth-weight babies are encouraged to keep them as close to their bodies as much as possible to take advantage of the natural, constant warmth.

If the heating used indoors produces a very dry heat the baby's breathing passages may be affected, and a humidifier should therefore be used, or a container of water placed in front of the heat source.

The baby's cot or pram may be preheated with a hot water bottle, but it should always be removed before the baby is put to sleep to avoid burning the child. Babies can get overheated, especially in summer, but also in winter if the room is overheated and they have too many covers. The baby will then develop a heat rash and be almost as uncomfortable as if he is too cold.

Attention should be given to the fibres used for the baby's clothing and bedding. Natural fibres such as wool and cotton are absorbent, soft and good insulators. Synthetic fibres can be non-porous, cold and clammy.

Sleep

A baby will get the amount of sleep he needs. Some babies seem to need more than others, but on average they spend about 60 per cent of the day asleep. They will have one or two regular waking periods during the day, usually during the afternoon or early evening. They will quickly develop a sleep pattern and routine, and should soon learn to sleep at night-time, especially if the parents put the baby to bed at a regular time in a quiet, warm, darkened room. As they get older they will require less sleep.

Babies will only waken if they are hungry, thirsty, disturbed by loud, sharp noises, in pain, or uncomfortable. After a nappy change, a feed or a drink, or being lifted out to get rid of wind or just to be given a cuddle, they should go back to sleep again. Restless, disturbed babies will often respond to being rocked, soothing music, or being sung to. A very young baby needs the security of being swaddled, i.e., tightly wrapped in a shawl or blanket. He prefers the warmth and comfort of being close to his mother, but this is not always possible. He will soon find his most comfortable position for sleep, which may be on his side or his tummy, but young babies should not sleep on their backs in case they are sick and choke.

Some parents are lucky and have babies who sleep soundly throughout the night. Other babies are wakeful and cry frequently, disturbing their parents who are then short of sleep. Parents should share the responsibility of getting up to a restless baby. It is very frustrating to be constantly disturbed at night and leads to a lot of stress, but if parents can try to relax and remember that this particular phase will not last for ever, they will get through much better.

Clothing

Another obviously essential requirement for the newborn baby is clothing. The sensible parents will have already bought the layette during pregnancy, so that everything will be ready when the baby arrives home. Some new mothers regard their babies rather like dolls to be dressed up to look pretty, but clothing for babies should be functional, and the main considerations are:

- comfort
- safety
- good design
- suitable choice of fabric
- economy
- protection
- washability.

The expectant mother will know the time of year the baby is due, and will buy summer or winter designs accordingly in suitable weight fabrics. The new baby grows very quickly so it is a waste of money to buy expensive first-size garments. Nightdresses, day dresses, Babygros, vests and jackets will all need washing nearly every day; it is therefore important that they are made from easy-care fabrics, needing little or no ironing.

Garments should be easy to get on and off, remembering that babies do not like being dressed and undressed. Wide-necked vests, long back openings on nighties, and popper fastenings along the legs and front of Babygros, all make the job quicker and easier.

It is essential that clothing is checked for safety. Many babies have choked with draw-string necklines or long ribbons used at neck and wrists. They can catch their toes and fingers in openwork lace jackets and shawls. Fluffy wool can be swallowed and be irritating, and some dark colours will run if they are chewed or get damp, which can be harmful. Some chemical dyes can cause an allergic reaction such as a skin rash. Buttons and decorations must be well stitched on or they can come off and be swallowed. Thick seams, bulky gathers, tight elastic, and belts tied round the waist, will all be uncomfortable for a baby who is lying down all the time. Baby wear can be attractive as well as functional, and most chain stores have a good selection of well-designed, safe and comfortable garments.

133

Love and security

The essentials we have discussed so far for the new baby have been physical requirements. Obviously without food, warmth and shelter the baby will die. He will survive if deprived of love and security, but his development will be impaired and he could grow up with severe emotional problems. Observation has shown that babies who do not receive love are unable to be loving people when they grow up, and mothers and fathers who have been ill-treated themselves when young are more likely to ill-treat their own children.

It is normal for a mother to love her child, though the length of time it takes for affection to develop varies. Affection grows during pregnancy and following the birth. Some women feel a strong emotional attachment immediately after the birth, but sometimes, especially if it has been a long, difficult birth, these reactions are delayed because the mother is exhausted. Some mothers experience deeper maternal feelings than others, and some have a very prolonged period of developing attachment. The mother should be allowed to hold her child next to her body and put him to the breast immediately after the birth. During her stay in hospital he should be in a crib at the side of her bed day and night ('rooming-in'), so that she can feed him as and when he needs it and pick him up and cuddle him when he cries.

If the baby needs special care because he is premature, or ill in some way, mother contact should be maintained by letting her care for the baby – cleaning him, changing his nappy, feeding him if possible, and stroking and touching him through the portholes of the incubator.

It has been shown that when strong bonding attachments have been made, babies thrive better, they breast-feed more successfully, their language development is more advanced and there is less chance of ill-treatment by the mother. The bonding is lasting and persists even during temporary separations.

The first person a baby becomes attached to is the person who cares for him physically and loves and cuddles him, and this is usually his mother. Within a few days he can recognise her shape, the outline of her face, her voice and the tones of her voice, and he is sensitive to her individual smell. He will respond to her moods; if she is depressed, angry or happy, he will be frightened, unhappy or content. The more she can keep him in close bodily contact, by using a baby sling when she is working and by nursing him whenever possible; the more eye contact there is; the more she talks and sings to him; the more loved and secure and content he will be.

Although the baby will usually become attached first of all to his mother and will always return to her when he can, after a short time he will form attachments to other people, usually his father and perhaps his grandparents or other relatives he sees frequently. The mother should guard against being too possessive; it is important that the bond between father and child is also given the chance to develop. He will begin to love those who show him love and who comfort him when he is distressed. A child who feels secure in the love and affection of his parents and family will have the confidence to explore other situations and relationships, knowing that his mother (or the person who cares for him in the same way) is always there to return to.

Follow-up exercises

Category 1

1   When the new mother returns home with her baby, how can the following people help her?
father
grandparents
the health visitor.

2   Plan a daily routine for the following families:
   a)   mother, father, new baby, three-year-old who goes to playgroup
   b)   mother, new baby, father who does shift work
   c)   mother, father, new baby, a five-year-old and an eight-year-old

3   Which of the following electrical machines would the new mother find the most useful? Place them in order of importance, giving your reasons.

deep freeze   toasted sandwich maker
electric toaster   washing machine
tumble dryer   microwave cooker
electric blender   food mixer
vacuum cleaner

4   From the dishes listed below plan two days' balanced menus suitable for a nursing mother:

green salad   cheddar cheese
beans on toast   beef curry
fresh milk   poached egg
macaroni cheese   coffee
liver and bacon   pickled onions
chicken casserole   fresh fruit juice
sprouts   crispbreads
wholemeal bread   tomatoes
stewed apple   sandwich cake
white cobs   rice pudding

5 If these letters had been written to the problem page of a woman's magazine, and you were Trish, how would you answer them?

a) Dear Trish,
   I have just returned from hospital with my new baby. Instead of being as happy as I thought we would be, my husband and I are always quarrelling about how to look after the baby, and then he goes out to the pub and leaves me all alone.
   What should I do?

b) Dear Trish,
   My mother-in-law is staying with me to help after the birth of my baby. She is very kind, but she will interfere and try to make me do what she did when she brought up her kids. I have my own ideas and ways. The whole thing is making me upset and weepy.
   What shall I do?

c) Dear Trish,
   I have a lovely new baby who keeps me very busy. I do not have as much time for my 2½-year-old, who seems to be especially naughty just now. I caught him pulling apart his new sister's teddy bear yesterday. How should I treat him?

6 Copy out and complete these sentences about the newborn baby:
   a) The average new baby weighs _____ .
   b) The average new baby is _____ in length.
   c) The eyes of the new white baby are _____ in colour.
   d) The baby's navel will have _____ .
   e) The hair of the new baby is _____ .

7 Give *four* reasons why a new baby could be crying and say what his mother should do about it.

8 Explain the meaning of the following terms:
   Sense receivers
   Test weigh
   Demand feeding
   Make up his birth-weight
   Four-hourly feed pattern
   Complementary bottle feeds.

9 Spot the mistakes! Copy out the following description of the bathing routine, and underline all the things that are *wrong* in it. There are at least six.

Get everything ready first including clean clothes and nappy, toiletries and the bath. Put the water in the bath, hot water first and then cold. Put on a plastic apron lined with towelling and undress the baby, putting the dirty nappy in a bucket of soapy water. Wrap the baby in a warm towel. Wash the baby's hair first, using a little baby shampoo, and pat the hair dry. Then wash the baby's face, starting with the eyes and using a piece of cotton wool for each eye. Clean his nostrils, his ears and round his mouth. Use a flannel and soap to wash his face. Dry well.

Unwrap the baby, place him in the bath and soap him all over. Take him from the bath and dry him well. Apply talcum powder; if the nappy area is sore apply cream and powder it well. Leave him to kick a little before dressing him.

10 Which is the correct answer, *i*), *ii*) or *iii*)?

a) If a baby cannot be bathed *every* day he can be
   i) given a bath once a week.
   ii) topped and tailed morning and evening.
   iii) powdered with a lot of talc.

b) To see if the bath water is the correct temperature the person bathing the baby should test it with
   i) his or her elbow.
   ii) his or her hand.
   iii) a thermometer.

c) Trimming the baby's nails should be done with
   i) a nail file.
   ii) pointed nail scissors.
   iii) round-ended nail scissors.

d) The stump of the umbilical cord will
   i) shrivel and drop off.
   ii) draw into the abdomen.
   iii) need to be removed.

e) A baby can be left in his bath unattended
   i) if the person bathing him will only be gone a few minutes.
   ii) if his small brother or sister is with him.
   iii) under no circumstances.

f) Breast fed babies need supplementary
   i) carbohydrate.
   ii) calcium.
   iii) vitamins.

11 Give the advantages and disadvantages of using:

- nappy liners
- sterilising solution for nappies rather than boiling them
- disposable nappies.

12 How would you recognise:

- a heat rash?
- nappy rash?
- a milk rash?

What treatment would you give in each case?

Category 2

13 *a)* What is the name given to the type of family who live at No. 1?

b) What is the name given to the type of family who live at No. 2?

c) What are the advantages of living in the type of family who live at No. 2?

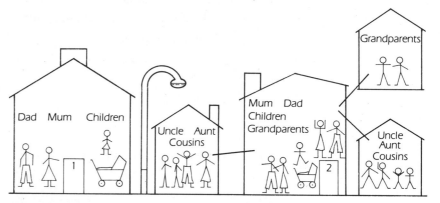

14 Write a specimen letter to your MP about the lack of facilities for nursing mothers in public places, suggesting what should be done about it.

15 Make a survey of the different types of dried milk for babies. Compare the prices, including those from the health clinic. Study the instructions on the tin and see if they are clear. How much would it cost to feed a 5.4 kg (12 lb) baby for a week on dried milk?

16 Write a paragraph about each of the following:

a) Keeping tiny babies warm.

b) The sleeping habits of young babies.

c) The choice of safe, comfortable clothing for young babies.

Category 3

17 Why are love and security so essential for a young baby? How can bonding be established?

SECTION D **Physical Development**

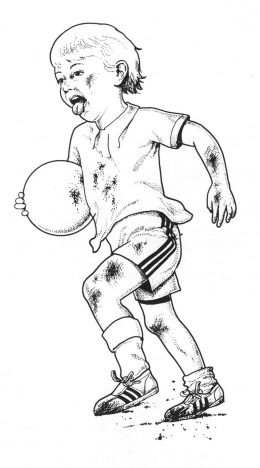

9 Stages of Physical Development

During the first twelve months of children's lives, they will grow and develop more rapidly than at any other stage. From being totally dependent babies they will, by the time they are one-year-olds:

- be able to crawl and possibly walk.

- be able to pick things up and offer them to other people.

- be able to say a few words and understand a lot more.

- be able to drink from a cup, put things in their mouths and join in normal family meal times.

- have several teeth.

- show pleasure in the company of other people, by cooing and gurgling.

- be exploring places and things and getting into mischief.

- be developing their own personality and basic temperament.

- like to sit and listen when pictures and objects are pointed out.

- be able to understand, and be upset, when people are cross with them.

Some children develop rapidly in one skill, such as walking and balance, and slowly in another, such as speech. This does not mean they are gifted in one and retarded in the other; it just means they are developing at their own pace. There are average ages at which children will be expected by their parents and the health clinic to have attained certain skills, but this is only a rough guide, and parents should not worry if their children appear slow at attaining these goals.

Development is likely to be quicker and fuller if children are given the correct environment, stimulation, facilities and physical necessities, as well as the right encouragement. If children are deprived of these things their development will be retarded, perhaps permanently.

For the sake of convenience the child's development is usually divided into four areas:

1 Physical development
2 Intellectual development
3 Social development
4 Emotional development

These areas are in fact all inter-related and dependent upon each other.

Physical development describes the growth and care of the child's body. This includes:

- height, weight, vision, hearing, teeth and bones.
- locomotion – sitting, crawling, standing and walking.
- co-ordination – muscular; manipulative; hand/eye.

Healthy physical development depends upon:

- a well-balanced diet.
- exercise, fresh air, rest and sleep.
- suitable clothing.
- well-chosen toys and activities.
- the prevention and treatment of illnesses and disease.
- safety in the child's environment.

All this is dependent upon the knowledge, good sense and care of parents and others who look after young children.

Height and weight

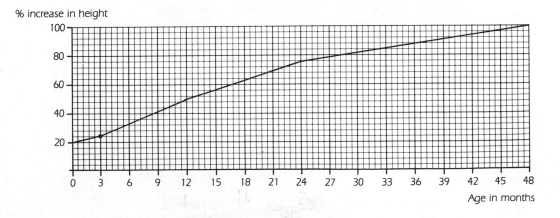

Average height increase from birth to four years

Height in cm

Height in inches

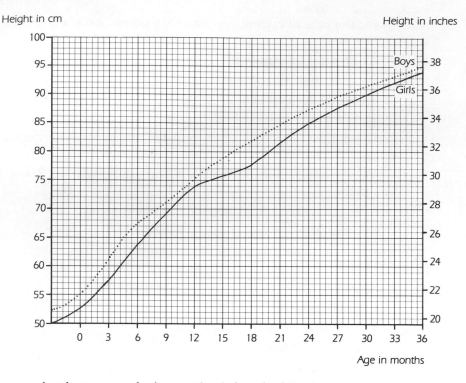

Age in months

Average height increases for boys and girls from birth to three years

- What does the second chart tell you about the difference in the rate of height increase of girls and of boys?

Immediately after birth the baby loses a few grams. This weight is put back on during the next one or two weeks.

This chart is only a rough guide, as children can lose weight through illness or overactivity. Weight increase is not necessarily a sign of health, however, since a thin child may be much healthier than a fat one.

% increase in weight

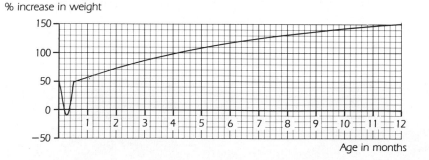

Age in months

Average weight increase from birth to one year

● Why do you think there is a difference in the rate of weight increase of girls and of boys?

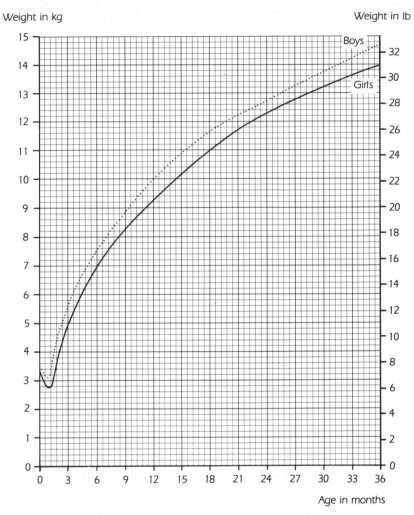

Average weight increase for boys and girls from birth to three years

Vision and hearing

Vision

It used to be thought that babies could not see very well and put no meaning to what they did see. We now know that babies, although short-sighted and unable to focus very well, can see quite adequately and can take an interest in the things they see. They will spend longer looking at something that is patterned, textured or moving than at a plain, untextured or static object.

The eye muscles of newborn babies are very weak, making it difficult for them to focus. They only see things clearly that are about 20 cm away from their faces. The images babies receive are blurred and flat, and, as they do not distinguish colour clearly, the colours are muted. However, even at only a few hours old, babies follow interesting objects with their eyes. Because they are more stimulated by pattern and movement, they enjoy looking at faces, and especially faces that soon become familiar to them, such as their parents'.

The general pattern of vision development

- *From birth to six weeks*   The baby can see things fairly clearly only at a distance of 20 cm, and will concentrate on objects that interest her (because they are moving, patterned, or have depth) for a few seconds. As the baby is unable to move her head easily, she will only focus on objects within her line of vision.

- *From six weeks*   The baby can focus on an object held about 45 cm away from her eyes. If the object is moved from side to side she will follow it with her eye movements – this is referred to as **tracking**. She will look at an object very seriously, but if she sees a person she is familiar with, she may respond with smiles and cooing noises.

- *From three months*   The baby will stare fixedly for several minutes at an object, so learning what familiar objects look like. She can control her head movements better and will be able to turn her head to look at things, and will therefore enjoy cot toys and mobiles. When she is in her pram at home or on a walk, she can be propped up to watch things that interest her.

- *From six months*   The baby will be learning to co-ordinate her eyes with her movements. She will reach out for a moving object; she will be curious about new sights and will concentrate deeply on new toys and objects. She will be very interested in her own hands and feet, examining her fingers and trying to grasp her feet as she waves them in the air.

- *From eight months*   The baby will be able to see very small objects and her eyes will be able to pick out fine detail. Her eyes will have the same range and abilities as an adult's.

The baby's vision can be stimulated right from the start by surrounding her with interesting pictures and mobiles, by moving objects across her pram and cot, and by putting a mirror on the nursery wall and on the side of her bed. As the baby uses her eyes she is learning.

Hearing

Research has shown that babies can hear well before they are born. When they are in the womb they listen to their mother's heart-beat and digestive noises, to blood being pumped through her body, and to her voice. After birth, a recording of these noises will help to calm a fretful baby. A young baby will react to a sudden, loud noise by first remaining still and widening her eyes, and then crying. She will respond to her mother's voice with more interest than to her father's, because she is generally more familiar with it, and seems to prefer the quieter, more musical tone.

The general pattern of hearing development:

- *From four months* As the baby begins to be able to move her head about, she will try to locate the source of a sound and turn towards it. She will also begin to recognise different sounds and will be able to associate them with pleasant or unpleasant experiences; for example, she will recognise the sounds associated with food. She will begin to respond to a familiar voice with cooing noises and then with babbling sounds; this is the beginning of developing language and conversation.

- *From seven months* The baby will turn her head sharply to locate a quiet noise and will quickly discover where the sound came from. She will associate different noises with things (for example, a rattle or musical toy and their sounds) and different voices with particular people.

- *From nine months* The baby will listen to quiet noises such as a watch ticking, and will understand simple commands and words.

Parents can soon discover the sounds that please and interest their baby and can use these sounds to soothe her, to interest her and to stimulate the development of language.

Teeth and bones

Teeth

Most people have two sets of teeth during their lives, some only have one set and very rare cases have been recorded of people having three sets.

The first set of baby teeth (or milk teeth) are formed during pregnancy. They usually start to come through the gums about six months after the baby is born, although it is not uncommon for a baby to be born with one tooth, and some babies, especially twins, triplets and premature babies, do not cut them until 10–12 months. Most children have their full set of 20 milk teeth by the time they are three years of age. The order in which the teeth appear is usually as shown here.

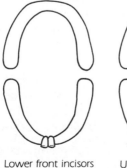  

| Lower front incisors (cutting teeth) | Upper front incisors | Lateral incisors |

6–8 months   1 year

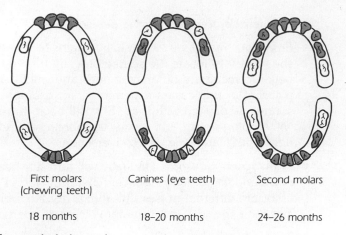

First molars   Canines (eye teeth)   Second molars
(chewing teeth)

18 months   18–20 months   24–26 months

Signs that show a baby's teeth are on the way include:

- fretfulness and grizzling.
- dribbling – very often there is an increase in the amount of saliva.
- chewing her fist or any hard object.
- a red cheek or cheeks.

Teething does not cause convulsions (fits), stomach upsets, fever, loss of appetite or bronchial complaints, as has been previously believed, but it can be painful and uncomfortable so a parent can help by:

- giving the child hard things to chew such as rusks, raw carrots, or a teething ring.
- seeing that the baby wears a hat to help keep her head warm when she goes out, and avoiding cold winds and draughts.
- giving the baby plenty of fluids to drink.
- only giving pain relief, such as paracetamol mixture, when really necessary. Commercial teething preparations are not advisable as they may have side-effects. Gentle massage of the gums with the little finger will give relief.
- giving the baby as much love and cuddling as possible.

It is just as important to protect these first teeth as the permanent teeth that follow. There are three important factors in the care of teeth: diet, cleaning, and prevention and treatment of decay by a dentist.

Diet
Sweet sticky foods will cause dental decay. A child's food should not be over-sweetened; she should not be taught to regard sweets as a reward; she should not be given a lot of sweet drinks; and she should not have a dummy which has been dipped in jam, honey or any other sweet substance.

A child's diet must include plenty of foods that contain calcium and Vitamin D, which are essential for healthy teeth and bone structure. These are the dairy foods such as milk and cheese, as well as eggs and cereals. Vitamin D is also formed in the skin by the action of sunlight.

Cleaning

As soon as the first teeth begin to appear, the child should be bought a small toothbrush with a small head and soft bristles and be taught how to clean her teeth. It is not necessary to brush just up and down; any rotating movement can be used as long as the teeth are cleaned regularly. A child can be encouraged to brush frequently by being bought a specially shaped toothbrush (some have bells in the handle), and flavoured toothpaste. If a child sees her parents and family brushing their teeth it will encourage her to do so, until a habit has been formed.

Fluoride is a mineral that is present in drinking water, either naturally or because it has been added, and helps to prevent tooth decay. If there is not much present in the drinking water in their area, parents can obtain fluoride drops or tablets that can be given daily to babies, or, when the children get older, fluoride toothpaste can be used. Too much fluoride, however, can harm teeth, so parents should get advice from their dentist on whether or not fluoride supplements are needed in their district. It is the plaque that forms on teeth that causes tooth decay. This plaque feeds on sugary foods and forms acids which eat into the tooth enamel, so it is important that the teeth should be cleaned after every meal.

Treatment by a dentist

Parents should try to select a dentist who is sympathetic to the needs of small children and specialises in preventative dentistry as well as corrective treatment. Even small children can benefit from going to the dentist's when their parents go, to get used to the dentist and to dental equipment. Parents should be as relaxed as possible as any nervousness will transfer to the child.

Sympathetic dentists will allow the child to ride in the chair and examine the equipment. They will begin to examine the child's teeth every six months from about the age of three years. A child should not require fillings if correct care is given to the teeth regularly from an early age.

Bones

Bones, like teeth, require sufficient Vitamin D and calcium in the diet to develop and become strong. A shortage of these nutrients will result in **rickets**, a vitamin deficiency disease that causes the bones to soften and results in bowed legs. It is rare in the UK now, although it is present in some Asian children, due to lack of sun on the body, and a diet that does not help the body absorb calcium easily.

Locomotion

To be able to walk means that the child has learnt and developed a whole range of skills. The brain triggers the nervous system to produce the necessary movements, as the reflex actions the baby is born with are gradually replaced by controlled actions. The baby's movements will appear jerky at first, but with practice co-ordination will become smoother.

The general pattern of development

- *A newborn baby* lies in the foetal position, curled up with arms and legs tucked in. Her head is floppy and she needs supporting.
- *A one-month-old*, if placed on her tummy, will attempt to raise her head and look around.
- *At two months* the baby will be able to raise her head and hold it up for a few minutes.
- *At three months* the baby's neck is stronger. She may prop herself up on her arms and when held will turn her head to look around.
- *At four months* she may be able to roll from side to side and on to her back.
- *At six to eight months* she will be able to sit up unsupported and bend her body round.
- *By nine months* she will push herself onto hands and knees when put on her front, and will eventually start crawling.
- *By ten months* she will be trying to pull herself up by the furniture.
- *By one year*, nine out of ten babies can walk by holding on to the furniture, and with a toddle truck three out of ten can take a few steps by themselves. They are still very unsteady and often revert to crawling for speed.
- *By eighteen months* most babies can walk quite well. They may also be able to bend down to pick things up, and push and pull their toys along.

These ages are only a guide. Many children are slower than this, or have longer gaps between each stage. Some babies are more adventurous and active than others, and they will be much quicker to walk than placid, cautious babies. Lazy babies can be encouraged to walk by putting desirable toys out of reach. The use of baby-walkers is discouraged because they can be very dangerous.

When they have reached the walking stage, children should be given opportunities to develop their walking and running skills. They should play in the garden or an open space such as a park, and be encouraged to paddle and make swimming actions at the baths. This is also a way of releasing some of their energy.

Once a child has mastered the skill of walking she will proceed to more complex activities in her own time.

- *At eighteen months* the child can usually walk well and is attempting to run. She can walk up steps holding someone's hand, and walk backwards. She can push and pull her toys along.
- *At two years* the child can run about well, without bumping into things. She can climb up and down stairs and climb on to furniture. She can kick a ball, but balance is still a bit unsteady.
- *At two-and-a-half to three years* the child can jump, stand on tiptoe, climb and swing. She can ride a tricycle and balance on one leg.

1

The new baby lies curled in a foetal position.

2 *Age three months*

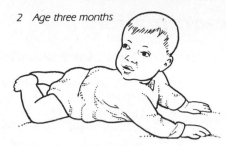

The baby can raise her head and look around.

3 *Age six months*

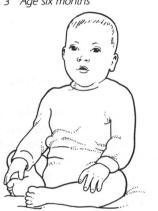

The baby can sit unsupported for a short time.

4 *Age nine months*

The baby can crawl quite well.

5 *Age ten months*

The baby can pull herself up by the furniture.

6 *Age twelve months*

The baby is beginning to walk.

Development of movement

Co-ordination

Muscular co-ordination

From making jerky, unco-ordinated, unreasoned movements, the young baby has to learn how to control her body so that the muscular movements will be controlled and finely adjusted. Messages from the brain, via the nervous system, make the muscles work and with constant trial and practice the baby acquires the necessary basic muscular co-ordination.

This co-ordination begins at the top – with the head, then the trunk, then the arms and finally the legs. The baby first learns how to control her head movements, how to raise her head and turn it from side to side. Then she learns to control her upper body, arch her back and sit up. After that, her arm and hand movements will become less wild and the movements will be used for a purpose. Finally she will be able to pull herself on to her legs and start walking.

These progressive steps in acquiring skills are known as **milestones** and parents usually watch eagerly for the various stages and are proud if their child achieves them early; but the baby will only progress from one stage to the next when she is ready to do so. It is no sign of superior intelligence if she achieves a physical skill a few weeks earlier than another child. Minor clumsiness or poor co-ordination can, however, be signs of minimal brain damage, and skills which come naturally to most children may have to be taught to a child who finds difficulty with them.

Manipulative co-ordination

A baby has to learn how to use her hands – how to develop manipulative skills.

- She is born with strong reflexes (see p. 110), one of which is the grasping reflex, which means that for the first eight to ten weeks her hands will be tightly curled up and will only open when touched. This reflex disappears by the age of three months and she will then hold open her hands loosely, and grasp and hold an object put into her hands for a few seconds.

- *By four to five months* the baby will reach out for an object and try to grasp it, at first awkwardly between two hands or between the palm and two fingers of one hand. This grasp gradually becomes more sensitive and she learns how to pick up small objects between thumb and fingers (**primitive pincer grasp**).

- *From six to nine months* the baby's hand movements become much more skilful. She will be able to pick up objects, hold them in front of her face, and transfer them to her mouth. She can transfer things from hand to hand and offer them to other people, and can separate her fingers and use them for poking and prodding. She enjoys the feel of things and the actions of grasping and exploring with her hands.

- *By nine to twelve months* the baby is using her hands much more precisely. She can squeeze, clap, grasp, pick up very tiny objects, slap and thump. She can pick things up between the tip of her forefinger and thumb (**mature pincer grasp**), she will enjoy playing with bricks and will be able to place one brick on top of another.

- *By a year to 15 months* the baby will be able to grasp a crayon and make a mark on paper. She will be able to imitate actions, such as hair brushing, and will be able to feed herself with a spoon and pick up a beaker of milk. She will be able to release objects as well as hand them to people.

- *By 15 to 18 months* the baby can build a tower of three bricks, turn the pages of a book, use a comb and toothbrush and enjoys toys where shapes are fitted into holes, such as a posting box.

- *By two years old* the baby is a much more independent character. She will attempt to dress herself; she can twist things with her hands; she can wash and dry her hands. She likes construction toys, simple jigsaws and building bricks.

- *By three years old* a child's co-ordinating skills are advanced. She can perform tasks that need fine muscular co-ordination, such as drawing with a pencil, painting, cutting paper, threading beads, undoing buttons, and precise use of pots and cutlery for feeding. She enjoys helping with household tasks and doing things independently. Parents can help and can show how things are done, but they should allow the child to try to do things for herself.

It is by this stage that the child will be showing whether she is right- or left-handed. This is often a hereditary characteristic and it is pointless to try to make a left-handed child use her right hand. Left-handedness can be a slight disadvantage, as most equipment and tools are designed for right-handed people, but trying to force a left-handed child to be right-handed can cause severe psychological problems, which could result in physical and emotional problems.

Hand/eye co-ordination

It takes several weeks for a baby to bring together the skills of sight and manipulation and to realise that the object she sees can be grasped with her hands.

- *At six weeks* the baby will be focusing on objects up to 25 cm (10 in.) away. She will not yet be able to control her hands and arms.

- *At two to three months* the baby can focus a little better and will be interested in watching her hands waving about.

- *At three to four months* the baby will start to reach out for moving objects, but will not yet be able to grasp them.

- *By six months* the baby can move her eyes in any direction and focus well, and she will reach out and try to grasp an object. She has learnt to co-ordinate eye and hand movements in order to pick up an object.

These stages of physical development cannot be rushed, but they can be helped and encouraged by sensible choice of activities, games and toys for the child. The section on play (p. 179) looks at the way physical development can be helped through the correct choice of activities and toys.

Developmental testing

The people in the best position to know whether a child is developing properly are the parents. They will soon become concerned if they think that their child cannot see or hear properly, cannot co-ordinate her muscles or is very slow at talking or walking. A good safeguard is to take the child to the local child welfare clinic. Here she will have regular checks from specialist doctors, who will check her physical, emotional and mental progress.

Routine developmental testing can be carried out at child welfare clinics, health centres, hospital clinics, day nurseries and special schools, usually at three months, six months, nine months and one year. The tests are carried out using simple equipment and observation, and with information from the child's parents, to assess the child's basic abilities and development. If any physical or mental abnormality is suspected the child will then be given a more detailed examination. A chart such as the one shown below may be used to check the baby's progress.

Month	Motor	Social	Hearing and speech	Eye and hand	Month
1	Head erect for few seconds	Quieted when picked up	Startled by sounds	Follows light with eyes	1
2	Head up when prone (chin clear)	Smiles	Listens to ball or rattle	Follows ring up, down and sideways	2
3	Kicks well	Follows person with eyes	Searches for sound with eyes	Glances from one object to another	3
4	Lifts head and chest prone	Returns examiner's smile	Laughs	Clasps and retains cube	4
5	Holds head erect with no lag	Frolics when played with	Turns head to sound	Pulls paper away from face	5
6	Rises onto wrists	Turns head to person talking	Babbles or coos to voice or music	Takes cube from table	6
7	Rolls from front to back	Drinks from a cup	Makes four different sounds	Looks for fallen object	7
8	Tries to crawl vigorously	Looks at mirror image	Shouts for attention	Passes toy from hand to hand	8
9	Turns around on floor	Helps to hold cup for drinking	Says 'Mama' or 'Dada'	Manipulates two objects at once	9
10	Stands when held up	Smiles at mirror image	Listens to watch	Clicks two bricks together	10
11	Pulls up to stand	Finger feeds	Two words with meaning	Pincer grip	11
12	Walks or side-steps around pen	Plays	Three words with meaning	'Holds' pencil meaningfully	12

People who may look after the child include:

- a paediatrician, who specialises in the general health of the child.
- a psychologist, who specialises in the child's emotional and mental development.
- an audiologist, who specialises in hearing problems.
- an ophthalmologist, who specialises in visual development.
- a speech therapist, who deals with assessing speech problems.

Baby clinics

These are known as child health clinics, child welfare centres, and well baby clinics. They are run by the local health authority, or may be part of the local health centre, run by the general practitioner. They may be held in modern, purpose-built accommodation attached to a hospital or health centre, or they may be held in a church hall or any available room. The health visitor will tell the new parents about their local baby clinic and the facilities it offers. It is sensible for all new parents to attend, especially with a first baby, as they will receive expert guidance. These are the services that are usually provided:

- Development is checked at regular intervals, and records of the development are kept.
- Advice is available on general matters, such as feeding, sleep and minor health problems.
- The baby will be weighed at each visit and a record of her weight kept.
- Any problems to do with the child's health will be referred to a specialist where necessary.
- The mother may obtain contraceptive advice or discuss family problems.
- An immunisation programme against infectious diseases will be offered.
- Milk powder, cod-liver oil, vitamin drops, perhaps Marmite, etc., will be on sale at cheaper prices than in the shops.
- Social facilities such as mother and baby groups, drop in clubs and crèches are advertised, and there are opportunities to get to know other mothers.
- Information is available about local activities and groups especially for mothers with young children, such as playgroups, the Church Young Wives' Group, La Leche League, etc.
- Very often there is a notice-board that advertises second-hand baby equipment and clothing, and the services of baby sitters and baby minders.

Parents may take their children to the baby clinic as often as they wish, without an appointment. They will receive a card on which will be recorded the baby's weight, details of immunisations and general progress. The clinic nurse or health visitor may be telephoned outside clinic hours, if advice is needed.

Follow-up exercises

Category 1

1 If a baby boy is 50 cm (20 in.) long when born, how long would you expect him to be when he is:

    a) six months?   *b)* one year?   *c)* two years?

2 If a baby girl weighs 3.2 kg (7 lb) when born, what might she weigh at:

    a) six months?   *b)* one year?   *c)* two years?

3 Copy out the words from the following list that apply to the vision of a new baby.

blurred
unable to see things beyond 20 cm (8 in.)
poor focus
poor distinguishing of colour
eye muscles weak

4 Give the approximate age at which a baby:

    a) can see very small objects.

    b) can turn her head to look at things.

    c) can co-ordinate eyes and movement.

    d) can focus on an object held about 45 cm (18 in.) away.

    e) has almost fully-developed vision.

5 Which of the following sounds will soothe and which will frighten a baby?

    a) a saucepan being dropped

    b) music on the radio

    c) the front door bell

    d) a dog barking

    e) mother's voice

    f) the vacuum cleaner

Give some further examples of soothing and frightening noises.

6 True or false?

    a) Red cheeks may be a sign that a baby is teething.

    b) A baby can have fits when teething.

    c) There are 22 teeth in a set of baby teeth.

    d) A baby who is teething needs hard things to chew on.

    e) To have good teeth children need plenty of iron in their diet.

    f) Fluoride helps to prevent tooth decay.

    g) A child needs a toothbrush with soft bristles.

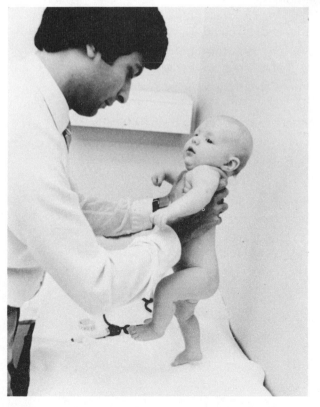

A baby clinic

7 Give three ways in which a child can be helped to overcome any fear of the dentist.

8 Draw pictures of the baby to show the stages of locomotion at three months, six months, nine months, and twelve months.

9 What is meant by 'hand/eye co-ordination'?
Describe the stages of development of hand/eye co-ordination.

Activities

1 Write a story which you could tell to a two- or three-year-old which would encourage her to care for her teeth.

2 Do a survey to find out the proportion of people in your class who are left-handed. Make up a questionnaire to find out what it is like to be left-handed. Include such questions as:

Did (or do) your parents try to encourage you to use your right hand?

Are you ambidextrous (able to use both hands equally well)?

What are the worst features of being left-handed?

What special equipment is there for left-handed people?

Make a summary of your findings.

3 Try to make a visit to your local baby clinic.

How many of the services described in this book are available there? Are there any others that are not on the list?

Which of the people listed here are there to help? Are there any others, not on the list?

Why would you advise mothers to go regularly to their local baby clinic?

10 Conditions for Physical Development

Food

To ensure good physical development, the child will need a healthy diet and proper food preparation.

A healthy diet

The only food a baby needs for the first few months is milk. **Weaning** is the term used to describe the process of gradually reducing the amount of milk feeds and introducing solid foods. This is the start of **mixed feeding**.

Very often a parent may be tempted to start weaning the baby too early, thinking that milk is insufficient. Although many babies feel the need for solid foods at about four months, breast and bottle milk contain sufficient nutrients for the first six months of life. The following are possible results of starting mixed feeding before the child needs it:

- It can reduce the baby's desire to suck and therefore cause less breast milk to be produced.
- As the child's digestive tract is not fully developed for the first three months the food will be largely undigested and digestive troubles can be caused.
- Strain will be put on the baby's kidneys.
- The baby may develop allergies to certain protein foods, or develop coeliac disease, due to an intolerance of the protein **gluten** which is present in some cereals.

When a baby shows obvious signs that his milk feeds are not filling him, if he keeps chewing his fists and cries for his bottle well before it is due, he will be ready to start on solid foods.

Weaning and mixed feeding should be very gradual processes. Choose the 10.00 a.m. or 2.00 p.m. feed to introduce the new food, before giving the baby his milk. Start straight away with spoon feeding, not by adding cereal to his bottle. Give one or two teaspoonfuls of rice cereal mixed to a runny paste with breast or bottle milk *or* fruit or vegetable purée *or* strained broth. All food given should be a smooth purée free from lumps.

The baby will probably not like it at first as it is a new experience. He should *never* be forced to eat. Take things slowly and go at his pace. If he obviously does not want to try it, give him his milk and try the new food a few days later.

Try to maintain a relaxed atmosphere – if the parent is tense at meal times then the baby will be too.

As the amount of solid food increases, the number of milk feeds decreases, and the baby will need plenty of fluid in the form of water and fruit juice.

As the baby becomes accustomed to the idea of solid foods, new flavours can be gradually introduced, although babies do not usually like highly spiced foods. After a time it will be possible to plan for the child to get a balanced diet from solid foods alone, including all the nutrients.

Healthy food habits start when the baby first begins mixed feeding. The diet must contain enough fibre to provide the roughage necessary for satisfactory bowel movements. This means using unrefined ingredients such as wholemeal flour and bread, wholemeal rice and pasta, and fibrous fruit and vegetables. The necessary protein can be obtained from cheese, milk, eggs and fish, with just small amounts of meat. There is an increasing trend in the UK towards a vegetarian diet, and babies and young children can thrive perfectly well on a balanced meatless diet that contains eggs and dairy products, pulses and vegetables, to provide enough protein. Salt and sugar should be avoided; babies are not born with a desire for them, and too much of either can damage health by leading to excess weight or higher blood pressure in the long term. When making up the baby food from fresh ingredients, the parent should choose ripe fruits (bananas, pears, dessert apples, peaches) which do not need sugar. Vegetables can be cooked and puréed without salt. If the parent is buying commercial baby foods, he or she should look on the label to see that they are free from salt and sugar. Parents should also avoid giving babies biscuits and cakes, fatty, fried foods, warmed up left-overs, and foods with a lot of additives and preservatives.

Babies love to use their hands to find out about food. From six months onwards they should be able to attempt to feed themselves, either with finger foods (which can include rusks, toasted crusts, sticks of carrot, peeled apple, etc.), or using a spoon or their hands. This is a messy stage, but worth it, to avoid feeding problems later.

By the age of six months a baby will be on to normal family feeding times with possibly an early morning and/or a nightly milk feed. He will be able to have ordinary cow's milk as long as it is boiled and cooled for him.

Food preparation

Hygiene

By the time a child is at the mixed feeding stage, it is not necessary to sterilise all the equipment used, as was the case with bottle feeding. It is still necessary, however, to be very careful with the preparation and handling of the baby's food, to prevent contamination with bacteria.

Hygienic food safety rules:
- Hands and nails must be thoroughly clean to start with.

- All equipment used must be washed in hot soapy water and dried with clean tea towels. It should not be cracked or chipped.
- All dish cloths, tea towels and pan scrubs need regular washing and sterilising.
- Food preparation surfaces must be cleaned well. They should not be cracked or chipped, as they would then harbour germs.
- Cupboards, the fridge and storage jars where food is kept should be kept clean.
- Frozen foods must be properly defrosted before cooking, especially poultry.
- Meat and fish should be thoroughly cooked through and never partly cooked and then reheated.
- Left-overs should be stored, covered, in a fridge, and kept for only one or two days.
- Some dishes can be made up in bulk and frozen in suitable sized portions to save time and fuel.
- Bacteria quickly multiply in milk and milk products. Left-over milk or milk dishes should not be reheated for use.
- If the peel is left on raw fruit or vegetables it should be well washed or scrubbed.
- The person feeding a child should never test the taste or temperature of the food or drink first, and then put the same spoon or cup to the baby's mouth.
- Food which the baby drops on the floor such as rusks, pieces of apple, etc., should be washed if possible, otherwise thrown away.

Making purées

When a baby first starts to take solid food, and up to about six or seven months, the food will need to be in the form of a purée, otherwise the child may choke. There are three main methods of making a purée.

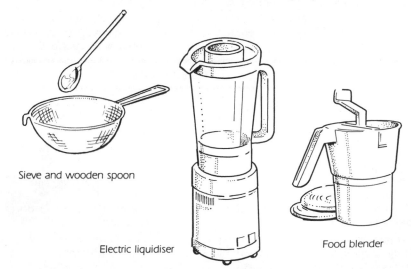

Sieve and wooden spoon

Electric liquidiser

Food blender

Equipment used in the three main methods of making a purée

For the first few weeks the baby will only be eating a few spoonfuls of the food prepared for him. The adults looking after him will have to decide whether to make the food themselves or to buy some of the wide range of commercial baby foods which are available. Most parents tend to do both, making the foods themselves when it is practical to do so and using commercial ones for convenience.

Commercial baby foods come in a wide range of sweet or savoury, either as one food or as a complete dish such as egg custard. They may be tinned, in jars, or dried (in packets). They are available as strained foods for the young baby, and minced or chopped ('junior meals') for the child from six months onwards. The cans, jars or packets may be colour-coded to distinguish types of foods and consistency.

A comparison of home-made and commercial foods

Home-made foods	Commercial foods
Advantages	
• *Cheaper if the family meals are suitable for the baby.*	• *Cheaper if the parent needs to buy special equipment and foods to purée.*
• *Food can be made up in bulk and frozen in portions.*	• *Involves much less work and effort – only needs warming up, if that.*
• *Parents know what is in the food.*	• *Manufacturers have prepared foods which are suitable for a baby.*
• *No additives, preservatives, artificial colourings, salt, sugar need be added.*	• *Large variety of food available.*
• *Not bulked out with too much cereal which has fattening effect.*	• *Useful when travelling, going on holiday or leaving the baby with someone else.*
• *Fresh foods can be used which may be of higher nutritional value.*	• *Useful if the parent is ill or very busy.*
• *Psychological satisfaction of making food for baby.*	• *Prepared under hygienic conditions which may be better than in the home.*
• *Baby is part of family meals, not eating something different.*	• *Parents do not feel as frustrated if the baby will not eat the food as they would if they had prepared it specially.*
Disadvantages	
• *Incorrect sieving could leave lumps which could choke the child.*	• *If only very small quantities are needed a lot may have to be thrown away, which is wasteful.*
• *Inefficient cleaning of equipment and food pre-paration could lead to tummy upsets.*	• *If baby goes off the taste or it disagrees with him the whole tin or packet will have to be thrown away.*
• *Parents may add sugar or salt to the adult taste, which is too much for a baby.*	• *Many brands have far too much sweetening or salt added.*
• *It is tempting to give the child unsuitable foods (e.g., fried or spicey foods) because the rest of the family are having them.*	• *Preservatives and other additives are often included.*
• *Time-consuming, messy job. Emotionally upsetting to parents if baby wastes the food which involves their time and effort.*	• *Too much cereal and other fattening ingredients may be present.*

Parents should always read the labelling on the tin, bottle or packet so that they know exactly what they are feeding to their baby.

1 Spoon the required amount into a cup or basin.

2 Warm the cup or basin in a bowl of hot water.

3 Test the food to see that it is not too hot.

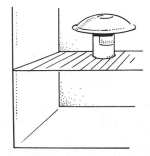

4 Cover the tin with remaining food in it with a plate or saucer.

5 Keep the tin in the fridge, for no longer than two days.

A suggested weaning guide

A nutritionally balanced diet for a child is similar to that for the expectant mother (see p. 58). The young baby should be allowed to experiment with new flavours and textures. As long as he is having a mainly milk diet he will be getting the nutrients he needs. As his intake of solid foods increases more attention should be paid to the nutritional content of the foods he is given.

Recommended daily intakes

		Age range (years)			
		0-1	**1-2**	**2-3**	**3-5**
Body weight	kg	7.3	11.4	13.5	16.5
	lb	16	25	30	36
Calories		800	1200	1400	1600
Protein	g	20	30	35	40
Thiamin (B1)	mg	0.3	0.5	0.6	0.6
Riboflavin (B2)	mg	0.4	0.6	0.7	0.8
Niacin	mg	5	7	8	9
Ascorbic Acid (C)	mg	15	20	20	20
Vitamin A	mcg	450	300	300	300
Vitamin D	mcg	10	10	10	10
Calcium	mg	600	500	500	500
Iron	mg	6	7	7	8

The five main food groups (see p. 58) are:

A	**B**	**C**	**D**	**E**
Meat Fish Eggs	Milk Cheese Yoghurt	Cereals Nuts Pulses (e.g., beans, lentils)	Fresh fruit Salads Vegetables	Fats Oils

A one-year-old child should have approximately these amounts from every group per day:

Group **A**   56 g (2 oz) portion or 1 egg

Group **B**   1 pint milk or 14 g (0.5 oz) cheese or a whole or half carton yoghurt

Group **C**   1 slice wholemeal bread or 85 g (3 oz) pulses or 56 g (2 oz) nuts (not whole)

Group **D**   1 piece of fruit or 56 g (2 oz) vegetables – serve some raw

Group **E**   14 g (0.5 oz) either butter or margarine

An example of a daily diet for a one-year-old could be this:

Early morning   Water or fruit juice

Breakfast   Cereal with milk; apple or banana

Lunch   Chopped meat or fish, potatoes, carrot; milk pudding or egg custard; fruit juice

Tea   Grated cheese and tomato sandwich; milky drink

By this stage the child will probably be eating the same meals as the rest of the family. Do not force the child to 'eat it all up' – he knows how much he can manage. Feed the child slowly and let him feed himself if he wants to. Let him play with the food a little. If possible let him have his meals with the rest of the family; it is good social training and he likes the company. Never leave a very small child alone to feed himself – he could choke.

Food manufacturers produce a lot of leaflets and booklets to help mothers with feeding information. Some even give free samples. Some literature is published in Bengali, Urdu and Punjabi, as well as English. Advice can always be obtained from the Child Welfare Clinic, or the health visitor.

Overfeeding is a much more likely problem than underfeeding. Children never starve themselves to death.

Suggested feeding pattern from 4–12 months

Stage/age	Early morning	Breakfast	Lunch	Tea	Evening
4 months	Breast or bottle feed (210 ml–7 fl. oz)	1 or 2 teaspoon-fuls baby rice Breast or bottle feed	Breast or bottle feed (210 ml–7 fl. oz)	Breast or bottle feed (210 ml–7 fl. oz)	Breast or bottle feed (210 ml–7 fl. oz)
4½ months	Breast or bottle feed	1 or 2 tsps baby rice Breast or bottle feed	1 or 2 tsps strained fruit or vegetable or both Breast or bottle feed	Breast or bottle feed	Breast or bottle feed
5–6 months	Breast or bottle feed	Baby cereal and/or egg yolk Breast or bottle feed	Meat or fish purée with vegetables Mashed banana or stewed fruit Fruit juice	Small portion yoghurt or fruit Breast or bottle feed	Breast or bottle feed
6–7 months	Breast or bottle feed	Baby cereal or porridge, scrambled or boiled egg, bread fingers Cow's milk	Minced meat or fish dish, chopped vegetables Milk pudding Fruit dessert Fruit juice	Cottage cheese or savoury sandwich Fruit or yoghurt Cow's milk	
7–8 months	Cup of milk or fruit juice	Cereal and/or egg Drink of milk	Minced chicken, liver, fish, beans, nuts, mashed vegetable Stewed or fresh fruit Milk pudding Fruit juice	Cottage cheese, egg sandwiches, fish sandwiches, fruit/yoghurt Milk	
9–12 months	Cup of milk, water or fruit juice	Grilled bacon egg or fish, toast, cereal Milk	Chopped meat, fish or cheese, dish Vegetables Egg custard, milk pudding Fresh fruit Fruit juice	Sandwiches, cheese on toast, or macaroni cheese Fruit Yoghurt Milk	

By the time a child is a year old he will be eating three meals a day, with a mid-morning and afternoon drink. Good food habits are started in childhood and if children are not given crisps, sweets and biscuits between meals, they will not develop a craving for them. Sweets and chocolate should be kept as a rare treat for a child – they only provide 'empty calories' and cause obesity and tooth decay.

During the coming two or three years when the child's body is developing rapidly and he is very active, he will need plenty of body-building and energy foods. He knows how much food he needs and his appetite may be erratic; one day he may be too busy to want to eat much, the next day he may eat a large amount. He will also be keen on some foods for a time and then go off them and refuse to touch them. This is all quite natural, and the sensible parent will provide a selection of nutritious dishes in small helpings, but not make a fuss if the child does not eat as the parent thinks he should. Children love to be the centre of their parents' attention, and will play on their natural anxiety to draw attention to themselves.

A toddler's food can be made to look attractive and desirable by using interesting tableware, and letting him use a bendy straw to drink through. Milk can be coloured, or have milkshake powder added to it. A child reluctant to eat may be encouraged to have a tea party with his toys, or may eat it if he has helped to make it himself. Sandwiches can be cut into shapes with biscuit cutters, or rolled up into sausage shapes. Vegetables can be arranged on the plate in a pattern, or a face can be made from potato, carrot and a sausage. Potato can be coloured and piped onto a dish, and potato crisps can be crumbled up to give a crispy coating.

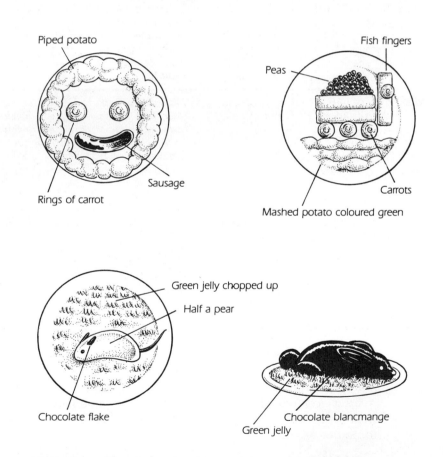

Making food attractive for children

Feeding cup and first beaker

Double handed
feeding beaker

Unbreakable mug,
bowl and plate set

Nursery set with cartoon
TV characters on it

Keep warm plate that can
be filled with warm water
to keep food warm-
divided into sections for
different foods

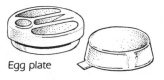

Egg plate

Dish with suction base

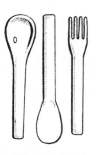

Plastic cutlery

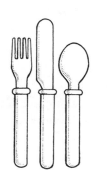

First-size knife, fork and spoon set

Moulded soft polythene bib
with special spill pocket

Feeding equipment

These dishes, bowls and beakers are made from unbreakable plastics such as melanine and polypropylene.

165

Feeding problems

Problems with feeding usually begin during the child's second year, when the novelty of trying out new foods wears off, and he becomes bored with meal times. He may develop food fads and become a food refuser simply to attract attention. As long as a child is healthy, active and not losing weight, parents need not be concerned about meal-time tantrums.

A child should not be given between-meal snacks because he did not eat his proper meal and is hungry. He should not be offered alternative foods if he rejects a reasonable choice, and he should not be given extra pudding if he will not eat his first course. If he does not want his meal, it should be removed without fuss – he will eat when he is hungry. A child should not be forced to eat.

Loss of appetite can be a sign of an oncoming illness. If it is accompanied by other symptoms such as a flushed appearance, crying, tiredness, etc., a doctor should be consulted.

One of the major feeding problems is **obesity**, i.e., being 20 per cent or more over the average weight. This is the result of eating too much food, or the wrong type of foods. The reasons for obesity include:

- a diet containing too many 'empty calories', such as sweets, biscuits, chocolate, ice-cream, or cakes.
- too many fatty foods such as chips, fried foods, or creamy cakes.
- too many snacks such as crisps, sweet drinks, ice-creams.
- developing the habit of eating more food than the body requires. Obesity tends to run in families because of this.
- lack of opportunities for exercise to burn off some of the fat.
- plump babies sometimes being regarded as attractive, so that some parents worry if they think their child is too thin.
- the introduction of solid foods at too early an age.

Obesity can cause:
- slow physical development. Overweight children have more difficulty in sitting up, pulling themselves to their feet and walking.
- mechanical disorders of the hips, legs and feet.
- difficulty with activities such as running, climbing, playing games.
- psychological difficulties because of teasing from other children.

Obesity should be prevented, or treated by adjustment to the diet of the child and keeping him actively occupied.

Stomach disorders that may occur include constipation and diarrhoea. Constipation is not uncommon. It can be corrected by giving more high fibre foods such as wholemeal bread, raw fruit and vegetables and plenty of water. Prunes or rhubarb will often produce a bowel movement. Diarrhoea is usually due to eating contaminated food, or to germs being passed from dirty hands. The child should be given only very plain foods and plenty of fluids whilst the attack lasts. If it persists he should see a doctor.

A child may be getting sufficient food, but he may still suffer from **malnutrition** (nutritional deficiency). This is because he is not getting a balanced diet and is being deprived of some essential nutrients. Very few children in Western countries suffer in this way, but children from families that have recently immigrated may develop a deficiency disease such as rickets, unless the family adapts to the climate and available foods of the new country.

Mineral elements and the effect of shortages

Mineral	Effects of shortage
Sodium (common salt)	May cause cramp (Excess of salt is more likely than shortage, and may make high blood pressure worse.)
Iron	Anaemia through lack of haemoglobin in the red blood cells
Iodine	May cause goitre
Calcium	Bones become soft and weak

Vitamins and the effect of shortages

Vitamin	Effects of shortage
Vitamin A	May cause skin disorders, vision disorders, and lower resistance to infections
Vitamin B	Deficiency disorders such as beri beri or pellagra General health may be affected
Vitamin C	Growth may be retarded Scurvy may result
Vitamin D	May cause rickets and tooth decay

Bowel and bladder training

A young baby cannot of course control when he passes urine or has a bowel movement. Control over the bowels and bladder do not come until well into the second year. Holding a child on a potty may have successful results, but it will only be a matter of luck, and potty training cannot be achieved until the child is physically ready for it. Bowel control is usually achieved between 15 and 18 months and the child may be dry during the day a few months later. By the age of two-and-a-half years approximately 90 per cent of girls and 75 per cent of boys have achieved bowel and bladder control throughout the day, but it may take another six months before they stop wetting during the night.

Important points

- Do not force the pace – the child must achieve control in his own time.
- Some children go straight from wearing nappies to using a toilet without using a potty at all.
- Allow a child to get used to his potty – let him play with it. Make sure it is comfortable, stable and hygienic.
- *Never* hold a child forcibly on the potty until he has performed. This will only create tension and fear, and may cause the child to be oversensitive to normal bodily functions when he is older.
- Encourage a child to use his potty, and praise him when he does, but do not scold or punish if he is unable to perform.
- Do not show disgust or repugnance towards the contents of the potty. A child will soon notice this and be puzzled at the reaction to his efforts.
- Do not be surprised if a child seems to be potty trained and then reverts to wetting and soiling his pants. It can be caused by illness, attention seeking or emotional problems and will need patient understanding, not anger and scolding.
- The child should not be compared with other children who may be quicker to obtain bowel and bladder control. It is not his fault and unkindness may make him stop trying altogether.
- Hygiene rules should be established during this stage. Children should be taught how to use toilet paper (front to back for a girl) and to wash their hands after every visit.
- Trainer pants (towelling pants with a plastic cover) can be a help when the child has almost got control. They are less bulky than nappies and easy to get up and down.
- Children are curious about what they have done and may wish to handle the faeces. This should be discouraged, but without a display of horror or disgust. It should not be implied that there is anything disgusting about the body's natural functions.

Children may find using a toilet a frightening experience and fear falling down. Two useful aids are a footstool, to help them reach the seat and to assist balance when they are sitting there, and a child-size lavatory seat which fits inside the adult seat and reduces the size of the opening.

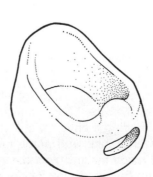

1 Plastic moulded potty with optional lid, integral handle, and curved interior for easy cleaning – comfortable and stable, with splash guard and back support

(continued)

2 Plastic or metal potty in
conventional shape – cheaper

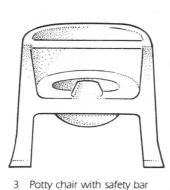

3 Potty chair with safety bar
and removable inner bowl –
comfortable, non-slip

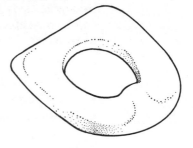

4 Toilet trainer seat

A range of potties

Exercise and fresh air, rest and sleep

Once the milestones of crawling and walking have been achieved, young children seem to be constantly active. This is a natural part of their physical development and opportunities should be provided for them to be active. Not only does it help with their physical co-ordination, but it is a release for psychological and emotional stress. A child who has been told off for being naughty will whack his hammer and peg toy; a group of small children released from sitting in a classroom will dash round the playground. In these ways they are releasing the build-up of energy.

Once a child is able to get about, he should be allowed to play outside in the garden as much as possible. Even in cold weather he can be well wrapped up and encouraged to go out. A child who is kept indoors and inactive for long periods will become naughty and grizzly; he will get to the stage where he becomes lazy and unwilling to exert himself.

Parents who do not have gardens must make an effort to get their child to a park or recreational area, every day if possible. Even a walk to the shops, pointing things out on the way, will exercise and educate the child. Children can enjoy water play at the local swimming pool or park paddling pool, and they can climb, jump, dig, etc. on visits to the country or to the seaside. The fresh air and exercise will help to make the child naturally tired and hungry and should minimise feeding and sleeping problems.

The young baby who is only a few months old will sleep about 60 per cent of the day, but as he gets older the number of hours sleep he requires per day will decrease gradually. He will not fall asleep almost immediately after his feed, and as he becomes more active and able to sit up and take notice his need for sleep will lessen. Young children vary a great deal in the amount of sleep which they require, but as a general guide:

- from about nine months the baby should be sleeping 12–13 hours at night with two long naps during the day.
- at 15–16 months he may only have one daytime nap and a rest period, with 12 hours sleep at night.
- by two years of age he should be getting 12 hours sleep at night and may only need an afternoon rest. This amount of sleep and rest continues until after he has started school when it again decreases gradually.

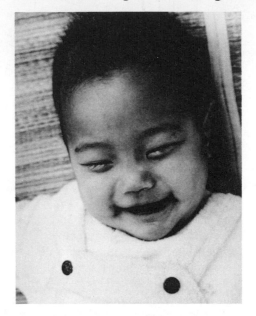

It is sensible to establish realistic bedtime routines right from the start, but these routines should be flexible and suit the child and the family. It is natural for babies and young children to want to be with their parents during the night as well as during the daytime, and there is no harm in letting a small child share his parents' bed if he finds difficulty in getting off to sleep. It is much better that they should all get their sleep in this way than that parents and child should suffer disturbed nights for long periods. Eventually he will want to be in a bed of his own, perhaps popping into his parents' bed sometimes for comfort. Some parents have their baby's cot or a single bed for him next to their own, so that he can feel close and secure. Some children will take quite happily to their own bed in their own room, or one shared with a brother or sister. Whatever the bedroom arrangements are, they should be as relaxed and pleasant as possible.

Most children prefer having a regular bedtime routine, very often starting with a bath and play, then a story and a cuddle before settling down for the night. If a child is put to bed early, about 5.30 or 6.00 p.m., he will probably wake up early, so parents must decide whether they want an evening to themselves and an early morning rising, or to lie in longer in the morning and have the child with them until 7.00 or 8.00 p.m. Very often, even if a child wakes early he will amuse himself for a while playing with a cot toy, watching a mobile, or singing to himself.

A child should never be left to cry himself to sleep. A small child can quite suddenly develop a fear of the dark, or of being left alone, and just leaving him to cope can cause worse problems such as nightmares, sleep-walking, or bed wetting.

These things will help a child who is experiencing sleeping problems:

- Make sure the bedroom is warm enough in winter and cool in summer, with some ventilation.

- The cot or bed should be comfortable, with light, warm bedding. Cotton sheets and pillow slips are cool and soft; cellular wool blankets are light and warm. Duvets should only be used by children over the age of two years, because of the danger of suffocation. Small children like to be wrapped up securely and quite tightly tucked in.

- Nightwear should be loose, comfortable and absorbent, preferably cotton or brushed cotton for warmth, with all-in-one feet and soft ribbing at cuffs and neck.

- The bedroom door should be left open so that the child still feels part of the family. Any noise made by the family should not disturb him, but will reassure him. Let him have a night-light, or leave the landing light on if he needs it.

- Do not let him watch anything frightening on the TV, or tell him a frightening story before he goes to sleep. He will enjoy hearing the same stories over and over again, and singing nursery rhymes or songs with repetitive noises.

- A warm drink will be soothing.

- Let him have a comforter if he needs one. This may be a dummy, his thumb, or an old piece of fabric which he sucks. He may like to cuddle a doll or his teddy.

- If a regular, relaxed, early bedtime routine is established, this will give the child a sense of security and he will know what is expected of him. Staying up late for something special can be given as a treat.

Bedtime problems

Problems that may have either physical or emotional causes include fear of the dark, nightmares, sleep-walking, wakefulness, talking in his sleep, wetting the bed, and disturbed sleep.

Check that:

- he is physically comfortable, not hungry, and has not had too much food before going to bed.

- he is not overtired and 'wound up'. If he has had too much excitement and insufficient rest during the day he will be unable to get off to sleep easily.

- he is not ill or sickening for some infection.

- he has not developed a fear of something in his room, or something happening outside.

- he has not been frightened by another child telling him about ghosts or 'things in the night'.

- he is not feeling insecure or unhappy, perhaps because of a new baby, or because he has been naughty and thinks his parents do not love him any more.

All these problems must be treated with sympathy and understanding. He should not be scolded or laughed at. If necessary the doctor or health visitor will give advice. They rarely prescribe sleeping tablets unless the sleep situation is really desperate, and then only to establish a sleep pattern. Usually if a child has a fairly active day, with plenty of opportunities for exercise and rest, a good diet, and loving care, he will sleep well.

Clothing

Clothing for the toddler and the pre-school child must be selected just as carefully as for the baby's layette, and the points given on p. 85 apply equally. Remember too that clothing for a small child must stand up to a lot of hard wear.

General points about clothing for a toddler

- Children grow very quickly so the size should allow for growth and for easy movement, but not be so large that it is dangerous. Trousers that are too long may catch on the child's shoes, or an over-large hat obscure the child's vision.

- Stretch fabrics allow for movement and activity.

- Unisex clothes are useful – they can be handed down to a brother or sister.

- Fastenings should be easy for the parent or the child to manage. Zip fasteners, velcro and popper studs are easier than buttons or ties. Elasticated waist bands, necks and wrists are easy and comfortable.

- Children love strong colours and simple patterns. Darker colours do not show marks as quickly as pastels.

- All clothing should be machine washable, dye-fast, shrink-resistant and minimum iron. As much clothing as possible, and especially nightwear, must be flame-resistant.

- The fabric should suit the purpose of the garment (e.g., denim for play overalls, polyester cotton for a summer nightdress). Natural fibres absorb perspiration and are healthier, but a small amount of synthetic fibre added to natural fibre will help the fabric to resist creasing and stains and be easier to launder.

- In cold weather children are warmer in several layers of light clothing rather than one or two heavy garments.
- If garments are bought from a reliable shop with a good brand name, they should wear well, be well designed and safe. The shop will replace faulty garments to protect its good name.
- Home-made garments can save a lot of money, but safety points must be observed when making them.

Children quickly develop an interest in what they wear and should be consulted as soon as they are old enough to understand. Battles about what they will or will not wear should be avoided!

Underwear and nightwear

The young child will need to wear a vest, with an envelope neck or a round neck. It can be made from ribbed cotton, terry stretch fabric or thermal fabric for warmth. Many vests can double as a summer T-shirt.

When the nappy stage is over the child will wear cotton briefs, in similar fabric to that of the vests. At a later stage boys can wear front opening briefs. For sleepwear the child can have a sleep suit, pyjamas, nightshirt or nightdress. The fabric should be soft and comfortable and suit the temperature, so at different times of year it could be a thermal fabric, stretch towelling, fleecy-lined cotton, cotton lawn, or polyester cotton. In every case it should be flare free and flame-resistant.

A fleecy dressing gown with a zip opening is also useful.

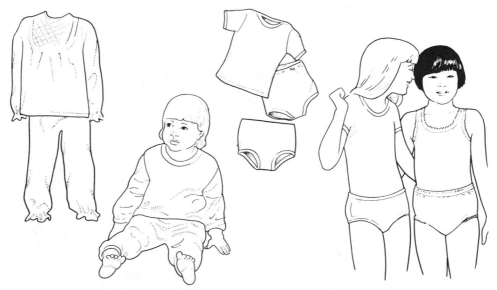

Nightwear and underwear

Top wear for playing

Fashions in children's wear change nearly as rapidly as adult fashion. Some children's garments look very cute but are not serviceable and are uncomfortable to wear. The most popular and practical are usually a top with trousers or pinafore, or an all-in-one suit. Examples of playwear include dungarees, tracksuits, pull-on play suits, jogging trews and top, denims, knitted jersey and trousers, pinafore dresses, skirts with waist elastic, knitted jumpers, T-shirts, blouses and sleeveless gilets.

Suitable fabrics include corduroy, velour, brushed cotton, fleecy-lined cotton, denim, knitted jersey fabric, Viyella, polyester cotton, stretch fabrics, and pure wool. Clever use of contrasting colours, appliqué, knitted motifs, etc., will make a garment attractive while it remains practical.

Clothes for playing in

Outdoor wear

These garments should be warm and protective without being heavy and bulky. Clothing that is lined, padded or quilted will give extra warmth. Outdoor clothing includes anoraks, pram suits, duffle coats, coats and trousers. Some coats and jackets have integral hoods and mittens. Knitted hats or helmets, scarves, and mittens or gloves are essential for cold weather.

Fabrics used can include woollen cloth, brushed cotton, fleecy-lined fabrics, corduroy and velour.

For rain and snow

To keep warm and dry in wet or snowy weather an all-in-one waterproof jump suit, snow suit or splash suit is ideal. The garment should be elasticated at wrists and ankles and round the hood (no draw-strings). Jackets, duffle coats, parkas and anoraks made from plasticised fabric, PVC or weather-proofed fabric can be teamed with similar trousers. Plastic capes and raincoats can be used in warmer weather.

Fabrics used are usually a mixture of polyester or nylon and cotton, given a weather-proof coating. Nylon, plastic or PVC clothing tends to restrict movement and keeps in perspiration. It should therefore have air holes under the arms. Most bad weather wear is given a quilted, sherpa pile or fur lining.

Outdoor wear

Outdoor wear for rain and snow

Make do and mend

Children's clothing is expensive, and it gets a lot of hard wear.

The following points should be observed:

- Looser fitting garments with raglan sleeves and no waistline allow for growth, and so do wide hems on sleeves and the bottom of garments. Decorative tucks can be put in the sleeve and skirt of dresses to provide extra length, and dungarees and pinafore dresses should have long straps, which can be lengthened as the child grows.
- Reinforcing elbows and knees of garments will prolong their life.
- Careful laundering and washing *before* the garment gets ingrained with dirt will make it last longer.
- Good quality fabrics usually wear better.
- Replace buttons, stitch up tears and darn small holes *before* they go beyond repair.
- Decorative patches can be placed over worn parts, contrasting fabric can be let in to lengthen or widen garments, and appliqué designs can cover stains or damage.
- Good parts of worn or outgrown garments can be made into something else. For example trousers can be made into shorts, jackets or blouses can be made into waistcoats, and long-sleeved shirts or blouses can be made short-sleeved or sleeveless. Outgrown sleep suits can still be worn with the hands and feet of the suit cut off.
- Children should be taught how to look after their clothing and encouraged to do so.

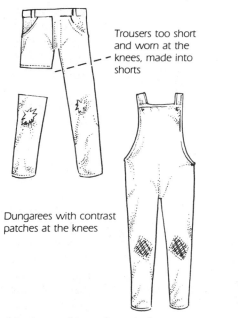

Trousers too short and worn at the knees, made into shorts

Dungarees with contrast patches at the knees

Summer dress lengthened with contrast fabric, with appliqué to cover marks

Jacket or cardigan with sleeves and neck cut out to make a waistcoat

Altering and mending clothes

Footwear

Suitable shoe designs

Babies and young children do not need to wear shoes. It is much better to allow the feet freedom of movement and fresh air. Socks or tights can be worn when it is cold.

Growing feet can easily be damaged with incorrect footwear, and this includes socks and tights as well as slippers, shoes, sandals, boots and wellingtons. It takes about 18 years for the foot to become fully formed, and if constant pressure is put on all the tiny bones as they are developing, it will lead to problems such as corns, bunions, ingrowing toenails and foot deformities. Some of these can only be corrected by surgery, and most of these problems are caused by badly fitted or badly designed footwear. The following points must be observed.

Shoes

Shoes should be bought from a good shoe shop where the assistants are trained to measure and fit children's shoes. The shoes must be fitted to leave 18 mm ($\frac{3}{4}$ in.) between the end of the longest toe and the end of the shoe. There should be only 3 mm ($\frac{1}{4}$ in.) between the heel and the back of the shoe. The width is important as well as the length. The shoes should be wide enough for the toes to lie flat on the sole of the shoe. The heels must grip quite tightly but not rub the child's foot.

A child's feet grow rapidly. They should be checked every three months. The shoe must hold firmly to the child's foot with laces, buckles, or velcro, and the fasteners should be adjustable. Leather is the best material for shoes. It is a natural product and allows the feet to 'breathe' (i.e., lets more air in and reduces sweat). Special footwear such as canvas shoes, trainers, plimsolls and wellingtons, which may be made entirely from synthetic materials, should not be worn for long periods as they make the feet perspire and encourage athlete's foot. The sole of the shoe should be pliable to allow the foot to bend, and should also be non-slip. The heel should not be more than 1 cm high ($\frac{3}{8}$ in.).

It is very unwise to allow children to wear second-hand shoes. The shoes will have taken on the shape of the previous owner and could deform the new owner's feet.

Slippers

These should be chosen as carefully as shoes. Although they should be warm and comfortable, they should not be too big or sloppy, but should be the correct size and fit. They should be fairly flat, and attach to the foot firmly but be fairly easy to put on and take off. They should be safe, with safe decorations, and hygienic, being cleanable or washable.

Wet weather and playwear

Wellingtons should be waterproof, large enough to take thicker socks, and fit snugly to the ankle and leg. They should not be too heavy, and have ridged soles. It is a good idea if the boots are brightly coloured or fluorescent so that the child can be seen in murky weather.

Shoes for playing in, such as trainers, sandals, or canvas play shoes, should be chosen and looked after in the same way as other shoes. They can be dangerous and unhealthy if allowed to get worn, dirty and damaged.

Socks and tights

These can cause just as much damage as badly fitting shoes. Many mothers would not allow their child to wear shoes that are too small, but are not so careful about socks.

The feet of the socks should be big enough without being stretched. There should be enough length for the toes and width for the foot. Socks soon shrink; the heel of the sock should never slip to the sole of the foot.

Fine wool or cotton or a mixture of natural and synthetic fibres are better than all nylon or acrylic socks. Natural fibres absorb moisture and perspiration, but synthetic fibres do not, and help to cause athlete's foot. Heels and toes may be strengthened with nylon.

Frequent washing and use of fabric softener should keep socks in good condition and extend their life. Buying several pairs of socks the same means that if one gets lost or damaged, the other one of the pair can be matched up with the rest.

Toys and activities

Progress in manipulative skills, muscular co-ordination and hand/eye co-ordination can be greatly assisted by the use of properly chosen toys, games and activities. The acquisition of physical skills is a very gradual process, and the rate varies from child to child. Presenting a child with a toy that is much too advanced for its stage of development is not only a waste of time and money, but will cause frustration in the child, often resulting in antisocial behaviour such as destruction and temper tantrums. The following chart shows the approximate stage of development at various ages, and the toys and activities that will help the child to progress to the next stage of development.

Toys and actvities for physical development

Approximate age	Stage of development	Toys	Activities	Comments
0–3 months	The baby can turn his head to a sound. He is beginning to hold his head up, straighten his back, and grasp things.	The baby likes objects that move and give a pleasing sound. Give him rattles, squeaky toys, pram toys, a soft ball with a bell in, bath toys, mobiles, and soft toys.	The baby's first clutching of an adult finger is the first piece of manipulative play. He can grasp things for a few seconds.	The baby can only focus at about 20–30 cm (8–12 in.) so toys should be within his range of vision. Harsh noises will frighten him.
3–6 months	The baby can sit up with some support. He can lie on his tummy and roll over. He will grasp objects put in his mouth.	As above plus large wooden blocks, large beads, a plastic teething ring, roll-along toys, and household objects such as wooden spoons. Soft cloth shapes that rattle, and a baby mirror, will fascinate him.	The baby will enjoy being sung to, and finger-play songs and games. A music box will please him.	Put toys out of the baby's reach so that he has to stretch or move to get them. Take care that toys are not small enough to be swallowed and will withstand chewing. Small wooden toys which he can grip will help with fine muscle control.
6–12 months	The baby can crawl and may be trying to walk. He can grasp and hold objects. He can say and understand a few words.	Toys, cars, push-along toys, stringing cotton reels, hammer and peg toys. Toddle truck.	Water play with squeezy bottles and beakers. Playing with sand and earth will give him experience of natural substances. He will enjoy 'peek a boo' games.	He should be allowed to experience different textures and shapes, sounds and sights. A playpen will be useful. (continued)

179

Approximate age	Stage of development	Toys	Activities	Comments
12–18 months	The baby can walk and balance quite well. He has a large vocabulary. He can control hand movements with precision.	Posting boxes, building bricks, nesting toys, small tricycles or sit-on toys. Pencils and crayons will help with fine motor control.	The baby enjoys ball games, and loves exploring and trying out his physical independence.	At this stage the baby will be climbing, but without controlled balance yet, so he needs careful supervision.
18 months–2 years	The child can run about, climbs, and goes up and down stairs.	Small jigsaws with large pieces, constructional toys, screw-in toys.	The child enjoys games of chase, hide-and-seek, jumping, running and skipping.	Outdoor play on a swing, climbing frame or small tricycle will help develop balance and muscular co-ordination.
2–3 years	Muscular control develops and improves.	Jigsaws, bead threading, lacing cards, modelling clay, Lego, and Meccano type models.	By the age of 3 the child begins to enjoy playing games with other children. Seesaws, cycling, (on a tricycle) swimming and ball games will develop his body and physical control.	The more experience the child gets, the more confident he becomes in the use of his own body. Opportunities should be given for adventure play in the garden or park with large scale equipment.
3–4 years	The child has good muscular control. He can run, hop, skip and pick up very small objects.	Pencil and paper games, dominoes, colour games, bicycle with stabilisers, scooter, swing, climbing frame.	Making things such as a collage picture or a bits-and-pieces toy, musical games, activity rhymes, games of ball, chasing, etc. with other children.	The child is now much more independent and sure of his movements.
4–5 years	The child's balance is good – he can balance on one leg. Hand/eye co-ordination is very precise	Throwing and catching toys, large-scale construction toys, intricate puzzles, household objects for baking, gardening, etc.	Team games, musical play, sand and water play, all forms of physical exercise.	The child is very active at this stage and may tire himself. Outlets are needed for adventure and independence.

Prevention and treatment of illness and disease

If a child gains weight at a constant and not excessive rate, is active and alert, eats and sleeps well and is developing steadily it can be assumed that he is healthy. He may, of course, throughout childhood, suffer from some minor ailments adults have, such as coughs, colds, influenza, respiratory problems, upset tummy and earache, as well as teething problems, etc. Most of these can be dealt with at home with simple treatments and sympathetic nursing.

Two points to remember are:

- Young children never pretend to be ill. When ill they show it with some of the symptoms described on pp. 184–7, but when they are better they immediately wish to be up and about.
- Children usually have very rapid powers of recovery. They can appear to be quite seriously ill and within a short space of time – a few hours or overnight – be better.

The best way of dealing with illness is to try to *prevent* it. This can be done by:
- having a healthy diet.
- keeping the child and his environment clean and teaching him hygienic habits.
- keeping him away from possible infectious contacts.
- regular medical and dental checkups.
- not ignoring suspicious symptoms.
- following a suggested immunisation schedule (see p. 183), which can be discussed with the doctor or health visitor at the clinic.

Disease and illness are caused by:

Bacteria   These are single-celled organisms, invisible to the naked eye, some of which live harmlessly in various parts of the body and our surroundings. When we are run down, our internal bacteria can multiply and give rise to infections such as sore throats, upset tummies, etc. It is more usual, however, for diseases to be caused by bacteria entering the body from another source. Diphtheria and whooping cough are caused in this way.

Viruses   These are parasites that live and reproduce in other living cells, breaking down these cells. They cause such infections as measles, influenza and the common cold, and cannot be treated with antibiotics.

Fungi   These are plant organisms, some of which cause such things as ringworm (a skin disease that appears in circular patches).

Metazoan parasites   These are such things as tapeworms, fleas and lice, which feed on the human body and can cause infections.

Infection can be spread in various ways. Droplets containing the bacteria or viruses can spread from infected people when they breathe out, cough or sneeze. Water contaminated by bacteria or viruses can cause diseases such as typhoid or polio, and food can be contaminated by flies, mice, rats, etc. Skin diseases such as impetigo (which causes infected sores) can be passed on by skin contact, and bites from insects can give infections such as malaria. Pets can transmit diseases such as rabies by biting victims, or pass on parasites such as tapeworms through their faeces. Inadequate diet will result in deficiency diseases, and constant damp and cold conditions will result in respiratory problems.

It is clear, therefore, that a consistently high standard of hygiene is needed to maintain good health. Children should be taught the basic rules of hygiene and healthy living from the minute they can understand, and these rules should be constantly reinforced by reminders and good example, until they become automatic.

Rules for hygiene and health should include:

- a daily bath if possible (or a good strip wash) with washing during the day whenever necessary.
- washing of hands after going to the toilet, blowing the nose, doing any messy jobs, before meals, etc.
- care of nails on hands and feet, and keeping them clean.
- frequent washing, brushing and combing of hair.
- cleaning and regular replacement of equipment needed for care of the body e.g., toothbrush, hair-brush, flannel, etc.
- regular changing and laundering of clothing, especially underwear.
- care with the preparation and eating of food and liquids. Food and drink which has already been partly consumed by other children, or dropped on the floor, or come out of dusty pockets, etc., should not be eaten.
- care with pets and animals. Avoid getting too close to an animal's mouth, or playing where animals may have urinated (e.g., in parks or on benches). Feeding dishes and equipment for pets should be kept separate from those of the family.
- avoiding contact with adults or other children who may have infections such as coughs, colds, skin diseases, etc.
- building up a good resistance to disease with a sensible diet and plenty of fresh air, exercise, rest and sleep.

A child should be encouraged to have a good mental attitude towards health, and be taught not to worry too much about minor aches and pains.

It is possible for a child to be protected from some diseases by being given some form of **immunity**. If he has some form of the disease naturally he will build up his own immunity by the formation of antibodies in his bloodstream, which attack and kill off the virus or bacteria that caused the disease. Immunity to some diseases will be passed on to a breast-fed baby for the first few weeks of life through his mother's milk.

Immunity can also be given by **artificial immunisation**. A vaccine is injected into the body, or taken in by mouth, to provide the necessary antibodies. **Passive immunisation** gives the child antibodies to the disease that have been developed in another human, or in an animal. Unfortunately this protection soon wears off. **Active immunisation** means that the weakened strain of the disease is injected into the child, so triggering off the body to form its own antibodies.

The infectious diseases for which a vaccine is available are diphtheria, polio, whooping cough, tetanus, tuberculosis, measles and German measles. Before the advent of immunisation most of these diseases were killers, or left the sufferer with a permanent weakness. Since immunisation became widely available, epidemics of these diseases are less frequent, with less drastic results. Unfortunately many parents feel that as their child is now less likely to have one of these infectious diseases, they need not bother to have him vaccinated. This means that there is more risk of epidemics starting. All parents should have their children immunised unless there are medical reasons against it.

It has been shown that an extremely small proportion of children given whooping cough vaccine have suffered permanent brain damage. The risk is very small: the risk of a child dying or suffering from convulsions, pneumonia, collapsed lungs or even brain damage as a result of whooping cough is far greater. In the ten years up to 1984, 82 children died from whooping cough in the UK. Parents who are worried should discuss the matter with their doctor or health visitor.

Immunisation Programme

Suggested age	Disease	Method of immunisation	Comments
3 months 5-6 months 9-12 months	Diphtheria/ Tetanus/ Whooping cough	Triple vaccine injection	The site of the injection may be a little sore, and the child may be a little feverish. The injection should not be given if the child is unwell, or to children subject to fits or epilepsy.
3 months 5-6 months 9-12 months	Polio	Oral (drops given by mouth)	These should not be given to a child who has an upset stomach.
14-15 months	Measles	Injection (one dose only)	A slight rash may develop at the place of the injection.
5 years	Diphtheria/Tetanus	Injection	A booster dose is given.
5 years	Polio	Oral (by mouth)	A booster dose is given.
10-13 years (girls only)	German measles	Injection	There may be some minor side effects. The effects of the vaccine may not be lasting – a booster dose will probably be needed later.
10-13 years	Tuberculosis	Injection of BCG vaccine if skin test is negative	The place of the injection may swell and be sore. It may leave a scar. It gives lifelong protection.
15-19 years	Tetanus	Injection	A booster dose is given.
15-19 years	Polio	Oral (by mouth)	A booster dose is given.

Parents should keep a record of the dates and type of immunisation given, so that they have a permanent checklist to refer to.

Common signs which indicate that a child may be ill are:

- listlessness and lethargy (having no energy).
- a raised temperature.
- headache or earache.
- crying and being miserable.
- going off his food, not eating.
- stomach ache, vomiting.
- diarrhoea or constipation.
- inflammation and swelling of glands and throat.
- pains and stiffness in joints.
- various types of rash on various parts of the body.
- a very flushed or very pale face.
- being hot and perspiring.
- laboured breathing, wheezing, or shallow breathing.

Many of these symptoms, although distressing for the child, are not serious and will soon clear up. Only if the symptoms persist or become severe is a doctor needed.

A doctor should be called *immediately* if the child:

- is unconscious – from a fall or any other reason.
- is bleeding and the bleeding cannot be stopped.
- turns a bluish colour, especially at the lips.
- has a fit or convulsion.

Infectious Fevers – Signs and Symptoms

Disease	Incubation period*	Symptoms	Treatment
Chicken pox	*14–16 days*	*May start with child feeling unwell and feverish, followed by appearance of an itchy rash of small red spots. These become blisters and crust over.*	*Itchiness may be relieved with calamine lotion.* *Infected spots may need antiseptic cream.*
Measles	*10–15 days*	*Starts with symptoms of a cold – runny nose, cough, high temperature. Rash of pink spots starts after four days behind the ears, then on the face, chest and limbs (Koplik's spots).*	*Paracetamol to reduce fever.* *Antibiotics only if chest or ear infection develops.*
German measles	*14–21 days*	*Slight temperature, enlarged glands in the neck. Rash of small pink spots develops on the face, then spreads to the rest of the body.*	*No special treatment.* *Child is infectious until rash disappears, so keep him away from pregnant women, as German measles can harm the foetus.*

(continued)

Disease	Incubation period*	Symptoms	Treatment
Scarlet fever	2–5 days	Sore throat, temperature, swollen glands, sickness. Rash of small red spots – skin flakes off. Tongue very red ('strawberry tongue').	Paracetamol to reduce fever. Course of penicillin (or other antibiotic if child is allergic to penicillin).
Mumps	17–21 days	Generally off colour. Fever, swellings behind the ears or under the jaw on one or both sides. Sore throat, difficulty with swallowing.	Paracetamol to relieve pain, soft foods, plenty to drink. Warmth applied to swelling.
Whooping cough	7–14 days	Cold and cough symptoms. Cough develops into continuous bouts with typical whoop. May cause sickness and vomiting.	Fresh air, frequent small meals, rest, mild sedative. Cough may last several weeks.

Incubation period This is the time between the child being in contact with the disease and showing the first signs of having it himself. Keeping a child totally isolated, i.e., **in quarantine**, with an infectious disease is very difficult and not usually necessary except in severe cases. It is sometimes thought best to expose children to some infectious diseases so that they can build up a resistance before they go to school. All cases of infectious diseases, even if very mild, should be reported to the doctor.

Other Common Ailments

Ailment	Symptoms	Treatment
Asthma	Breathing difficulties because air passages are temporarily narrowed. May be caused by an allergy or infection. Many children grow out of it.	Anti-allergy and other drugs and inhalers.
Bronchitis	Inflammation of the bronchial tubes. Causes cough, excessive mucus.	Consult doctor who will probably prescribe antibiotics.
Cold sores (herpes)	Caused by a virus which makes the skin itch and causes a watery blister. Easily passed from person to person. Blister will dry and scab over.	Cold sore lotion or ointment from a chemist's. See doctor if sore is severe.
Colic	Usually occurs after feeds with some babies and disappears after the first six months.	Severe cases can be treated with drugs.
Con-junctivitis	Inflammation of the eye, making the eye red, sore and itchy.	Very contagious, so use separate towels for the child. Doctor will prescribe drops or ointment.

(continued)

185

Ailment	Symptoms	Treatment
Constipation	*Usually caused by poor diet. The child may pass hard stools with blood in.*	*Give child more roughage, fresh fruit, prunes, and more liquid. See doctor before giving any laxatives.*
Convulsions (fits)	*Usually accompany high temperatures and fevers. Child becomes unconscious and twitches violently. Must not be left as he may vomit and choke.*	*Call a doctor.*
Coughs	*Usually a sign of bronchitis or an infectious disease.*	*See doctor.*
Cradle cap	*A thick layer of scurf which forms on the scalp of some babies. It is harmless but unsightly.*	*May be softened with warm olive oil and removed.*
Croup	*Affects the child's breathing, giving him a barking cough and a tight chest.*	*Consult doctor.*
Earache	*May be after-effects of a cold or infectious disease. Results in inflammation of the tubes of the ear.*	*Doctor will give immediate treatment with antibiotics. Hearing must be checked when the infection is cleared up.*
Eczema	*Infantile eczema is related to hay fever and asthma and seems to run in families. It produces a scaly, red rash on the face, behind the knees and elbow creases. It is very itchy and children make it worse by scratching.*	*There is really no cure, but it is generally outgrown after three or four years.*
Epilepsy	*There are two main types – **petit mal** and **grand mal**. During a petit mal attack the child may lose consciousness for a second, become vacant and pale, then continue as if nothing has happened. With a grand mal attack, the child has convulsions, falls unconscious and may bite his tongue, shake violently and grind his teeth.*	*There is no cure for the complaint, but medication does help to control it, and is generally very successful in preventing convulsions.*
Meningitis	*This condition is the result of inflammation of the **meninges** (covering of brain and spinal cord), caused by a virus or bacterial infection. Symptoms include fever, convulsions, sickness and apathy.*	*Treatment with antibiotics must be quick as the acute illness is dangerous. It can leave permanent deafness.*
Nose bleeds	*These are usually caused by the child damaging the nose whilst playing, or picking his nose.*	*The head should be held over a bowl and the nose firmly pinched at the sides to stop the bleeding. If there are frequent nose bleeds the child should see a doctor.*

(continued)

Ailment	Symptoms	Treatment
Pneumonia	*This is the infection of the tissues of the lungs. The child will have a high temperature, a cough and difficulty with breathing.*	*Usually responds to antibiotics.*
Stomach upsets	*Usually caused by unsuitable food or bacteria which has infected the food.*	*The child should be given plenty of fluids to avoid dehydration, and special attention given to personal hygiene.*
Thrush	*This is caused by a fungus and affects the mouth and sometimes the nappy area. It appears as a thick white fur on tongue and gums.*	*It is easily cured with Nystatin preparations, which will be supplied by the doctor.*

These are just some of the ailments which a small child can suffer from. Usually they are not serious and many can be cleared up with simple home remedies. Exceptions are pneumonia, meningitis, epilepsy and convulsions; a child with any of these must see a doctor.

N.B. Aspirin or any medicine containing aspirin or salicylates should not be given to any child under 12 years of age unless it is prescribed by the doctor. Product contents are printed on all packs of home medicines, so before giving a child under 12 a medicine that has not been prescribed, check that it does not contain aspirin or salicylates. These substances may be linked with Reye's Syndrome, a rare but often fatal disease.

Care of the sick child

It is usually possible to tell by observation when a child is ill, but some parents like to take a child's temperature to help them to assess how serious the condition is. The temperature of the body usually remains constant at 36.9°C (98.4°F), but a child's temperature may vary between 36.4°C and 37.5°C (97.5°F and 99.5°F) depending on whether he has been very active, has eaten a big meal or had a hot bath. Taking a child's temperature is not, therefore, a completely reliable guide to illness and should be considered along with other symptoms.

To take a child's temperature, use either a **clinical thermometer** (most reliable), or a **heat strip**.

A heat strip is a strip of material sensitive to heat, which is pressed to the forehead. A colour change indicates the level of body temperature. It is quick and easy, but not very accurate.

A clinical thermometer is a thin tube of glass with a bulb of mercury at one end and a very fine inner tube up which the mercury passes when it is warmed. The tube is marked with the temperature readings. The thermometer is usually placed (mercury end first) under the tongue and kept there for two or three minutes, with the patient breathing through his nose. Before the temperature is taken the mercury must be shaken down into the bulb with a sharp flick. After it has been read the mercury must be shaken down again.

Small children and babies cannot have the thermometer placed in their mouths as they may bite it. It can be placed under the arm or in the groin and kept there for two or three minutes. When you read it after taking a temperature like this, 0.5 °C (1 °F) should be added to the reading. The temperature may also be taken by placing the thermometer in the child's rectum, but great care is needed not to snap the thermometer if the child moves, so this should only be done by a doctor.

A low temperature can be just as serious as a high one. A temperature below 36.3 °C (97.4 °F) must be reported to the doctor, as a child can quickly suffer from hypothermia (the temperature of the whole body dropping abnormally low, so that the child gets extremely cold).

A clinical thermometer

If the doctor has to be sent for, make sure the child is resting comfortably. Parents should have a list of the symptoms and a note of the child's temperature if they have taken it. Hand-washing facilities should be ready for the doctor – the sink or bathroom is all that is needed. The child should not be given any medication; if aspirin or anything else has been given beforehand the doctor should be told. Once the doctor has been, his instructions should be followed, and the full course of any prescribed medicines should be given.

Medicines for children are usually made up as a syrup. A correct measuring spoon can be obtained from the chemist. Most children do not like taking medicine, so persuasion and even bribery must be used if necessary, although bribing a child may cause problems later. A dropper may be used for babies.

The following points must be observed when giving medicines:

- Wash your hands first.
- Read the label on the bottle to check that it is the right one, and to check the correct dosage.
- Shake the bottle if necessary.
- Hold the child's arms firmly, and place a cloth under his chin.

- Speak to him gently, and explain what is being done if he is old enough to understand.
- Fill the spoon to the level required.
- Tip the medicine into the child's mouth – into one of the cheeks, not pushing the spoon in so that he chokes.
- Hold his mouth closed until the medicine is swallowed.
- Reward him with extra attention, perhaps in the form of his favourite food, or a story, or a small present.
- If tablets are prescribed they can be crushed between the bowls of two spoons and then mixed with jam or honey.

When a child is ill he will need a lot more attention and loving care. He tends to become clinging and want his mummy, or the person who usually looks after him. Housework will have to be left until the child has his rest, or until someone else is prepared to sit with him.

The child who is really ill will want to stay in bed or in his cot, but as he begins to recover there is no need for him to be forced to stay in his room. He will much prefer to be wrapped up, lying in an armchair or on the settee where he can see his family and watch TV. He must not be allowed to overtire himself and should have a rest period morning and/or afternoon.

A child who is ill needs:

- to be in a room with a fairly constant warmth – about 22°C (72°F). If the room is too hot he will become flushed and uncomfortable.
- plenty of fluid (but food can be gone without until his appetite returns).
- to be kept clean and comfortable, with his bed freshened often.
- to be given plenty of opportunity for undisturbed rest and sleep.
- contact with his mother and the rest of the family. His bedroom door should be left open so that he is aware of their presence.
- his medication given to him as prescribed.

He is likely to be irritable and revert to babyish ways, so parents must be patient.

As he gets better he will need amusing much more as he will feel bored and lonely. His appetite will need to be tempted with small, attractive, nourishing meals, and he should get some fresh air – a short rest in the garden or a ride in the pushchair if the weather is suitable. A few special treats, and something to look forward to, such as a day at the zoo or the seaside when he is better, will help.

Amusing the sick child

A sick child needs activities which are slightly below his normal capabilities, and he has a shortened span of interest. TV and the radio are very good but it is more fun if someone else is there too – Mother or Father could be doing a household job whilst keeping him company. A large tray or bed table will form the base for jigsaws, building bricks and construction games, felt shapes, lacing and threading games; and children will spend a long time crayoning, painting or drawing, especially if the picture is hung on the wall afterwards, or sent to grandparents. The young child will enjoy making odds-and-ends toys with the help of an adult. Bits of wool, string, beads, empty cartons, foil, cotton-reels, squeezy bottles, etc., can be made into different fun objects.

The child will enjoy simple games of picture dominoes, noughts and crosses, ludo, picture lotto, word and number games – according to his ability.

Books are invaluable when a child is ill. Children always love being told stories, shown picture books or having rhymes and songs sung to them. Older children will spend some time looking at books and comics by themselves.

As the child becomes more active he will enjoy helping in the house. He can help with the baking or dusting. If he is with one parent all day he will enjoy the company of the other parent or brothers and sisters when they are at home. Grandparents and other relations or friends can be encouraged to visit and keep him company for a while.

Going into hospital

Sometimes a small child needs to have a stay in hospital. Almost half of all children under five will need to go to hospital for one of the following reasons:

- accidents at home such as poisoning.
- infections of the chest or stomach.
- surgery to deal with broken bones or special conditions.
- treatment of congenital conditions.

If possible the child should be prepared for the situation. It can be very traumatic and a serious emotional shock, and no child should just be delivered to the hospital and left. The child should go to a hospital which has special wards for children with specially trained staff. There should be unlimited visiting hours and if possible accommodation for the parents of children, especially those under the age of two. The DHSS has made these recommendations and parents should if necessary form pressure groups to see that their local hospitals carry out these recommendations.

The National Association for the Welfare of Children in Hospitals (NAWCH) is concerned with the comfort and care of children in hospital and helps to fight for the rights of parents.

A child should be prepared for going into hospital by:

- discussing the matter with him fully, if he is old enough.
- showing him books and telling him stories about being in hospital.
- explaining about the staff and the jobs that they do.
- if possible, visiting the place beforehand.
- playing games of doctors and nurses, letting him have a toy stethoscope and bandage up his teddy.

- letting him help pack his suitcase, and buying him new pyjamas or a new toothbrush. Let him take his favourite toy, his teddy, and his comforter if he has one.
- leaving his favourite soft toy on his bed, ready for when he comes home.

When he goes into hospital his parents should take him, undress him, show him where the toilets are, and stay with him as long as possible. One of them should visit as often as possible – several times a day – and friends and relations should be encouraged to visit. Take a small present each time, but not food or drink. Keep reassuring him that he is loved and missed at home, and how much everyone is looking forward to his homecoming. Try to be there when he comes round from an operation.

Parents should keep a check that the child is being well looked after and should be prepared to make enquiries if they think he is not.

When he comes home, he will probably cling to his mother or father and may act in a babyish way. He will need patience and understanding as it will have been a traumatic experience.

Parents can expect a few problems. He may be aggressive or withdrawn, he may start to wet the bed, or he may develop a stammer. These are all results of psychological upset, and will disappear when he readjusts.

Medication and follow-up checks and any special care instructions must be attended to.

A child who needs a long-term stay in hospital, or frequent stays, may develop long-term psychological problems and will need special care and attention.

Safety in the child's environment

Accidents, both inside and outside the home, are the main cause of death to children under five. The nought to five age group and the over 65s are the groups most at risk, as they are the ones who are least able to look after themselves. One in three accident patients in hospital is a child.

Young children are not aware of danger, and they do unexpected things. They do not know that if they eat certain things they will be poisoned, if they fall downstairs they may break bones, or if they touch a gas flame they will be burnt. It is therefore the responsibility of adults who look after children to try to foresee how accidents can happen and try to prevent them.

Safety in the home

No home can be totally accident proof, but most accidents in the home could be prevented with a little care and forethought. Children are more prone to non-fatal accidents than to fatal ones, but non-fatal accidents can leave permanent scars and damage. During an average year 230 000 children in the under-five age group will have an accident at home. The main types of accidents are:

- choking and suffocation
- scalds and burns
- falls
- poisoning
- cuts
- drowning
- electrocution.

Some of the causes of these accidents happening in the home are described below.

Choking and suffocation   Playing with plastic bags; cat lying on sleeping baby; swallowing small objects such as buttons, small toys, tiny sweets; leaving a baby to feed himself from a propped-up bottle; plastic bib blown over the face of a sleeping child; allowing a baby to have a pillow; cord or ribbon fastening at the neck of a garment; a dummy on a long string round baby's neck; food which is not suitably chopped or puréed for a small child, or has bones or gristle left in.

Scalds and burns   Having small child on lap when drinking a hot drink; bath water too hot and not tested first; open fires left unguarded; using fabric for children's clothing (especially nightwear) which is not flame-resistant; leaving matches or burning cigarettes lying about; leaving a teapot of tea on the edge of the table, or leads of electric kettles where toddlers can pull them, or saucepan handles overhanging the top of the cooker, or a washing machine containing hot water without its lid or with its door open.

Falls   Falling down stairs and steps; not using safety gates; poor lighting on the staircase; leaving things on the floor for children to fall over; leaving small children unstrapped in high chairs or prams; the drop-down side of a cot not being secure; babies rolling off surfaces such as beds, tables, or changing worktops; windows left open; cots placed under unbarred windows in the nursery; falls from the balconies of flats.

Poisoning   Swallowing pills the child thinks are sweets; drinking medicines for someone else or in the wrong quantities; drinking disinfectants and cleaning fluids; eating cosmetics, which he finds in unlocked drawers and cupboards. Babies will also chew newspapers, paper bags, magazines, etc., which can be harmful, and they will chew painted woodwork, which can cause lead poisoning if the paint is not lead-free. Petrol, lighter fuel, turpentine and rat poison have all been known to cause accidental poisoning to children.

Cuts   Broken glass; broken crockery; sharp edges to toys; sharp knives; razor blades; scissors. Children walking or running with a tumbler or mug in their hands can fall and break it; they can run into glass doors or they can ride or push their toys into them and break them. Small children will pick up sharp household instruments and tools, not knowing that they can cut themselves.

Safety room by room

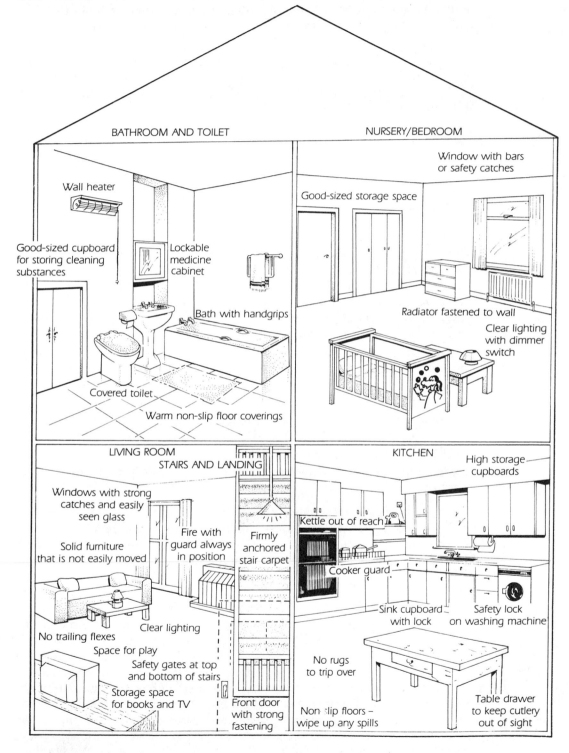

BATHROOM AND TOILET

Wall heater

Good-sized cupboard for storing cleaning substances

Lockable medicine cabinet

Bath with handgrips

Covered toilet

Warm non-slip floor coverings

NURSERY/BEDROOM

Window with bars or safety catches

Good-sized storage space

Radiator fastened to wall

Clear lighting with dimmer switch

LIVING ROOM STAIRS AND LANDING

Windows with strong catches and easily seen glass

Solid furniture that is not easily moved

Fire with guard always in position

Firmly anchored stair carpet

Clear lighting

No trailing flexes

Space for play

Safety gates at top and bottom of stairs

Storage space for books and TV

Front door with strong fastening

KITCHEN

High storage cupboards

Kettle out of reach

Cooker guard

Sink cupboard with lock

Safety lock on washing machine

No rugs to trip over

Non-slip floors – wipe up any spills

Table drawer to keep cutlery out of sight

Drowning   Being left alone in their bath, even when only for a few minutes. Children have also drowned in washing machines when left alone in the kitchen. A young child can drown in only a few centimetres of water.

Electrocution   Unsafe wiring or electrical appliances; small children poking knitting needles down the holes of sockets, or chewing through the trailing flex of an appliance, or pulling the back off an appliance or poking their fingers into the live parts.

Most of the accidents described above can be prevented by parents not allowing these circumstances to arise. Accidents can also be prevented by:

- making sure that *all* members of the family are safety conscious. This should include visitors to the house such as grandparents, relations and friends.
- never leaving a child alone unless he is completely secure, i.e. strapped in a pram or playing in a playpen; and even then frequent checks should be made to be sure he is safe.
- making sensible use of safety equipment such as a cat net on the pram, safety gates at the top and bottom of the stairs, a cooker guard, plastic plug-in socket covers, plastic film to cover glass doors and windows and hold glass in place if it is broken, window bars and safety catches, and cupboards with locks for keeping dangerous substances or articles.
- making sure that the home and garden are as safe as possible and carrying out regular checks on anything that may become dangerous. Repairs should be carried out immediately; damaged furniture, toys, worn carpets and damaged appliances have caused injury to many children.
- teaching a child how to cope with danger and how to be aware of it, without making him too timid. There should be a happy medium between recklessness and overprotection.
- setting a good example. Children will follow the example set by their parents.

There are lots of leaflets, booklets and posters available (some free) from the Health Education Council, the Royal Life Saving Society, RoSPA (the Royal Society for the Prevention of Accidents) the Electricity Council, and the British Standards Institution. These all give useful information about home safety and accident prevention.

A child will be very lucky indeed to avoid having any accidents at all, and parents should make as sure as possible that any accident is only a minor one, and that they have some idea of what to do in an emergency. All parents, especially the main person looking after the children, should have a basic knowledge of first aid, and there should be a well-stocked first aid kit easily accessible in every home. Either buy a special first aid box and contents, such as those supplied by Boots, or use a clean biscuit tin with a well-fitting lid, clearly labelled. Check the contents regularly to clear out old items and replace used ones. The box should be kept in the kitchen or bathroom out of reach of children.

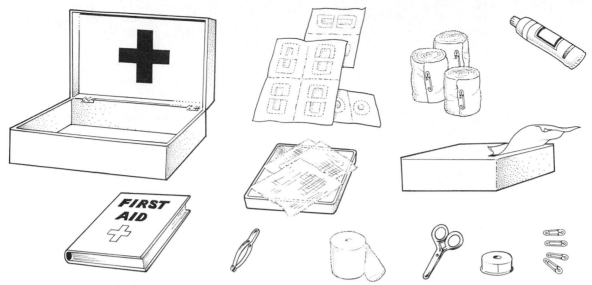

Contents of the first aid box

Contents should include adhesive dressings in various sizes; assorted bandages, including crepe bandages for strains; a packet of gauze dressings; a tube of antiseptic cream; a roll of cotton-wool; paper handkerchiefs; a roll of adhesive tape; safety-pins; blunt-ended scissors; tweezers; medicaments such as paracetamol, milk of magnesia, insect repellent, calamine lotion, TCP and Burn-eeze; and a first aid manual.

It is sensible to keep a special cupboard for storing medicines. It should be cleared out regularly to get rid of old medication.

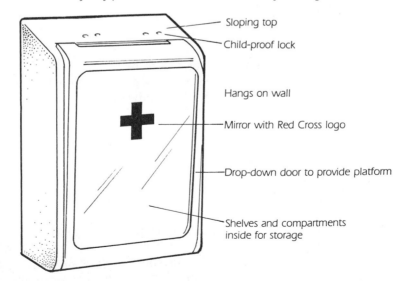

A medicine cabinet

Contents should include all medicines prescribed for anyone in the family; pain killers, such as aspirin (*not* for the under 12s – see the note on p. 187); laxatives; kaolin mixture (for stomach upsets); antiseptic creams; eye and ear drops; nasal sprays; medicaments for cold relief; cough mixtures; medicine spoons; a medicine glass; and a clinical thermometer (or a heat strip).

General points

- Everyone in the house should know where the first aid box is.

- There should be a list of telephone numbers that may be needed, i.e., those of the doctor, ambulance, hospital, fire service and police.

- In an emergency try not to panic. Even if feeling panicky the parent should try to appear calm, and think clearly.

- Remove the child from the source of the accident, e.g., switch off the electricity, heat or gas, remove the child from the water, remove knife or tablets, etc.

- In the case of poisoning try to keep some of the poison (tablets, medicine, bleach, plant, etc) to show to the doctor.

- Stay with the child, or leave someone with the child and get help as quickly as possible.

- Do not administer any first aid unless you know what you are doing. Badly applied first aid can make matters much worse.

- Do not give the child anything to eat or drink. Keep the child warm, check that he is able to breathe, and get help.

- If the accident only appears to have minor effects, e.g., a fall, the child should be carefully observed for some time afterwards to check for delayed reaction. A check-up with the doctor or hospital is usually necessary.

- A little bit of blood goes a long way. What may appear to be a severe cut may only be a minor scratch when the blood is wiped away.

- The child will be frightened and will need calm reassurance and soothing, certainly not being shouted at or scolded.

Treatment for specific injuries changes from time to time as improvements are made. It is wise to keep up to date. First aid courses are often arranged by local hospitals, health centres, the St John's Ambulance Association, the Red Cross Society or local education centres. Knowing what to do in an emergency will give confidence and help to reduce panic.

Treatments for specific injuries

Injury	Treatment
Burns and scalds	Use only cold water to treat burns or scalds. Hold the burn in cold water for several minutes – under running water if it is a small hand burn. This will reduce the heat in the skin. Remove any tight clothing, and any fabric that is soaked in boiling water or a corrosive chemical such as bleach. Do not remove any burnt fabric. Do not apply ointment, cream or butter. Do not prick blisters. Medical treatment is usually needed.
Bleeding and cuts	For minor wounds the bleeding will soon stop of its own accord. The wound should be cleaned and a plaster put on. For severe bleeding, press firmly on the wound with a pad of cotton-wool, pressing the edges of the cut together. Lay the child down and raise the affected limb; this helps to stop the bleeding. Apply a clean dressing and take the child to hospital for stitches. A wound that pierces the flesh, such as a dog bite, or one that happens in the garden, will make a tetanus injection necessary.
Broken bones	Do not move the child if you think a bone may be broken, unless he has to be moved from danger. If the leg is broken, tie the uninjured leg gently to the injured one, putting padding between. Put an injured arm in a supporting sling if possible, and get help as soon as you can.
Choking	Do not try to remove the object with your fingers – you may only push it further in. Hold a baby or small child upside down by the legs and give sharp slaps between the shoulder blades. A larger child should be held round the waist and tipped well forward over the parent's arm, then slapped sharply on the back between the shoulder blades.
Drowning	Remove child from water, lay him on his back and give **mouth-to-mouth resuscitation** immediately, even if the child appears dead. *Mouth-to-mouth resuscitation* 1 Clear the child's mouth of any dirt, vomit, etc. 2 Push the child's head back and chin upwards to clear the airways. 3 Put your mouth over the child's nose and mouth and blow gently (20 breaths per minute) so that the child's chest moves. 4 Continue doing this until the child starts to breathe again. 5 Place child in the recovery position, by turning him half over on to his stomach with one arm slightly behind him and the other arm bent in front. Bend the lower leg up to support the lower body and turn his head to one side.
Poisoning	If the child has swallowed pills or medicine get him straight to hospital, taking some of the substance with you. Do not try to make him sick. If he has swallowed household or garden chemicals including corrosive substances (such as bleach or weed killer), give him milk or water to dilute the poison, then get him to hospital.
Electric shock	Switch off the current immediately, at the mains if it can be reached quickly, or if not by pulling out the plug. Do not touch the child until you have done so or you may also get a shock. If you cannot switch off the current, stand on a box or rubber mat and push the child away from the source of the electricity with a chair or broom handle. Make sure your hands are dry. If he has stopped breathing give *mouth-to-mouth resuscitation* (see 'Drowning' above). If his heart has stopped, immediately begin **CPR** (cardiopulmonary resuscitation). *CPR* 1 Put the heel of one hand on the child's breastbone, just above the notch where the ribs meet it, and place the other hand on top of that. Keep your fingers lifted off the child's chest. *(continued)*

Injury	Treatment
	2 Kneel beside the child with your shoulders directly over his breastbone.
	3 Push down with straight arms so that the child's breastbone goes down about 2.5–3.0 cm (1–1½ in.) then release it. Repeat this five times.
	4 Quickly lean towards the child's head and push his chin up. Put your mouth over his nose and mouth, and blow gently once.
	5 Go on giving five compressions and one breath like this until the child's heart starts. Then give *mouth-to-mouth resuscitation* (see 'Drowning' above) until the child starts breathing.
Suffocation	Remove the cause of suffocation, usually a plastic bag or a pillow, and give *mouth-to-mouth resuscitation* (see 'Drowning' above) if breathing has stopped.
Falls	Children fall down frequently and usually recover very quickly. If, however, a short time after the fall the child is sick, drowsy, bleeds from the ears or becomes unconscious, he may have damaged his skull and needs immediate medical attention.

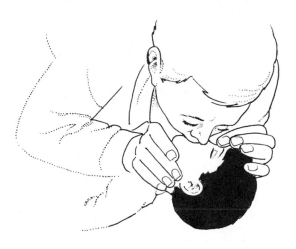

Mouth-to-mouth resuscitation for a child

Safety in the garden

Most of these points are obvious, but unfortunately many children have accidents in the garden because it is not regarded as needing the same security as the home.

- Cover any ponds, water butts or paddling areas with wire mesh or a lid.
- Fence the whole area, and keep the fence in good repair. Have child-proof catches on the gates and make sure people visiting or delivering post, milk, etc., do not leave them open.

- Keep all garden tools and substances in a locked shed.
- Fence off rubbish bins and garden refuse. Remove animal droppings as soon as they are spotted.
- Always use a fine mesh pram safety-net when leaving a baby outside in his pram.
- Keep garden toys in good repair and see they are of a safe design. The hard edges of swings should be padded with soft material such as old rubber tyres.
- Teach children how to climb trees, climbing frames, etc., safely and carefully, without reducing their sense of adventure.
- If any DIY jobs are being done, such as building or repairing walls or greenhouses, toddlers must be kept well away.
- Barbecue equipment or fuel and garden lights can be very attractive to small children.

The flowers and other plants shown here are poisonous and should never be grown in a garden where children play.

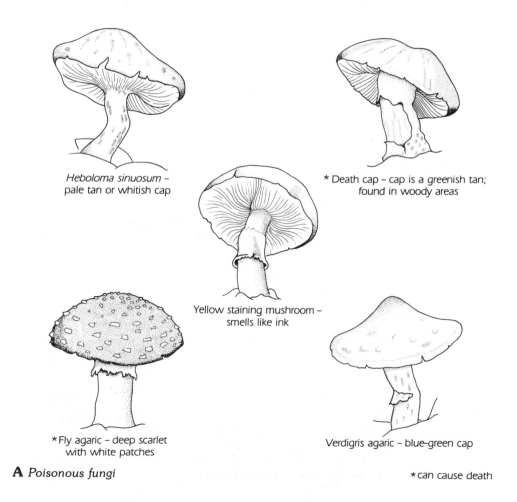

*Heboloma sinuosum –
pale tan or whitish cap*

* Death cap – cap is a greenish tan;
found in woody areas

Yellow staining mushroom –
smells like ink

*Fly agaric – deep scarlet
with white patches

Verdigris agaric – blue-green cap

A *Poisonous fungi*

*can cause death

B *Poisonous flowering shrubs*

*can cause death

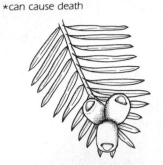

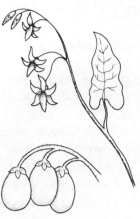

* Yew – pink berries; very poisonous

Woody nightshade – clusters of
poisonous red berries; shiny leaves

*Laburnum tree – seeds can kill;
commonest cause of poisoning
by plants in the UK

C *Other poisonous plants*

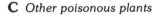

* Deadly nightshade – berries look
like small black cherries

Wild arum – clusters of red berries

Black bryony – hundreds of
bright red berries

* Thorn apple – seeds can cause death

* Hemlock – leaves look like parsley;
seeds cause death

Safety on the roads

On average, nearly 500 children a year are killed in road accidents, and nearly 50 000 children a year are injured in road accidents. Many of those who are injured are left with permanent scars and disabilities.

There are thousands more minor accidents which could have been worse. The young and the elderly are those most at risk. The risks can be lessened by:

- parents teaching children road safety as soon as they are able to understand.
- constantly reinforcing road safety drill.
- never letting young children out by themselves until they understand and can cope with dangers on the roads.
- adults showing a good example, and never taking risks themselves or allowing a child to take risks.
- teaching children the Green Cross Code when they are able to understand it.

The Green Cross Code

1 **Find a safe place to cross, then stop.**
2 **Stand on the pavement near the kerb.**
3 **Look all round for traffic and listen.**
4 **If traffic is coming, let it pass. Look all round again.**
5 **When there is no traffic near, walk straight across the road.**
6 **Keep looking and listening for traffic while you cross.**

The following points are important:

- Walking reins or harness should be used for small children when they are out shopping or near a busy road, or when mother is pushing a pram or looking after other children.

- Children should only play on scooters, bikes, tricycles, etc., in their own garden or in play parks, not on open roads. This type of large equipment must be kept in good working order.

- Ice-cream vans attract children. They should never play near them or run over to one.

- Use of fluorescent materials (colour-glow treated) helps to make children more easily seen in dim conditions. Garments such as jackets or trousers can have fluorescent strips stuck on; fluorescent socks, wellingtons, bags, can be bought; and fluorescent wool can be used for hats and mittens.

- Children should be warned not to answer anyone in the street if they do not know them, and certainly not to go away with them for any reason.

- There may be a Tufty Club in the area where the child lives. These teach the over-threes road safety in a way that is fun.

- Parents should teach their children how to cross roads safely by using pedestrian crossings, pelican crossings, footbridges or underground causeways. They should know that policemen and the lollipop lady or man will see them across.

Always remember: small children run rather than walk, do things on impulse, soon forget instructions, and are not aware of danger. That is why they are so much at risk on the roads.

Safety in cars

Children should always be fastened in. It is against the law to hold a baby or child on your lap in the front seat. They should never stand on the floor or the seat at the back, and they should not be allowed to lean out of the windows or wave from the windows. All doors should have child-proof locks, and special harnesses should be fitted as follows:

Stage 1   *Carrycot restraint harnesses* are strong webbing straps attached to the back seat, which fit round the carrycot to prevent it sliding and being thrown forward.

Stage 2   *Car safety seats* are special safety seats that clip to attachments in the back of the car. They are suitable for children of 9–18 kg (1st 6lb–2st 12lb).

Stage 3   *Car safety harnesses* are adjustable waist and shoulder straps with quick-release fasteners. They fit on to the back seats and are suitable for children of 18–36 kg (2st 12lb – 5st 10lb).
Booster seats, to be used on an adult's lap or the back seat of the car and with a diagonal seat belt, raise the child and make him comfortable and able to see out of the window.

Safety harness

Safety seat

Carry cot restraint harness

Safety equipment for cars

Safety at play

In a public park or playground

Many of the points discussed under garden safety apply here also.

As there is more space and more people about, it is easy for the child to wander off and get lost. Parents should never lose sight of their child and should supervise his play. Open stretches of water, dogs, ball games, toy equipment, other children on bicycles, suspect strangers, dirty sweets and food to be picked up, are all possible hazards in a public playground. Parents should check the large-scale play equipment for safety before they allow their child to go on it, and the under-fives need supervision when playing on swings, slides and roundabouts. Most public parks have a first aid centre and parents should know where it is. It is also wise to carry a mini first aid kit ready for emergencies, composed of medicated wipes, antiseptic cream, plasters, antiseptic dressings and sting cream.

A playground for children should have a soft surface such as grass, sand or loose gravel, not concrete, and the equipment should not be too high. There should be plenty of room around the swings and roundabouts. Dogs should be banned, or there should be a fence round the play area. Slides should be built into a slope, and there should be frequent inspections to check the safety of the equipment and to carry out repairs. There should be an age restriction, and the park should be supervised.

Water and ice

Many children are drowned each year, either at home, in ponds or rivers, in swimming baths or at the beach. Small children should never be left unsupervised near water, even if it is only a few centimetres deep. Observe the following rules:

- Teach children to swim at as early an age as possible.
- Teach them to respect water but not to fear it.
- Use water wings, safety floaters and rubber rings to give them early confidence.
- Do not let them paddle in a dirty river, pond or paddling pool, especially if there is a danger of broken glass or sharp stones.
- Do not let them paddle or swim in any water where there are strong currents.
- Never allow a child to use an air bed, rubber boat or water toy if there is any risk of it being blown out to sea.
- Do not let a small child get out of his depth in the sea or at the baths.
- Children should not play on ice – even if it is thick enough to bear their weight at the edges, it gets thinner towards the middle, and immersion in icy water can kill within seconds.
- Life jackets must always be worn by children when holidaying or living on boats.

There are many other points about safety, too numerous to include, but the main point is this: **never leave a child at risk.**

There is a Safety activity on p. 274

Follow-up exercises

Category 1

1   What could be the possible results of:
   a)   introducing mixed feeding too early?
   b)   giving foods to a baby that contain a large proportion of sugar?
   c)   parents getting tense and anxious at meal times and trying to make the baby eat?

   d)   giving a baby insufficient fibre in his diet?

   e)   reheating left-over milk from the baby's bottle to give to the child again?

   f)   parents tasting the food and using the same spoon to feed the baby?

2 True or false?

   a)   Weaning begins when the baby is about four months old.

   b)   The best time to introduce solid food is at the 6.00 p.m. feed.

   c)   It encourages bad habits to allow a baby to play with his food.

   d)   The more solid food a baby takes, the fewer milk feeds he will need.

   e)   From the age of six months onwards babies can be given boiled cow's milk.

   f)   A purée is food which has been well chopped up.

   g)   It is all right to give a rusk which has fallen on the floor back to the baby, as long as it has not been there very long.

3 *a)*   Make a list of things which will help a child get off to sleep and have a good night's rest.

   b)   Approximately how much sleep is required by a child aged:

       i 4 weeks?   *iii* 16 months?

       ii 9 months?   *iv* 2–5 years?

4 What would you consider when buying bedding for a cot, and sleepwear for a toddler?
Illustrate your answer and give details of fabric and cost.

5 Why are the garments worn by this child totally unsuitable for most of the activities in a child's life?

6 Discuss the advantages and disadvantages of pure wool when used for a hand-knitted sweater for a child.

7 Match the fabric to the garment:

Fabric	*Garment*
Stretch towelling	Raincoat
Flame-resistant polyester cotton	Tracksuit
Corduroy	Nightdress
Pure wool	Dungarees
Denim	Boy's shirt
Fleecy-lined cotton	Child's dress
PVC	Sleep suit
Lawn	Trousers
Viyella	Cardigan

8 Suggest several ways in which parents could save money when buying clothing and footwear for children.

9 Describe some of the symptoms which could lead you to think that a child has an infectious disease.

10 Describe the rash which is a symptom of:
measles

chicken pox

scarlet fever.

11 What simple remedies would you keep in the house for the following common ailments in children?

cradle cap   insect bite

headache   an itchy rash

constipation

12 How would you take the temperature of a small baby who is feverish and restless?

13 Why should:
a) the full course of any antibiotic be given to a sick child?
b) the medicine bottle be shaken before the dose is given?
c) medicine be poured into the cheek of a small child?
d) the label of the medicine bottle be read?
e) a correct measuring spoon be used?
f) the bottle be wiped after use and the cap screwed on firmly?

Category 2

14 Make a chart that shows the difference between the daily diet of a child of six months and one of a year.

15 Explain the meaning of the following terms:

obesity   vitamin deficiency

malnutrition   empty calories

16 Plan the food for the following situations:

a party for a small group of two- or three-year-olds

a picnic lunch for a child going on a playgroup outing

a Sunday lunch for a family consisting of mother, father, grandmother, a five-year-old and a nine-month-old baby.

17 Explain how and why the following things will help with a child's toilet training:

a well-chosen potty

trainer pants

a relaxed attitude from parents

ignoring the age at which other children are toilet trained

a child-sized lavatory seat

18 How can parents who live in a block of high-rise flats with balconies ensure that their chidren have sufficient opportunities for outdoor play?

19 Copy out this diagram of the sole of a shoe into your notebook.

a) Draw in the line where the end of the big toe should come, the line where the back of the heel should come, and the natural shape of the foot.

b) Name three suitable types of fastening for the shoes.

c) What should they be made of if they were for winter? And for summer?

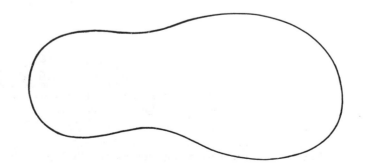

20 From the group of toys illustrated select those which would be useful in developing:

hand/eye co-ordination

locomotion

manipulative skills.

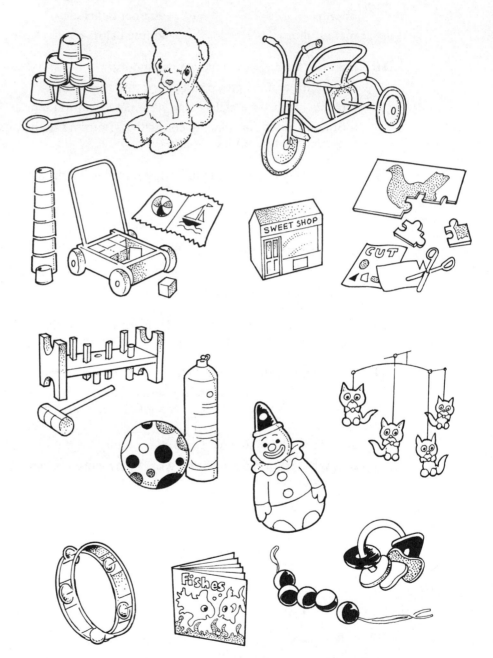

Toys to promote physical development

21 *a)* Draw a simple design, and the plans, for a wooden toy which a parent could make that would help with a child's physical development.

   b) Make a list of the safety features you would consider.

22 How do large-scale garden toys, e.g., a climbing frame, contribute to physical co-ordination and development?

23 How can the following things contribute to a child's ill-health?

poor food hygiene

cold, damp housing conditions

a family pet

24 Explain the meaning of the following words and their connection with disease.

bacteria   viruses   fungi   parasites

25 Explain the difference between passive and active immunisation.

26 What factors might influence parents in deciding whether or not to have their child immunised against whooping cough?

27 You are looking after a four-year-old for the day. He is recovering from an attack of measles.
Write down your time plan for the day to include meals, rest times, etc., and suggest several ways in which you could amuse him.

28 How can a child be helped to readjust after a long-term stay in hospital?

Category 3

29 *a)* Suggest the ways in which a child might show that a new toy was too advanced for his stage of development.

   b) How would you deal with a situation in which a child's grandparents had bought him a much too advanced toy, e.g., a difficult jigsaw or a large bicycle?

30 What features would you look for in a hospital that specialises in looking after sick children?

Activities

1 Make a list of the advantages and disadvantages of the three main methods of making a purée. (These are shown on p. 159). Practise making some food purées using cooked fruit, vegetables and meat. Remember: use the minimum amount of sugar or salt. Try all three methods. Which is easiest? Which gives the best result?

2 *a)* Make some suggestions, with illustrations, of ways of making some sweet and some savoury dishes attractive to a child.

b) Make a survey of commercial baby foods. Work out the price of a portion of different foods (for example, a mixed fruit dessert) when bought in a tin, bought in a packet (dried), and homemade.

c) Study the list of contents on various brands of baby foods. Which manufacturers use the most additives and what are they?

d) Make a recipe booklet of dishes suitable for a toddler. Put down the main nutrients each recipe contains.

e) Make a large bib for a baby, using perhaps the best part of an old towel. Bind the edges, line it with plastic and stitch an appliqué motif on the front.

f) Make a table mat specially for the young child. It must be washable and quite thick.

Plastic-lined towelling bib with appliqué design

Towelling cover-all with back button fastening and decorative pocket

Recipe book for the under-fives

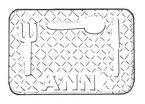

Quilted table mat with appliqué cutlery and child's name

Coloured felt fish-shaped table mat with lines of coloured embroidery or binding

3 Copy these sketches into your book. Draw in the design features for each garment, such as pockets, appliqué, fastenings, etc. Put details of fabric, sizes, cost and other features as though these were designs for a catalogue of children's clothes.

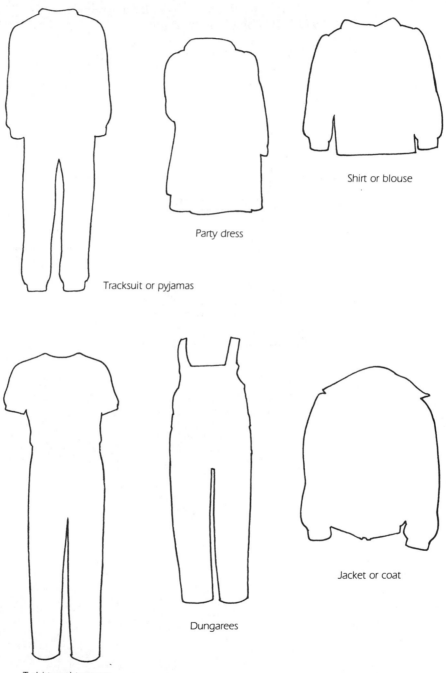

Shirt or blouse

Party dress

Tracksuit or pyjamas

T-shirt and trousers

Dungarees

Jacket or coat

4 A sweater top can be made for a child simply by knitting four rectangles of plain or stocking stitch. You will need 180 g (6 oz) of double-knitting wool and a pair of 4 mm (size 8) needles. Odd balls of wool could be used up to make a striped sweater. Follow the diagrams.

Knit a pom-pom hat to go with it, again using a straight piece of knitting, gathering up the top and putting a pom-pom on. (Mittens from the same wool will complete the outfit.)

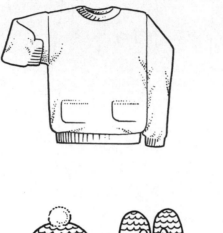

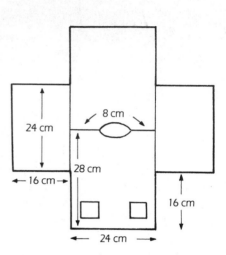

SECTION E **Intellectual Development**

11 Stages of Intellectual Development

It is easy to understand the process of physical development and how the child's body grows and matures during those first important years, because we can see those developments taking place. It is not so easy to understand the development of the intellect and the growth of understanding, because these are invisible and not so obvious. Physical and intellectual development, however, take place side by side, and from the moment the child is born she is absorbing knowledge through her senses (sight, sound, smell, touch and taste) from all the things going on around her.

Because, during the first few weeks, the baby's senses are not fully developed and she spends much of her time sleeping, she absorbs stimulation passively and does not appear to give much response. However, her brain and nervous system are accepting her various experiences and building up **concepts** (patterns of ideas). Intellectual development takes place in natural stages from early babyhood to adulthood (**maturation**), but this rate of development can be increased by providing visual and verbal stimulation and a rich environment from the start. We have seen that the average age at which a baby can reach out and grasp an object with accuracy is about five months, but experiments have shown that by enriching the child's environment this stage can be achieved by three and a half months. The enrichment in the experiment consisted of:

- increasing the amount of physical contact with the children.
- placing the children on their stomachs so that they could look round.
- replacing plain bedding with patterned.
- hanging an interesting mobile over the babies' cots.

It was noted that the babies took no notice of the mobile until after they were two months old, showing that they had to reach that stage of development before they could make use of the stimulation, but they then progressed more quickly because of the external stimulation.

Professor Jean Piaget

One of the most important people to have studied the intellectual development of the child is Professor Jean Piaget, a Swiss psychologist, whose work forms the basis for most modern studies on the subject. His experiments and studies led him to believe that the sort of person we become, in our behaviour and our personality, depends upon the events and influences of our early life. This is why parental influence and guidance is so important during the first formative years – the earliest part of a child's life is crucial in determining what sort of mature adult she will grow into.

Cognitive development

There are five stages of **cognitive** (intellectual) development through which a child must pass before she reaches maturity. The normal age at which each phase takes place is given in the chart that follows, but this will be influenced by two factors, **nature** and **nurture**.

- *Nature* means the internal factors that influence the child's development – her genetic make-up, the characteristics she receives from her parents, etc.
- *Nurture* means the external influences coming from the child's environment and the people she is in contact with – verbal and visual stimulation; a healthy environment and diet; feelings of love, security and confidence inspired by family and friends, etc.

Both of these factors will influence the rate at which development takes place.

The five main stages of intellectual development

Stage	Age (approximate)	Description
1 **The baby** Sensori-motor period	Birth to 2 years	*This is an intellectually experimental stage. The child is dependent upon the adult looking after her for all her needs and is totally **egocentric** (self-centred). It is a mainly non-verbal stage, the baby making known her requirements by crying or shouting. During this stage the child learns through sight, sound, touch, smell and taste to recognise objects; first of all her own fingers and hands and feet, then objects such as her feeding bottle or toys. She then begins to realise that objects removed from her sight are still there and will return. She is building up a series of experiences and linking them together.*
2 **The toddler** Pre-conceptual period	2–4 years	*At this stage the child is still egocentric and only capable of seeing things from her own point of view. She is learning to speak and to put her ideas into words, and will often speak her thoughts out loud. She may like the company of other children but is not yet capable of co-operation or playing together. She gains experience by trial and error.*
3 **The infant** Intuitive period	4–7 years	*During this stage the child is acting through intuition and previous experience, not through concrete ideas or logical reasoning. She begins to play with other children in a social way and is becoming a more independent character. Gradually she begins to associate objects with each other and to be aware of numbers. By the age of five she can understand mass (e.g., that several sections will make a whole), by the age of six she understands weight, and by seven she understands volume.*

(continued)

Stage	Age (approximate)	Description
4 The junior Concrete-operational period	7–11 years	*Logical thought and operations begin. The child begins to understand the basic ideas of mathematics, can classify groups of objects logically and can arrange objects in order. She becomes self-reliant and desires to be independent of adults. Children at this stage form into gangs of their own age and sex, strong friendships are formed and the good opinion of their **peer group** (people around them of their own age) is desired.*
5 The adolescent Abstract thinking period	11 years onward	*This is the stage when young people begin to deduce and to consider concepts which are not necessarily concrete ideas. They think on a hypothetical level and reason problems through. It is a period of great mental development when a fund of factual knowledge is gathered and the skills of language, numeracy and reasoning are built up.*

We can see that it is useless to try to force a child to learn a certain intellectual skill, such as reading or numeracy, if she has not yet reached that stage of development. If, however, she misses out on a skill, she can catch up at a later stage, but it may be more difficult for her to do so. For example, most children learn how to read between five and eight years old, and being unable to read by then makes learning harder later on.

Patterns of learning

Human infants have a long period of learning before they can become independent. Puppies and kittens are quite independent after only a few weeks, but it takes a child at least eight or nine years to achieve any sort of independence. The usual pattern of intellectual development and the stages of learning are as follows.

During the first month the baby is conditioned by the reflex actions with which she is born. She is exploring the very small world around her, and will gradually learn from her limited experiences, both those which bring her pleasure and those which bring her pain. Bathing, for instance, is a strange and frightening experience and at first she will scream with fear. As her experience of bathing increases she will learn not to be afraid and will eventually feel pleasure and enjoyment.

During the second and third months the baby's activities will begin to stretch beyond her own basic reflexes for survival. She will stretch out and grasp for pleasure. Her eyes will follow a moving object, and she will smile briefly at a person she knows well.

During the fourth month her actions are far more purposeful. She will reach for specific things, respond to a voice, show pleasure by smiling, and cry from anger and frustration as well as from fear or pain.

During the following few months the baby builds upon the many learning patterns which she has formed during her first months. She will be able to grasp objects and put them to her mouth, and will learn through sucking, taste and smell. She learns how to become mobile and can, therefore, explore and investigate.

After about nine months the baby will realise that an object may still be there even if she cannot see it – until then she is only interested in an object if she can see it. She may now look for it in the place she last saw it, but it is not until she is 18–20 months that she can use her mind to reason that the object may be elsewhere and she may find it by searching. The development of language means that she is able to communicate and to understand what other people want.

By the time she is one year old:
- she will recognise her own name and respond to it.
- she will understand many words and commands and will be trying out language for herself by putting together sound such as strings of repeated syllables ('mamama' and 'dadada').
- she will not be using her mouth so much to examine things, but will use her hands more.
- her memory is developing. She will remember, for example, that if she bangs her table with a spoon it makes a noise, and she will repeat the action again at a later stage.
- she is beginning to reason things through. For example, when she hears her food being prepared and her bib is tied on, she gets excited because she reasons that her food is coming.
- she enjoys looking at herself in a mirror and will sometimes kiss the reflection.
- she loves games of peek-a-boo, singing and anything which makes people laugh.
- she likes stacking objects, placing things in containers, and noisy activities.
- she is very inquisitive and will try to find how things work. She will sit and look at a picture book and listen to a story. She will be associating words with objects and building up her vocabulary

The second year of a baby's life is one of intensive learning, when she is building upon her experience and learning new things. She makes rapid advances in language and mobility. She is at an age when she can understand the idea of toilet training. She is still very dependent upon her parents, usually her mother in particular, and she needs lots of loving and reassurance. Her curiosity and constant activity can make it a very dangerous period, because she is as yet unaware of hazards.

By the time she is two years old:
- she has left babyhood behind and is developing her own personality. The degree of her intelligence will be becoming apparent.
- she has learnt that objects exist even when she cannot see them.

- she can remember objects or people and recognise them when she sees them again.
- her speech is well developed and she chatters incessantly. At this stage she must have people around her who talk to her so that her vocabulary will increase.
- she realises that she is a separate being from the things and people around her, and that she can manipulate objects.
- she may be very changeable as she starts to try to achieve more independence. She may go through a negative phase, constantly saying 'no' and indulging in food fads and temper tantrums, while still craving affection.
- she enjoys lots of physical activities, but will also sit and enjoy stories and children's TV.
- she will think about a problem or situation and size it up and then may be able to foresee an answer. This is a great step forward from her previous acceptance of situations.

During the third year the child develops much more independence. From being a 'troublesome two' she develops into a 'thoughtful three'. The aggression and negative attitudes of a two-year-old can be channelled into more acceptable ways. As the child's world becomes wider and she gains confidence in her physical and linguistic abilities she becomes less dependent upon her parents and more willing to socialise.

The three-year-old:

- is constantly seeking for information and experimenting.
- knows her own age and understands the concept of time, past, present and future.
- has a good command of speech and can explain her wants and needs.
- is developing a good memory and may remember things from several months back.
- is very good at imitating and enjoys pretend and make-believe games.
- has an increasing span of attention and will concentrate and listen for quite long periods.
- enjoys creative activities, constructional toys, and helping with household jobs.
- is prepared to share her things with others and wants other friends to play with apart from her family.
- knows what sex she is and that boys and girls are different physically.

Over the next two years the child will spend much of her time investigating her surroundings, forming friendships, developing her vocabulary, and beginning to understand numeracy. She is so active and develops so quickly that she gets tired and needs plenty of rest. Her parents often expect more of her than she is capable of and she can rebel and revert to childish behaviour, or become rude and truculent.

The average five-year-old can usually count up to 15 and understand the idea of numbers, can write a few letters, and may be learning to read. She can say rhymes and understand stories, and she knows her name, address, birthday and telephone number. Her powers of concentration and memory are much improved, and she will be prepared to stick at a job until it is finished.

She is, however, still a child, and although she enjoys the company of other children and other people, she still very much needs the love and security of her parents and her home.

Follow-up exercises

Category 2

1   Write down the five stages of intellectual growth, beginning with the sensory motor period. To each stage, match one of the sentences given below.

   a)   The child's interests are centred upon herself, and she often talks to herself for quite long periods.

   b)   By this stage the child can reason things out and think on a hypothetical level.

   c)   The child becomes self-reliant at this stage, and forms gangs with children of the same sex and age.

   d)   The child becomes aware of mathematical concepts, and is ready to socialise with other children.

   e)   The child is learning through her five senses. Everything will be explored with her mouth if possible.

2   Why do you think that the term 'troublesome two' could be a good description for an active two-year-old?

Category 3

3   Imagine identical twins had been brought up separately in families with very different social and economic backgrounds. What might be the effects of nature and nurture?

Activities

1   Write a description of an average five-year-old and her abilities, including examples of any children of this age whom you know. Try to visit your local infant school. You may be allowed to help with lunchtime activities, or perhaps you could invite a small group to your school for a picnic tea. Notice how much more independent and mature an infant schoolchild is compared with a three-year-old.

12 Conditions for Intellectual Development

Steady and progressive development depends upon:

- providing a stimulating environment for the child, with parents, friends and teachers who will encourage the learning process.
- providing opportunities for the child to listen to speech and develop his own linguistic abilities.
- providing the toys, games and activities which are going to encourage learning during its various stages.

The child's environment

If a child is constantly kept in his pram or cot, quiet and away from other people, very rarely spoken to and with very little to observe, he will have nothing to stimulate his natural curiosity and learning abilities. He will become bored and show his frustration by crying, or as he gets older by becoming aggressive to get attention. Babies who are constantly ignored and left to themselves (which sometimes happens when they are left with uncaring child minders who try to look after too many children) will eventually become apathetic and just sit where they are put, with no desire to move. Their development will have been severely retarded.

Even a child only a month old will benefit from being propped up in the pram so that he can watch people doing household jobs. He will move his head so that he can watch and listen. He should be talked or sung to, and will also enjoy music on the radio, the sound of the vacuum cleaner and other household noises. When he is put outside in the pram he will watch leaves blowing, or the washing on the line. His span of attention is short, however, and he needs changes of activity and scenery. This is why a walk to the shops or in the park, pointing things out along the way, is intellectually as well as physically good for him. Pram and cot toys, mobiles and an unbreakable mirror, are all good during these early stages to provide stimulation.

The child does not need stimulating activity all the time and will enjoy quiet periods cuddling a toy, playing with a rattle, or, as he gets older, being shown a book. Books do not need to be bought –they can be homemade, relating specially to the child and the things around him.

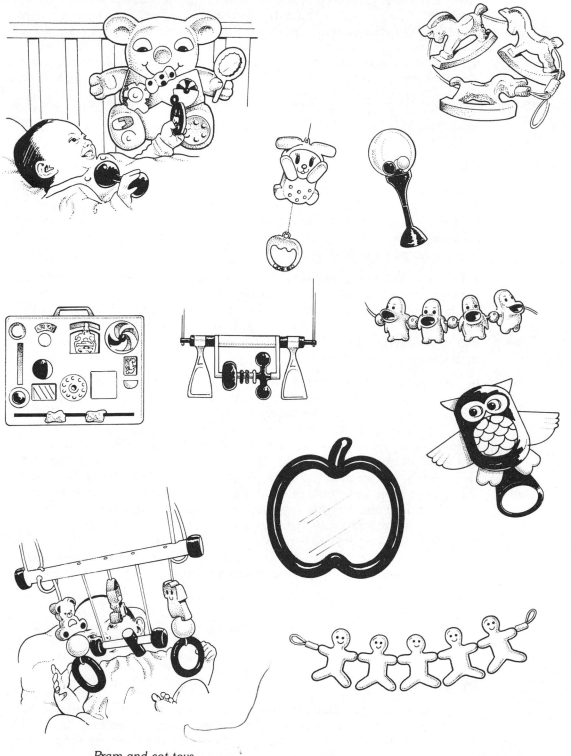

Pram and cot toys

Small children enjoy the company of other people, just as adults do. They like being with their mother or father, but they also enjoy watching other children, or adults, doing things and eventually will want to join in. It is good for them to be taken to the park to watch other children playing or games of football, tennis or bowls taking place. They like to sit on a beach and watch the water or the other children playing. They will enjoy the bustle of the market, going on a train, going to the public library or being taken to the swimming baths. They will be learning and building up different experiences all the time, ready for when they are older and can themselves be involved in the activity.

Groups for parents and young children

It is easy for a parent, usually the mother, with young children to become isolated, especially if she is living away from her original home town and has left her family and friends behind. There are several groups and organisations in existence that help to bring parents and young children together for friendship and social activities.

Many local churches have Young Wives Groups where mothers and children get together for discussions and activities. Meet-a-Mum Association (MAMA) has branches in various parts of the country to provide friendship and support, especially for new mothers. Some areas have One o'Clock Clubs, which open during the afternoons, and sometimes there is a Drop-in Club, which is open most days for coffee and a chat.

In many parts of the country there are Mother and Toddler Groups, which are set up by social workers, health visitors, the Women's Royal Voluntary Service, the Playgroup Association, or just by a group of mothers themselves. These groups provide a meeting place where mothers can discuss and obtain information about some of the problems of bringing up children, meet and make friends with other mothers and get together in social activities, and bring children together for play and activities. Mother and Toddler Groups usually welcome mothers with children under three, and the mother stays with her children. Sometimes there is a speaker or an organised discussion, but it is usually a very informal get-together, set up and paid for by the mothers themselves. These clubs are very valuable in widening the horizons of mothers and children; they provide toys, space and facilities for children to play that may not be available at home. The meetings usually last about two hours.

These activities allow a child to get used to the idea of meeting and being with other children and adults. As the child nears the age of three, he becomes ready for the next step, which is the more formal organisation of the playgroup or nursery school.

Playgroups

Many children benefit enormously from attending a playgroup, especially if they live in an area where there are few opportunities for meeting other children and no play parks nearby. All children, however, are not ready for a playgroup at the age of three and the parent should check that the child:

- has sufficient self-confidence.
- is accustomed to being with other adults.
- will not mind being without his parents for a few hours.
- can play with other children without being very aggressive or shy.
- will not be frightened by all the new experiences and surroundings.

The best course is to introduce the child into a playgroup when he is three. The parent should be prepared to stay with him for several mornings. If, after a while, he is prepared to venture away from his parent's side and begin to join in the activities and talk to the other children, the parent can then try leaving him for half an hour. If he is not happy, cries when he is taken and is obviously not enjoying it, it is best to leave it and try again at a later stage.

The advantages of going to a playgroup are that:

- the child learns to mix with other children and share things.
- he learns to be more independent and begins the process of learning some independence from his parents, especially his mother.
- he has the space to play which he may not have at home.
- he will have the benefit of a large selection of well-chosen toys and activities, including large-scale ones, which he will not have at home.
- there will be the encouragement and guidance of an experienced and qualified playgroup leader who will know how to encourage all aspects of development.
- it will be good preparation for the more structured life of the infant school.
- many playgroups organise special outings to zoos, parks, paddling pools, pantomimes, etc.
- both the children and their parents may benefit from a few hours' separation. The parents have a short time to pursue their own interests, meet friends or go shopping, knowing that the child is safe. Parents may have more patience and energy to give to their children because of this brief separation.

A playgroup does not try to teach a child traditional subjects such as reading, writing and arithmetic. The child is not old enough to comprehend these concepts and these are best left until he goes to infant school. The playgroup aims at learning through play, providing the stimulation and situations required for good intellectual, physical, social and creative development.

Playgroups first became popular in the 1960s, and the Pre-school Playgroups Association was formed to help women to get together and organise a playgroup in their own area. A playgroup is set up by a group of mothers, but by law it must then be registered and comes under the jurisdiction of the local authority. It is mainly financed by the parents themselves, but some local authorities and councils make contributions. It is a good thing to have parental involvement and there is usually a rota. The committee that organises the playgroup will fix the charges and arrange the accommodation and the times the group will meet. They usually welcome the help given by the children from local secondary schools and colleges, especially those on Child Development courses, and the system should be beneficial for the students who help, for the playgroup organisers, and for the children who attend the playgroup.

There is a Playgroup activity on p. 277.

Nursery schools

Parents may have the opportunity and prefer to send their children to a nursery school, rather than a playgroup. Nursery schools may be run by the State as part of the education system or may be privately owned. They are usually run along more formal lines than a playgroup and are staffed mainly by trained teachers or qualified nursery nurses. The number of places available in State-run nursery schools is very limited, and they are usually reserved for those children with special needs (whose parents both have to go out to work, who come from one-parent families, whose parents have mental problems, etc.).

The Plowden Report in the mid-1960s recommended State provision of nursery schools for all three-to-five year olds, but finance is still insufficient for this plan. State-run nursery schools may be run as a separate unit, or may be a nursery class attached to the infants' section of a primary school. The children may go every morning or only a few times a week, and the class is run by a specialist teacher and perhaps one or two helpers. The children spend some time in informal play and activities, but quite a lot of time sitting at tables in their own places. The atmosphere tends to be different from the more relaxed learning through play methods of the playgroups.

Care should be taken in the choice of privately run nursery schools. The fees charged should give some guide to their quality: but high fees do not necessarily mean a good school. The school should have plenty of suitable equipment, be kept in good repair and have trained staff, and to pay for this the parents should expect to pay a reasonable sum. Parents looking for a good school should visit the school beforehand and look for:

- spacious, well-maintained buildings with an outdoor play area.
- plenty of play equipment with room for movement and activities.
- a pleasant atmosphere and happy children.
- caring, well-trained staff.
- good standards of safety, hygiene, heating, lighting and toilet arrangements.

Information for parents

Many children benefit from attending a playgroup or nursery school, but if a child is happy at home, with plenty of other children to play with and parents who understand his needs and are able to give him plenty of time, he will develop just as well and be ready for compulsory schooling at the age of five. It is useful if parents have some knowledge of the way their child develops and how they can help, and there is a lot of valuable information available for parents and children. This includes:

- Open University courses on 'The First Years of Life' and 'The Pre-school Child'.
- TV and radio educational programmes that deal with pregnancy, birth and bringing up children.
- adult classes run by Local Education Authorities or health centres.
- information published by the Health Education Council, the British Association for Early Childhood Education, and the Advisory Centre for Education.
- videos and home computer programmes.
- postal play packs such as 'MacDonald 3/4/5' and the Humpty Dumpty Club, and postal catalogues such as those from the Early Learning Centre, Galt's and Hamleys offer advice on the choice of toys and activities.
- magazines designed for parents and children such as *Mother, Mother and Baby* and *Parents*, and lots of books on every aspect of child development. There is a list of some useful magazines, books and catalogues on p. 226.

Speech and language development

The acquisition of speech is one of the most important aspects of development. We have a need to communicate from the moment we are born and speech development will take place even if a child receives no encouragement; but progress will be better and more rapid given the correct conditions and stimulus.

Language is the key to learning. Without language a child cannot understand other people and cannot communicate with others. The child's first form of communication is usually with his mother, and happens when the newborn baby is picked up and spoken to. The child responds by looking into the face of the person holding him, and perhaps moving his head. He will continue to listen to the person's voice and watch her face, and eventually will begin to respond with smiles and coos and gurgles. The baby will communicate his needs, or his distress, by crying at first, but will also show pleasure with babbling and cooing noises. This interaction between parent and baby is very important as a first stage of language development. The baby learns quickly, especially if his parents talk to him a lot, maintain eye contact, vary their voices and use head and arm gestures to indicate their meaning. He will begin to imitate these expressions and sounds, until they are holding quite a conversation between them!

From babbling the baby will begin to produce the easiest of the speech sounds, which are the groups of vowels such as 'aa' or 'oo' and consonants such as 'mmm', 'ddd' and 'ppp'. It is a natural stage of progression to make these into the familiar 'da-da-da' and 'ma-ma-ma'.

Rate of progress

The rate at which the child progresses will depend upon:

- his own ability.
- the encouragement given by his parents.
- whether or not he has brothers and sisters.
- his contact with external stimulus.

This is the average rate of progress:

Up to 7 weeks The child cries, makes cooing noises, responds to noises and voices.

2-4 months The child starts to produce the simpler vowel sounds and some consonants.

4-6 months The child produces two-syllable words such as mama, dada.

6-9 months Babbling continues, but with more meaning. The child will be joining up more and more syllables (**jargoning**).

9-12 months The child will be able to say two or three words and understand some simple commands. He will say the words that indicate things that are important to him, such as 'mama', 'pussy', 'cup'.

18 months The child chatters a lot, can say six to twenty identifiable words, and has good comprehension.

18 months–2 years The child will be forming two-word phrases and short sentences such as 'me want apple'.

3 years The child chatters incessantly, has a vocabulary of at least two hundred words and understands many more. He is constantly asking questions.

By the time a child is five, he will have mastered the basics of language. He will be able to put his thoughts and ideas into words and should be able to understand at least two thousand words.

Conditions for progress

Children are not taught how to speak their own language; they are surrounded by people speaking it – in the home, in the street, on television, on the radio. The child realises that putting different sounds together expresses a meaning. His curiosity is aroused, and with increasing physical development, he sees a need to communicate. He imitates those around him, and each success gives him the confidence to try out more.

The adults around the child should:

- provide a source of natural, easily understood conversation.
- provide opportunities for him to experiment with language.
- listen to the child and try to understand his attempts at speech.
- respond to the child, praise his attempts and make him feel clever.

A child who is praised and encouraged will learn more quickly than a child who is constantly corrected, ignored or laughed at. Parents can help their child in his early attempts at speech by:

- speaking to him clearly and slowly, in a way that the child can understand and that suits his vocabulary.
- listening to the child, answering his questions, and giving him encouragement.
- being patient and not saying things for him or allowing his older brothers and sisters to speak for him.
- not showing obvious concern if the child appears to be slow at learning how to speak. Children develop in their own time.

Reasons for slow development

A child may be slow to develop language because:

- he is not often spoken to, or put into situations where conversation is taking place.
- he has psychological problems, such as word deafness (associated with **dyslexia** – inability to distinguish letters) or **autism** (extreme withdrawal and unresponsiveness).
- he has a physical defect such as deafness or a cleft palate. About five in every 2000 children are quite severely deaf.
- he is mentally retarded or has a handicap such as **cerebral palsy**.
- he is suffering from a disturbing emotional experience or physical ill-treatment.
- he has brothers and sisters who do it for him.
- he is not interested in speaking, and is a slow learner.
- he comes from a quiet, uncommunicative family.

If a child is not showing signs of speech – single words or jargon language – by the time he is 18 months, the clinic doctor or family doctor should be consulted and the child will be tested. It may be necessary for him to see a speech therapist, who will try to find the cause for the slowness.

Books, television and radio

One of the best methods of teaching language and communication skills is by using books. Looking at picture books, having a story read from a book and having words and pictures pointed out will all help a child to associate objects and language, and eventually lead to the desire to read and write for himself.

Even a small baby will enjoy sitting on his mother's or father's knee while his parent turns the pages of a book, pointing at the pictures and saying simple words. At first the baby is just enjoying the closeness of his parent, the cuddling and the voice, but quite quickly he begins to enjoy looking at the colourful, simple outlines and will start to imitate the word sounds.

First books should be bright and colourful, have simple pictures of familiar objects with uncluttered background, and be made of thick board or be rag books, so that the baby can clutch them or chew them. Examples are the first set of Ladybird books, which show simple everyday objects. It is very easy to make such a book from stiff card and thick coloured pens. The pages can even be given a clear plastic finish and then joined together concertina fashion. If you cannot draw very well, pictures can be cut from catalogues.

The next stage may be alphabet and number books, again with clear pictures and letters. From just looking at pictures and identifying them, it is easy to start telling stories about people and things. From about 18 months, the baby will love looking at pictures of nursery rhymes, having them said or sung to him and joining in the activities. Babies like the physical and verbal activity which accompanies such rhymes as 'One, two, three, four, five, once I caught a fish alive' or 'Sing a song of sixpence'. Traditional stories such as *The Gingerbread Man'* or *Three Little Pigs* are full of action, and the child will quickly learn how and when to join in.

By the time a child is two he will be willing to sit still for longer periods and listen to quite a long story. The books still need to have pictures to focus his attention, but the subject matter can be very varied. All children enjoy stories about animals, and like fantasy stories about people and things that could never exist, such as giants, gnomes, fairies and space men. They also enjoy tales about everyday life, and they can get reassurance from books that deal with normal problems such as going into hospital, going to the dentist, or having a new baby in the family. Some books deal with specific teaching topics, such as road safety, care of teeth, and telling the time.

The three- to five-year-old will sit for a long time looking at a book and being read to. He will be able to choose books for himself and will know a lot of the stories off by heart. Even when a child starts reading, he should still be read to by adults to provide close companionship and encourage an interest in books.

The preschool child may have quite a collection of books and he should be taught to take care of them. Many books are inexpensive, but some are beautifully illustrated and produced and made to be treasures, and are therefore more expensive. Books may be made at home, bought cheaply from jumble sales or book sales, or exchanged with other children. It is a good idea for parents to take their child to the public library when he is quite young. Most libraries have sections for very small children with special chairs and tables and activities. Often they hold special story-telling sessions, and give advice to parents on the choice of children's books. There are lots of different types of novelty books that may help to interest a child, such as books that squeak, pop-up picture books, jigsaw books with removable parts, books that float in the bath, and books with moveable pictures; but the main things to look for when choosing a book are these:

- Are the pictures colourful and clear and do they suit the text?
- Is it suitable for the child's stage of development?
- Is the language used simple enough and is the story of a suitable length?
- Have you chosen the book just because you like it, or because you think the child will enjoy it?

For the child who enjoys listening to stories on his own, or who is ill in bed, there are talking books. These are packs containing a picture book and a cassette that tells the story of the book.

Television and radio can never take the place of books, but they can be used to encourage children to learn and to discover the pleasure of books for themselves. Many of the characters in children's TV are also to be found in book series, such as Postman Pat, Paddington Bear and the Mister Men. Often if a child hears a story on the radio or sees it on TV, he will be encouraged to buy or borrow the book to read.

The best way to encourage a child's interest in books is for him to see his parents enjoying them. If he is surrounded by all forms of book, magazine, newspaper, etc. and is read to frequently he will accept it as a normal part of pleasurable learning.

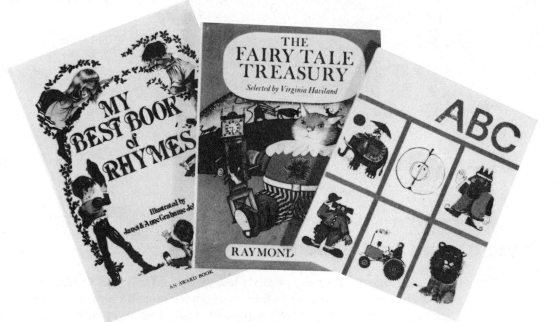

A selection of books

Toys, games and activities

We have seen that a baby of just a few weeks old will start to play, at first with his own fingers and toes, and then with objects around him. These objects are his toys: they may be modern, expensive, purpose-designed playthings or an old saucepan and a wooden spoon, but they will all be giving him the opportunity to learn. All toys, therefore, are educational.

Toys should be chosen to give the child the opportunity to investigate and experiment, and to develop skills. These skills may be physical, creative or imaginative, or the intellectual skills of numeracy and literacy, and of finding out facts. Parents should provide the child with the opportunities and the materials for developing intellectual skills, and also be prepared to give him their time, to answer his questions and to teach him these skills.

Suggested toys and activities for intellectual development

Age (approximate)	Stage of development	Toys and activities	Comments
0–6 months	*The senses are being developed. The baby is curious to know what is going on around him.*	*Toys that move and attract his gaze and hearing, such as mobiles and musical rattles; objects that are interesting shapes and have different textures and colours. Activity centres in the cot, and floating bath toys.*	*The nursery should have interesting wallpaper and objects such as pictures, collages and an alphabet frieze to stimulate curiosity.*
6–18 months	*The child is becoming mobile and grasping the first essentials of language.*	*Building bricks, pop-up toys, tough books, posting box; toys that involve sand and water play. Nesting and stacking toys encourage the child to think about order and how things are done.*	*The child needs toys that will encourage him to find things out for himself.*
18 months–3 years	*The child is very curious and requires constant and varied activities.*	*Drop-in jigsaws, picture dominoes, playboards, felt shapes, mosaic sets; word and picture games; constructional toys.*	*The child is learning from everything and everyone around him. He may even damage his toys to try to find out how they work. He may be destructive if the toys are beyond his capabilities*
3–5 years	*A time of concentrated learning. Concepts of letters and numbers are becoming under-standable. The child has a longer span of attention and is prepared to go back and try again.*	*Books, jigsaws; word building games, alphabet and number sets, reading and counting games; clockface with moveable hands, calendars, height charts; pretend shop with money; Lego, railway constructional sets; toys and activities that involve weighing and measuring of liquids and solids, such as measuring jugs, tape measure.*	*Toys and games must be sufficiently demanding to encourage the child to develop his abilities and make progress; but not so advanced that he loses interest and confidence. He needs constant help and attention from the adults around him.*

For imaginative and creative development

Closely linked to the toys and games that develop the intellectual skills are those that help to develop a child's imaginative and creative abilities. Opportunities for creative and imaginative play are important for teaching self-reliance, developing the imagination, and giving the child the opportunity to act out his fears and aggression.

In the early stages a child's mind is accepting and building up a store of information and ideas. He discovers that he can use these to create new ideas, make up stories, and imagine new experiences. He learns to differentiate between truth and fantasy, but often, in the early stages, his imaginary ideas and activities are so strong that he confuses them with reality. That is why a child who tells you that there is a witch living in his wardrobe should not be accused of telling lies, because he really believes it. The small child will often create an imaginary playmate, who acts as a very useful companion. Sometimes the playmate is made responsible for the naughty things which the child has done and parents have the delicate task of helping the child to sort out fact from fiction! Children who are not allowed, or encouraged, to use their imagination and creative abilities can grow up into dull and uninteresting people, who may be unable to cope with the problems around them.

Creative imagination can be encouraged by:

- providing an interesting environment that contains books, pictures, music, flowers and food that stimulate the senses.
- listening to the child when he tells you his stories and ideas and about his imaginary companions.
- suggesting imaginative games and activities, and joining in games of 'let's pretend'.
- providing paints, crayons, clay, playdough and sand, from which the child can create pictures and objects.

A child can sometimes create bad images in his mind because he has not fully understood some situations. The death of a well-loved granny, for instance, may make him think the same thing is going to happen to him; or some frightening aspect of a story may take on reality in his mind. Parents must carefully explain facts and fantasy, so that he realises that 'let's pretend' is enjoyable but is not real life.

Up to the age of two the child is busy mastering the basic skills, learning about everyday objects, and imitating sounds and activities around him. These form the basis for his creative activities. The young child will enjoy the feel and the texture of sand, clay and water, and as he gets older he will begin to use them to construct and create things. A small child will imitate his parents polishing the table or washing the car, but the older child will assume the role of mother or father, doctor or nurse, in role play games of make-believe.

The two- to five-year-old can be helped to develop his *imagination* by being given:

- dressing-up clothes. These may be old hats, shoes, dresses, trousers or shirts discarded by the family or bought from jumble sales; or shop-bought dressing-up kits such as Indian sets, Superman, a doctor's outfit or a space suit.
- old make-up, or special make-up sets produced for children.
- face masks, bought or homemade, to look like a witch, clown, etc.
- small places for the child to play, such as a Wendy house, toy shop or space ship, or large cardboard boxes which the child can make into a castle, hospital or train.
- toys that imitate the equipment used by adults, such as gardening tools, baking sets, sewing machines, post office sets, tea sets, etc.

All these will allow the child to act out the roles which he may have to take in adult life; and to investigate some of the situations which puzzle him. Dolls are very important in this type of play, for dressing up, for becoming the baby to be loved or the patient, or simply the naughty child who has to be smacked!

Toys for imaginative play

Things that will help to develop the child's *creative* skills include:

- materials for drawing and painting, such as crayons, paints, finger paints, plenty of paper (even newspaper will do), felt-tip pens, posters to colour, pencils and charcoal.
- materials for modelling, such as modelling clay, playdough (this can be homemade), Plasticine and plaster of Paris.
- materials for making collages, such as coloured paper, tissue paper, gummed shapes, scissors, glue, scraps of fabric, dried seeds, lentils, small nuts and different textures and colours of thread and yarn.
- sewing and knitting sets, craft kits, models to make, printing sets, templates, stencils, design and doodle boards, art straws and pipe cleaners.

It is not necessary for creative work to be expensive. All kinds of household odds and ends, such as silver foil, empty cartons, old buttons and cotton reels, can be used to make attractive objects and pictures.

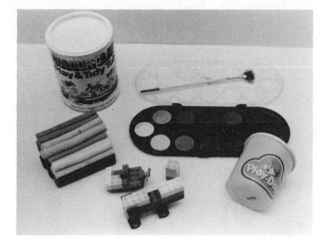

Toys for creative play

Creative play is usually messy, and parents must resign themselves to the fact that the child and his working area are going to get very untidy. If the child is restricted to just colouring in pictures in books, to avoid making a mess, then he will not be able to express himself as he should and his enjoyment will be lessened. A child loves to smear and blotch on paint; cut pictures from old catalogues and make a scrap book; paint a large picture on the bedroom wall. Does it matter if he makes a mess in the process? He will have learnt a great deal. He can wear protective clothing and the floor can be covered over.

Music is another valuable way of developing a child's creative instincts. It is noisy, of course, but the child gets a lot of pleasure from making music, and it is a good way for him to release aggression – better for him to bang a drum than to scream with rage. Musical instruments like the ones shown on the next page are useful, but instruments can be made at home by sealing some dried peas in a clean tin box, making holes in a wooden tube to blow down or using a wooden spoon and a plastic bowl.

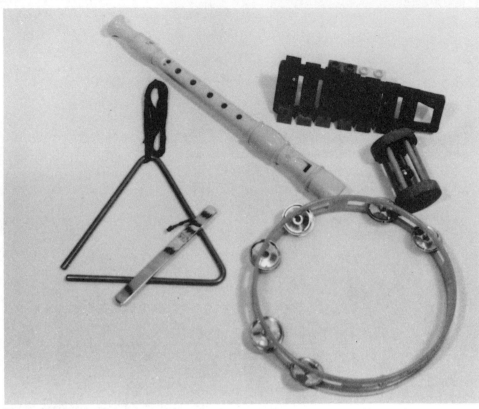

Musical instruments

Safety of toys

All toys can be dangerous, so they must be chosen carefully. These general points are important:

- If the toy is not suitable for the child's abilities, age or size, it could cause an accident. For example, a bicycle that is too big for the child will be unmanageable, or a baby could chew and swallow very small toys.
- Safety regulations for toys made in the UK are very strict, but those imported are not so strictly checked. The buyers must therefore check for themselves.
- Homemade and second-hand toys must be carefully checked before being given to a child.
- All toys should be regularly inspected and repaired, especially large-scale toys such as bicycles. Outdoor toys such as swings and climbing frames can corrode and wear.
- Look for the Kite mark (see p. 88) when buying toys, and buy good quality.
- If a toy is given to a child as a gift, and it could be unsafe or unsuitable, it should be put away, even at the risk of offending the giver.

There are many potential hazards. Here are some of the more common ones:

- rough or sharp edges.
- brittle plastic that will break and splinter.
- dressing-up clothes or soft toys that are flammable.
- paint that is not lead free.
- unsmoothed wood that could cause splinters.
- small easily removed parts that can be put in the mouth.
- soft toys with eyes that can be pulled off or internal wire that can push through.
- rattles with tiny beads inside.
- marbles and beads a small child could swallow or push into ears or nose.
- crayons, pencils or paints that could be toxic.

Having chosen sensible, safe toys, the major rule is this: never leave a child to play alone; give him constant supervision.

Follow-up exercises

Category 1

1   Give five advantages of attending a Mother and Toddler Group, and a playgroup.

2   True or false?
   a)   Babies can understand speech before they can speak themselves.
   b)   A baby will begin to respond to his name at six months old.
   c)   A child can be encouraged to speak by being spoken to slowly and clearly.
   d)   It is wrong to use baby talk to a child and it should never be used.
   e)   A child should be corrected every time he makes a verbal mistake.
   f)   If a child is not showing signs of speech by the time he is two years, a doctor should be consulted.
   g)   Picture books can be a great help when teaching language.
   h)   A child will begin to put short sentences together by the time he is nine months old.

3   Toys can very quickly become a jumbled-up mess at the bottom of an old carton, especially those that consist of several pieces such as jigsaws and constructional toys and games. Look through furniture and DIY catalogues to get ideas, and then list some ways of storing toys neatly and cheaply. The list could include plastic vegetable racks, clear plastic storage jars, etc.

Category 2

4 Below is a graph which shows how language develops. Copy it in your book, and add some more comments to explain the stages at each age.

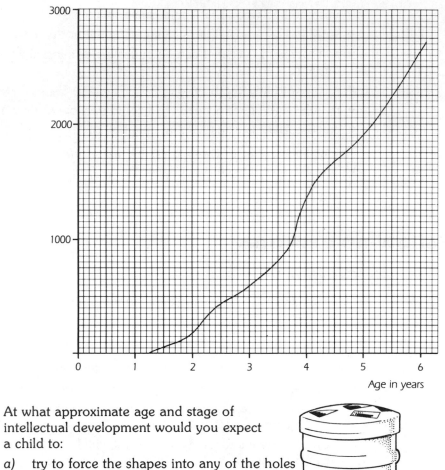

Average number of words understood

Age in years

5 At what approximate age and stage of intellectual development would you expect a child to:

a) try to force the shapes into any of the holes in the posting box?

b) if the shape does not fit the hole, try it in another hole?

c) think before trying to match the shape and hole and then place it in?

6 Which of these patterns would a young baby find the most interesting (that is, look at for the longest period of time) and why?

7 *a)* Divide the selection of toys that follows into four groups under the appropriate heading:

Physical   Imaginative   Intellectual   Creative

Some of the toys may come into more than one group. Add other suggestions to the lists of toys you think would help that type of play.

crayons	hammer and pegs	coloured cotton reels
Action Man	stencils	coloured pipe cleaners
plastic ducks	drop-in jigsaw	counting frame
Wendy house	finger paints	Plasticine
face paints	watering can	letter bricks
cuddly doll	tea service	post office set
beads and lace	drum	nesting building set
tricycle	Cindy doll	nurse's outfit

b) From the selection of toys, choose those you think are suitable for the following situations:

a three-year-old in bed recovering from measles.

the toys that would help to develop literacy skills.

activity play at the play group.

things to occupy a four-year-old on a wet afternoon.

a toy for an aggressive two-year-old.

something to develop the manipulative skill of an 18-month-old.

imaginative play in a group of four-year-olds.

8 If you were making the following toys (see illustrations on p. 240), which use felt, wood, fur fabric, paint, glue, etc. in their construction, how would you ensure that they were safe for the children in the age group for which they are designed?

a) Punch and kick toy (2–9 months)

b) Teddy bear (1 year onwards)

c) Threading toy (18 months–3 years)

d) Pop-up clown. (3–5 years)

Large fur fabric teddy bear with glass eyes, plastic nose, jointed limbs and removable clothes

Large felt ball with bell sewn on to base, to be suspended above baby's playpen or cot.

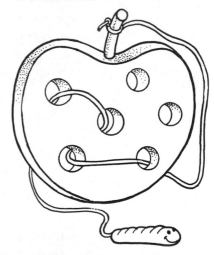

Apple shape made from wood and painted red, with several holes drilled through and a wooden worm attached to the stalk with string

Clown with a pingpong ball or felt head, scraps of fabric and wool for features, and a stiff card cone round dowelling or a lollipop stick

Category 3

9 'Toys are the tools with which a child learns.' What does this statement mean, and why are toys of such value to a child?

Activities

1 *a)* Try making a book suitable for a toddler you know. It could be called *Myself* or *David's (the child's name) Own Book* with a photograph of the child on the front. Inside put:

some pictures of the child's favourite toys and clothes

photos of grandparents, brothers and sisters, and parents

a picture of his house and garden

a picture of the family's car or bicycle

a drawing of the child's bedroom or playroom

pictures of his friends

drawings which he has done

Christmas or birthday cards he has received.

b) Another type of book that enables a child to learn in a way that is fun is a texture book. Small children love to feel different surfaces with their fingers and compare the different textures. This book could contain simple outline pictures with a textured filling, such as:

a snowman made with cotton-wool a robin with feathers

a saucepan made with shiny foil an apple made with felt

a doll with a velvet dress a box with sandpaper.

Underneath each picture, write a simple sentence describing the texture of the object.

Homemade books

2 Try to visit a Mother and Toddler Group, a playgroup, a nursery school and an infant school. Compare the more structured routine of the last two with the informal atmosphere of the first two.

3 Compose:
an action rhyme (like 'Incey wincey spider').
a number rhyme (like 'One, two, buckle my shoe').
A rhythm poem (like 'Round and round the garden').

4 Produce and tape a programme containing an introduction, a poem, a story and an activity suitable for a toddler and his carers to listen to together.

5 Design a selection of protective aprons a child could wear when painting, playing with playdough, playing with water, etc. Suggest a suitable material (such as PVC or denim) and appliqué designs to make them attractive.

SECTION F **Social and Emotional Development**

13 Social Development

From being totally egocentric (self-centred) during the first part of her life, the child has to learn how to accept and get on with other people, and how to fit into the pattern of the society into which she is born.

She is able from the start of life to distinguish people from objects. Her first demands are for food, warmth and comfort, which are usually supplied by her mother or the adult who looks after her. If this person readily responds to the child's needs in a loving, caring way, a warm relationship will be built up which will help the child later to establish friendly relationships with others. The baby that cries for food or comfort and is neglected for long periods may develop into a demanding child and an uncaring adult, unable to give love and affection because she never had any herself.

The baby's first social contact is with her mother (or adult carer) and if this is a happy, loving contact, good habits will be set from the start. As the child gets older she will imitate the ways of her parents and family. If they give affection to her and to each other, and if they welcome others into the family circle, she will learn to do the same. The child will need a model upon which to base her future actions. She will learn that to get love and affection, she has to be willing to give it: it is a two-way process.

The stages of socialisation

As with all development, although the stages of socialisation follow a regular pattern, the age at which each stage occurs may vary with the child's background and the stimulation given.

In the first few weeks the person a baby gets to know is the one who looks after her physical needs. This is usually her mother, but it could be father or any other caring adult. Eventually she will begin to recognise the sight, sound, smell and touch of this person, and will respond with a social smile and a gurgle.

By the time the child is **3 months old** she will enjoy the company of others and show distress if left alone. She will recognise the adult who looks after her most, and show pleasure by waving her arms and legs and cooing. She will turn her head to respond to her carer's voice.

By 6 months the child will recognise her parents, who are now very important to her, and she will gain security from their presence. She is beginning to distinguish between familiar and unfamiliar figures and may be anxious and shy in the company of strangers. She shows a different reaction to a scolding and a pleasant voice. She is beginning to lift up her arms to be picked up.

By 6 months to 1 year the child is making emotional ties with her own family. She wants the company of her parents and brothers and sisters, and may still be suspicious and frightened of strangers. This is the stage when she begins to imitate speech sound and makes babbling noises to attract attention and to communicate. It is an important progression as language is a most valuable form of social contact. She is beginning to acquire some of the social skills, such as drinking from a cup, using a spoon, and helping to dress herself.

By 1 year to 18 months the child is developing her own personality and should be encouraged to do so. She is still shy with strangers and clings to her mother or other carer. She needs lots of support and security and often wants a comfort object such as an old teddy, a piece of cloth, a dummy or her thumb to suck. She is becoming mobile and strikes out for independence, but must still return to a familiar adult for reassurance. She needs close contact with one special person to develop her own stable personality.

By 18 months to 2 years the child can communicate quite well and is very demanding. She alternates between independence and clinging, and will show frustration in temper tantrums, which need patience and understanding. She will be ready to learn more social skills and will become better at feeding herself and at toilet training. This is the time to begin forming good habits of personal hygiene.

By 2 to 3 years the child is becoming more self-confident and rather less dependent upon her parents. She will be more ready to accept strangers and is becoming more sociable towards other children. She is not yet interested in playing with children of her own age but likes to play alongside them – this is known as **parallel play**. She will have developed feelings of security, if she has been handled correctly, and will be more prepared to stay with strangers for short periods, knowing that her parents will return soon. With this developing awareness of other people comes an attitude of caring for others, not just for herself. She will really love her parents and family, will be sad if they are upset, and will want to share her pleasure with them if she is happy. She is beginning to understand that other people have different ideas from hers, and to discover how the outside world works and how she fits into it. These concepts should be encouraged, so that the child will think of other people's needs and feelings apart from her own.

By 3 to 5 years the child should have developed into a friendly, sociable person ready to socialise with children of her own age. This is the stage of **co-operative play** or **group play**, when children play together without requiring an adult. It is at this time that the child is ready for the companionship offered by a playgroup or nursery school. She will have her own best friends and be less under the influence of parents. The necessary skills should be well developed to make her socially acceptable to others and ready for school. She may be becoming less receptive to adult guidance, and begin questioning and answering back. She is ready to share her possessions and to take turns in getting adult attention. She is usually very compassionate and likes to comfort others in distress.

By 5 to 7 years the child is quite independent, with her own personality. She is ready to embark upon school life, knowing that there is a secure and loving home base, will become involved in group activities, and is keen to have the approval of her peers.

By the age of 7 to 8 years the child will be very much aware of sexual differences. Boys at this age usually prefer to be involved in traditional masculine games and activities, keeping mainly in the company of boys. Girls likewise tend to keep with their own sex, although they are rather more flexible than boys. This separation generally continues until adolescence.

Studies of children's behaviour have shown that there is a recognisable pattern that alternates between periods of stable, acceptable behaviour when the child gets on well with others, and difficult, unstable behaviour when the child seems to be at odds with everyone. These periods alternate throughout childhood, but eventually bring about a socially well-adjusted adult.

Social behaviour and social training

A child's social training begins at home and parents can help their child by:

- providing a secure and loving background.

- encouraging independence in the child as she becomes ready for it.

- providing a good example for the child to copy – a satisfactory father-figure or mother-figure.

- giving the child opportunities for mixing socially with:

  her family – at meal-times, family outings, and family activities;

  relations and family friends – allowing her to be present when they visit, and taking her to visit them;

  strangers – letting her get accustomed to talking to the shopkeeper or the postman or postwoman, and having casual contact with people on buses, in the park, etc.; but the child must be made aware of the dangers of talking to or going away with people she does not know;

  her peers – letting her mix with other children, finding others for her to play with, attending Mother and Toddler Groups, organising birthday parties and trips out with other children, and letting her go to a playgroup, or dancing classes, swimming clubs, public library sessions and other social activities.

- making her aware of the need for consideration for others. This involves teaching and enforcing good social habits such as table manners, politeness and good personal habits, so that other people are not offended. A visit to a snack bar or restaurant can be a treat, but will also provide valuable social training.

- encouraging the child to share her belongings and to be willing to take turns with the attention of her parents, teachers and other adults.

- never forcing a child to socialise if she is not ready for it. Some children are naturally shy, or may be going through a difficult stage when they do not wish to meet other people. Gentle encouragement can be given, but ridicule or force will only make the child withdrawn.

One factor that influences social development is the child's environment – if she lives in a remote country area or a block of high-rise flats it may be difficult for her to find companionship, while living in overcrowded conditions with poor amenities can lead to poor social contacts. Another is the size of the family and the child's position in it. The children in a large family may not get as much parental time and guidance in social training, but an only child may be over-protected and prevented from associating with other children. The middle child in a family may be aggressive and engage in antisocial behaviour such as quarrelling with siblings, arguing and answering back, because he or she has to fight for a place in the family. The older and the younger children tend to be better adjusted. A third factor is the financial situation of the family. Children from a very well-off family may be given everything they want and therefore be spoilt, which can result in an inability to share with or care for others. Children of poor families may resent the material possessions of others and become jealous.

A great deal will depend upon the personality of the child herself. Much can be done to guide and help the child (nurture) but this cannot completely change the basic character (nature) which she inherits. Some children are naturally shy and **introverted** (inward-looking) whilst others are **extroverted** (outgoing). Watch the children at a playgroup and you will quickly be able to spot examples of both types. The shy ones can be encouraged to come out of themselves and to make friendly approaches to others, and the extroverts have to learn how to conform and become less boisterous; but children should be allowed to develop their own personalities, emphasising the good characteristics and controlling the bad.

Discipline

To become a socially acceptable adult a child must be taught how to control herself and especially the less acceptable aspects of her personality. A child cannot just be left to do as she likes, and it is the parents' duty to exert control over their children in the form of discipline, to show that they approve of some types of behaviour and disapprove of others.

How and when this control is exerted depends to some extent upon the parents' expectations of the child, and on the way they themselves were disciplined. It also depends upon the expectations of their society as a whole and upon the particular culture into which the child is born. Some communities, for instance, exert a firmer discipline than the traditional British one, and this can lead to conflict in the minds of some children in ethnic minority groups.

Discipline is not just a matter of rewarding good behaviour and punishing bad behaviour. It should be based on loving guidance and it should be consistent and truthful. It is almost useless if the parents punish a child severely on one occasion and not at all another time, just because of their own moods, or threaten a punishment and then fail to carry out the threat because they cannot be bothered or forget. Parents should never set higher standards for one child than for another – for example, a father feeling that he needs to be stricter with his son than with his daughter. The parents' own behaviour is important, as children follow their example, so they should not have one set of rules for the child and follow a different set themselves. For instance, if they find something and do not hand it in to the police, how can they expect their child to be honest? However, parents are not perfect and they sometimes administer punishment unfairly. If they have a good relationship with the child, she is more likely to be able to accept the unfairness and not bear malice.

Discipline does, nevertheless, involve rewards and punishments. Some parents rely on praise as a reward and withdrawal of affection as a punishment, while others give material rewards (such as presents) and physical punishment. A child must be praised for good behaviour or she will not know what is expected of her, and similarly she must be made aware of being naughty. If she can be reasoned with and shown why she cannot have any sweets, or must not touch that hot teapot, then this is the best course of action. If she is in a tantrum and beyond reasoning with, it may be best to ignore her. Children need to know what to expect – that their parents disapprove of their bad behaviour, but that when it has been dealt with, their parents will still love them.

Parents should try to understand why the child is behaving badly. It may not just be bad temper or naughtiness, but it could be that:

- she is overtired and needs more rest.
- she is not well or perhaps is sickening for some illness.
- she is jealous of the arrival of a new baby or feels left out in some way.
- she is anxious about some new experience, such as starting school or going into hospital.
- she is bored and needs something to occupy and interest her.
- she is being teased by older brothers or sisters, or playmates.
- she feels insecure and is testing the affection of her parents.

In these instances a child needs love and understanding, not punishment. Very often naughty, unacceptable behaviour can be channelled into something good by distracting the child and offering an alternative occupation. For example, a toddler who resents the new baby and tries to destroy the baby's toys could be encouraged to help bath and play with the baby instead.

If punishment is too strict and administered too freely the child will feel unloved and insecure and will eventually lack confidence in herself. She may herself resort to bullying and aggression and in turn become a bullying, repressive parent. If punishment is too lax or inconsistent, however, the child will become spoilt and demanding and will expect to be able to do as she pleases at anyone else's expense. Correct discipline needs patience, tact and common sense, but it should result in an independent, self-disciplined, well-behaved person.

Toys, games and activities

There are many toys and games that will encourage a child to play and share with others, will help to prepare her for her role in adult life, and will give her experience in social activities. When she is a toddler she should be taken to the park, the paddling pool or the beach and allowed to mix with and observe the other children playing. As she gets older she will join in ball games, go on the climbing frame, play cowboys and indians, and take part in other group activities. At playgroup a child will play in the Wendy house, have a tea-party, play doctors and nurses – all things which will train her for adult life. She will take turns on the slide, help to build a tower of bricks, play a game of picture dominoes, and so on, and these activities will make her realise the value of co-operation, of helping other people and letting them help her. She will also learn that she cannot win every time and some children are better at some things than she is.

Toys and games for social development

Follow-up exercises

Category 1

1   Most children require some kind of comforter, which may be a dummy or a thumb to suck. What are the advantages of using a dummy, and what are the possible dangers? When and how would you try to wean a child from using a dummy? Give five points about the hygienic use of a dummy.

Category 2

2   a)   What are the baby's first social advances towards the person who cares for her?

b)   At what age or stage does a baby really recognise her parents?

c)   How long does the shy, clinging stage go on, and when is the child more willing to go to strangers?

d)   At what stage is a child beginning to think of others, rather than just thinking of herself?

e)   When does the child begin to question the attitudes of her parents and wish to become more independent?

f)   At what age or stage do children begin to prefer playing with groups of children of their own sex?

3   What is the difference between parallel and co-operative play? Give examples of each.

4   How would you make a child aware of the possible dangers of strangers whilst still encouraging her to be friendly?

5   What could be the possible effects upon a child of:

an over-protective mother or father?

a very strict mother or father?

being the middle child in the family?

coming from a very well-off background?

6   Give a brief description of an outgoing, extroverted child, and a shy, introverted one (from your own observations if possible). What are the disadvantages of both conditions and how can they be helped?

7   These are some of the actions which may be taken when a child misbehaves. Suggest which of them are not advisable, which are only suitable in some situations, and which are sensible. Give reasons for your selection.

a)   Telling the child to stop it and not do it again.

b)   Explaining to the child why she must not do that.

c)   Providing the child with an alternative occupation.

d)   Shouting at the child.

e)   Giving the child a little slap (on bottom or legs).

f)   Giving the child a good telling off.

g)   Sending the child to bed.

h)   Depriving the child of something she likes, such as sweets or a favourite toy.

i)   Threatening to tell the child's daddy.

j)   Threatening to call a policeman.

k)   Pulling the child's hair, kicking her, etc. 'to let her know what it feels like'.

l)   Giving the child a good hiding.

How can hitting a child easily turn to child abuse (baby-battering)?

8   If you were buying a toy for your four-year-old to help her mix with other children in the neighbourhood, what would you choose for:

outdoor play in the garden?
indoor play?

Category 3

9   Select from the following descriptions the things you think are important when choosing a friend for yourself. Put them in order of importance. Then make a second list picking out the important things you would look for if you were choosing a friend for your young child. Compare the difference.

loyal	lives close by	attractive or handsome
extrovert	of similar age	has similar interests
quiet	speaks nicely	wears nice clothes
same sex	introvert	has plenty of money to spend
caring	well-mannered	of similar social background
assertive	fun-loving	shy

10   How would you deal with the following problem situations?

a)   A child demands sweets in the middle of a busy supermarket and has a temper tantrum.

b)   A toddler keeps slapping or scratching her baby brother.

c)   A child at playgroup bites and pulls the hair of other children.

d)   An infant schoolchild brings home other children's possessions.

e)   A child has scribbled with felt pens all over her bedroom wall.

f)   A child refuses to share her crisps with her brothers and sisters.

g)   A child swears at the neighbour.

14 Emotional Development

Emotions are the feelings we have within us. They may be pleasant or unpleasant, good or bad. It is quite easy for a child to describe a physical condition (for example, if he has a pain or is uncomfortable), but it is much more difficult for him to describe how he is feeling emotionally, and why.

Here are examples of some emotions, listed as positive or negative; but some of them may be both, depending on the circumstances in which we experience them. Emotional states can be very complex, and we can all have mixed up feelings.

Positive emotions		Negative emotions	
contentment	curiosity	impatience	jealousy
eagerness	happiness	uncertainty	annoyance
humour	delight	anger	fear
joy	love	suspicion	depression
pleasure	excitement	anxiety	sadness
		guilt	hate

We can feel these emotions strongly, and they can be shown in different physical ways – if we are happy, for instance, we may laugh out loud, or if we are frightened we may scream. You would not be surprised if you heard a child in a supermarket yelling and shouting with anger because he could not have any sweets; you would be very surprised if you heard an adult doing the same thing. This is because we are taught from early childhood to control our emotions. We all have to live in a community, and it would be impossible if everyone expressed all their emotions exactly as they wished. We often conceal our emotions so that we do not hurt or upset other people.

Tradition and social attitudes teach us the degree to which our emotions may be shown or talked about. According to British social traditions, for example, it is expected that males are brave and do not show fear; it is acceptable that females may cry when they are distressed, but not males; small children may jump about and scream out when excited, but adults should not; and so on. Different communities have different expectations. These are the modes of behaviour accepted by society and taught to children from generation to generation.

Some communities, and some families within any community, are less inhibited than others and show their feelings more openly. Children coming from families with strict emotional control may find the pressures too great and may develop emotional problems in childhood or adult life. Keeping the emotions too bottled-up and repressed is like keeping the top on a bottle of fizzy lemonade; eventually, given certain conditions, there could be an explosion. Without being too restrictive, the parents' aim should be to produce an emotionally well-balanced child, able eventually to solve his own problems and make his own decisions; able to mix with, and have consideration for, other people.

Emotional development is closely linked with physical and intellectual development. The child cannot begin to control his feelings or have consideration for others until he realises that he is a separate individual and is able to think beyond his own basic physical needs. As with all the other areas of development, his emotional progress will depend a great deal on the example shown by the people with whom he comes into contact. This will be his parents and family first, followed by other relations, friends, teachers, other children and strangers; but his own family will be those with the strongest influence. Parents should guard against making their child emotionally dependent upon them, and should allow him to make his own decisions and set his own standards as soon as he is ready to do so. They should also not become emotionally dependent themselves upon their children. This happens most frequently when there is only a single parent who is very close to the child and finds difficulty in letting go.

Many children have their physical needs looked after perfectly but are emotionally neglected, and the results can be even more traumatic than those of physical neglect. Unfortunately they may not show themselves for many years, or may show themselves in forms of antisocial behaviour for which the child is blamed rather than the parents.

Conditions for emotional development

For proper emotional development, a child needs:

- the love and affection of his parents, family, teachers and friends.

- a feeling of being wanted and having a place in his family, his school and his community – a feeling of belonging.

- the opportunities to feel a sense of achievement and satisfaction in his own work. He should be given jobs of work and things to do, at school and at home, and be praised for the results. He needs encouragement if he fails, not ridicule; a child who is constantly criticised will give up trying.

- the opportunities to be independent and to make his own decisions, with the chance to try again if he fails. He must learn how to take the lead as well as how to follow; and how to share with others.

253

- to feel secure in his relationships with others; to be given social approval for good behaviour, and disapproval for antisocial behaviour.

- to be given confidence in himself and to be made aware of his own good qualities. He should learn how to value himself as a person.

- to be treated as an individual – not just as part of a family or a group, but as a person with his own identity.

Sensible, understanding adults will give the children in their care opportunities in work and play activities that will help to fulfil these needs. Simple responsibilities such as use of pocket-money, household tasks and care of pets are all valuable to achieve these ends. Through these carefully graded experiences a child will learn the basics he will need in order to deal with the situations he will meet in adult life.

Emotional contact can start immediately after birth, when the newborn infant is given to the mother. If the father is present he too will be involved in this initial contact. The tiny baby needs the constant care of at least one parent (or other adult carer) during his first few months, to satisfy his basic needs for warmth, food, protection and security. If these needs are satisfied without stress, a feeling of trust is established. A parent who is anxious and tense will soon transmit these feelings to the child, who will respond by becoming distressed. Gentle but firm handling will make a child feel secure. The child will also soon recognise his parent's tone of voice, and a constantly aggressive tone will upset him, whereas a pleasant, loving voice will reassure him.

By the time the child is six months old he is more aware of himself as an individual. Depending upon the type of contact he has had with other people, he will be developing feelings of trust, love and security – or of anxiety, aggression and fear.

By the age of one year he will be struggling through the first stages of independence, beginning to feed himself, taking his first steps, and saying a few words. This increasing independence should be encouraged by giving him constant praise and reassurance. Many of his first attempts will fail and he will become angry and frustrated, and the temper tantrums of the two- to three-year-old are the results of this rather than of naughtiness. Parents should respond with patience and support not with anger and punishment; praise rather than punishment should be the rule.

The way in which a child develops emotionally will be based upon his own character and the genes he has inherited (nature). Basically he may be quiet, shy and reserved, or noisy, boisterous and outgoing, but the influence of his family, friends and environment (nurture) will mould his personality along good or bad lines. By the time the child is five, he has his own personality, which has developed through his early emotional experiences. Good experience should produce an emotionally well-balanced child; but experiences cannot all be good, and he should be learning how to cope with unpleasant happenings as well.

Emotional disturbance

Most children go through periods of emotional disturbance, which are not usually serious and can be treated with parental understanding. These disturbances may show themselves in the following ways:

Antisocial behaviour   The aggressive child tries to draw attention to himself by bullying, hitting, spitting, biting, boasting, or temper tantrums.

Withdrawn behaviour   The insecure child shows lack of confidence, is usually quiet, has irrational fears, is shy and withdrawn, and clings to the adult he is most used to.

Retarded physical and intellectual development   The child may be so emotionally disturbed that he cannot cope with the normal development of learning and physical skills, and slows down in these areas.

Phobias   This occurs when a child cannot cope with a real fear, whether of a thing, a person, or a situation, and transfers the fear to another situation or object. A child may develop a totally irrational fear of spiders, for instance, and react hysterically to them; but his real fear may be of starting school, or the death of a pet, or some other traumatic experience.

Physical habits   Habits such as nail-biting, head-banging, hair-chewing, pulling out hair, or excessive thumb-sucking are often developed by lonely, neglected, bored children who are seeking attention.

Emotionally aggravated illness   The child may suffer from physical illnesses that are caused or made worse by emotional conditions. Such illnesses are asthma, skin rashes, eczema, tummy upsets, fainting, muscular tics, or allergies.

Emotional disturbances can be triggered off in many ways, by any of the following:

- a violent home background, where there is always quarrelling and fighting, and the child may be used as a pawn between one parent and the other.
- physical and/or emotional neglect, by parents who are too concerned with their own interests to bother with their child.
- immature parents who are not ready for child rearing and do not understand a child's needs.
- parents who expect too much from their child, putting pressures on him that the child cannot cope with, which result in his constant failure.
- lack of stable parenting in early life, so that the child is unable to form a close attachment to an adult, due to frequent separation. This sometimes happens when both parents go out to work and the child is left with a variety of child minders.
- parents who are unable to love their child, possibly because they themselves were never loved. They may look after the child very well physically, but be unable or unwilling to supply his emotional needs.
- jealousy, caused by the arrival of a new baby that makes the child feel pushed out and rejected, or by one child in a family being constantly compared unfavourably with another.

- new situations that the child cannot cope with and is not developmentally ready for, or that he has not been prepared for in advance. These may include starting playgroup or infant school, going into hospital, or a short stay away from home.
- bullying, teasing or unfriendliness from other children.
- adults such as playgroup leaders, teachers or nurses getting impatient and ridiculing or shouting at a child instead of giving praise and encouragement.
- a physical disability, or a disfigurement such as facial scars, a hare-lip or large birth marks, which make a child different from other children. These can cause emotional disturbance as well as physical problems.

It is often difficult for parents and child carers to realise that these problems have deep-rooted emotional causes and are not just naughtiness or the normal problems of growing up. If treated quickly many of the minor conditions can be cured simply, but more complex, deep-seated problems will need specialist treatment.

Treatment of emotional disturbance

Treatment by *parents and family* will depend entirely upon the problem and the individual child. The first step is to discover what is bothering the child, and the next to examine their own attitudes and way of life. Are they giving their child enough love, a secure background, enough attention? Are they expecting too much from him, comparing him unfavourably with other brothers and sisters, being too strict and punishing too severely? Do they need to change their own attitudes and adjust their ways to the needs of the child?

Playgroups, social groups and schools are sometimes understaffed, over-concerned with administration and finance, and too busy to notice the problems of the individual child. Do they make each child feel welcome and part of the group? Do they look out for bullying, and do they discuss a child's unacceptable behaviour with the parents? Do they provide stimulating and interesting activities with plenty of opportunities for success and praise, and do they set standards and rules which are easily understood and not too severe or too lax?

All the *people who are professionally responsible* for young children, such as social workers, health visitors, GPs and baby minders, should constantly be looking for suspicious signs that may indicate the emotionally disturbed child. The child who is over-aggressive, bullying, clinging, very quiet, or extremely over-active, or whose physical and intellectual progress is abnormally slow, could be needing treatment. Contact should be maintained, parents consulted, and help given where necessary. Sometimes it is the parents and the home conditions that need help. Parents who are under stress because of a large family, marital or financial problems, loneliness or poor health, may be too busy with their own problems to worry about those of their chidren. The social worker or health visitor may be able to give the advice needed to help the whole family.

Specialist treatment may be needed for the child who becomes very deeply disturbed. He will be referred by the child's doctor or school to a child guidance centre or a school psychological service, where he will meet the child psychiatry team. This consists of the **psychiatric social worker**, the **clinical psychologist**, and the **psychiatrist**.

The psychiatric social worker is a social worker or nurse with special training in all aspects of mental health.

The clinical psychologist tests and measures the emotional and psychological responses of the child.

The psychiatrist is medically trained and qualified in the medical conditions of mental disorder. The child's problems will be diagnosed and special care programmes suggested.

If emotional distrubances in childhood are ignored, they can emerge in later years, producing adults who are unable to make lasting relationships, and have difficulty making and keeping friends. They may be unable to provide love and security for their own children, because they did not experience it themselves, and be unable to cope with stress. This can result in nervous breakdown, emotional trauma and suicidal tendencies.

It is clear that to prepare a child for adult life parents and child carers must concentrate on all aspects of a child's development, because all aspects are equally important. It is a very daunting task and we make many mistakes, but fortunately children are very resilient; and they amply reward all the time, interest, love and affection that adults give them.

Follow-up exercises

Category 2

1   Compare the ways in which a child and an adult would react and behave if they wanted something and could not have it. Why would the behaviour of the adult differ from that of the child?

2   Give four examples of ways in which parents and teachers can help to develop emotional stability in the young child.

3   Why is emotional contact important to parents and child during the first few days of life, and how can it be established?

4   What is hypochondria, and why may it be an indication of emotional disturbance?

5   Suggest three ways in which emotional disturbance during childhood can show itself in adult life.

Category 3

6 Discuss the following statement: 'Experiences within the family affect the emotional development of the child.'

7 What is meant by 'emotional deprivation', and what can its effects be upon the child?

8 A child may feel jealous in the following situations:

having an elder brother or sister who is much cleverer at school.

having a brother or sister who is much better looking.

having a friend who has more toys and expensive clothes.

In each of these cases, how may this jealousy show itself, and how would sensible parents deal with the situation?

Activity

Discuss with your friends any phobias (irrational fears) you or they may have, and try to suggest some possible causes.

APPENDICES

APPENDIX A *Professional Carers*

This lists the professional people who look after the expectant mother, and the mother and child.

Audiologist	A specialist in hearing problems
Geneticist	A doctor who specialises in genetic problems
GP	The general practitioner or family doctor
Gynaecologist	A doctor who co-operates with the obstetrician, and who specialises in diseases and disorders of the reproductive system. The same doctor may be a gynaecologist and an obstetrician.
Health visitor	An SRN with extra training in looking after young families and the elderly
Midwife	An SRN with the extra qualification of State Certified Midwife
Neonatologist	A doctor (usually a paediatrician) who specialises in the care of the newborn child
Obstetrician	A doctor who specialises in looking after women during pregnancy and childbirth. The same doctor may be an obstetrician and a gynaecologist.
Ophthalmologist	A specialist in visual development
Paediatrician	A doctor who specialises in the treatment of children up to the early teens
Psychiatric social worker	A social worker who specialises in helping with the problems caused by mental disorders
Psychiatrist	A doctor who is trained to deal with medical conditions of mental disorder
Psychologist	A doctor who specialises in emotional and mental development
Social worker	A specialist who helps with family problems and care
Speech therapist	A specialist in speech problems

APPENDIX B *Special Services and Clinics*

This lists the special services and clinics that help prospective parents, the expectant mother, and the mother and child.

Antenatal clinics

Clinics that specialise in giving care and advice during pregnancy

Child guidance centres, school psychological services and centres for autism

Centres that mainly care for the child with mental or intellectual disorders and difficulties

Family planning clinics

Clinics where birth control methods are explained and supplied, and screening for cervical cancer is carried out

Genito-urinary medicine

Special treatment clinics for STD

Postnatal clinics

Clinics that give care and advice to mother and child after childbirth

APPENDIX C **Voluntary and Other Organisations**

This lists the voluntary societies and other organisations referred to in this book, and gives their addresses.

Advisory Centre for Education (ACE), 18 Victoria Park Square, Bethnal Green, London

A non-profit-making educational charity which gives information and advice about education

British Association for Early Childhood Education, Montgomery Hall, Kennington Oval, London

Gives advice and information specifically about education for young children

British Standards Institution, 2 Park Street, London, W1A 2BS

Sets standards of safety and efficiency for manufacturers to follow, and issues a trademark (the Kitemark) that shows goods have been tested and are in accordance with British Standards

Children in Hospitals (NAWCH), Argyle House, 29–31 Euston Road, London

A group set up in 1961 to help to improve the standard of care given to children in hospitals, and to give practical help such as visiting, fund-raising, and lectures to parents' groups

Design Council, Woolworth Building, Harewood Row, London NW1

Has its main showrooms, the Design Centre, in London (28 Haymarket, SW1), where it exhibits all types of products that are well-designed and functional. Issues a label that is awarded to well-designed products

Health Education Authority, 78 New Oxford Street, London, WC1A 1AH

A national body with local offices throughout the UK. Supplies educational literature, films, slides and speakers to schools, colleges, hospitals and other groups, on all aspects of health care

Meet-a-Mum Association (MAMA), c/o 2 Railway Terrace, Pontrilas, Hereford

Helps to organise social groups, or mother-to-mother meetings, especially for young mothers suffering from postnatal depression, isolation and other problems

Mother and Toddler Groups

Formed on a local basis, organised by social workers, health visitors or other local bodies. Usually very informal meetings of mothers and young children

National Childbirth Trust (NCT),9 Queensborough Terrace, Bayswater, London

A national organisation run with the aim of educating people for parenthood. Runs antenatal classes on childbirth and feeding

National Society for the Prevention of Cruelty to Children (NSPCC), 67 Saffron Hill, London

Founded in 1884 to protect children from abuse. A voluntary society with a force of about 240 inspectors who follow up reported cases of abuse and give advice and assistance

Royal Society for the Prevention of Accidents (RoSPA), Cannon House, The Priory, Queensway, Birmingham.

An independent organisation concerned with all aspects of safety in every environment. Supplies information, publications, posters, advice and training on all matters of safety

Pre-school Playgroups Association, Alford House, Aveline Street, London

An association that aims at providing an opportunity for children under five to get together for play and companionship, and to involve parents in the planning and setting up of playgroups

Many of these, and other organisations, will provide free information about their work upon request. There are hundreds of voluntary societies and organisations which are committed to helping children and young families. More information will be found in Volume 2 of this book.

APPENDIX D **Useful Sources of Information**

There are a lot of manufacturers, government sponsored bodies and voluntary organisations that will supply leaflets, booklets, catalogues and samples free upon request, or for a small basic fee. This information is very useful for work on activities. Do not forget to send a stamped addressed envelope with your request.

General health

Family Doctor Publications, BMA House, Tavistock Square, London, WC1H 9JP
Family Planning Advisory Service, 27–35 Mortimer Street, London, W1N 7RJ
Macleans Dental Health and Educational Service, Beecham House (BHA/4), Great Western Road, Brentford, Middlesex
Sterling Health, 1 Onslow Street, Guildford, Surrey GV1 4YS

Safety

General safety: RoSPA, Cannon House, The Priory, Queensway, Birmingham B4 6BS
Car safety: Kangol, Norfolk Street, Carlisle, Cumbria

Food

Cow and Gate Ltd, Trowbridge, Wiltshire
Dairy Produce Advisory Service, Milk Marketing Board, Thames Ditton, Surrey
Heinz Baby Foods Advisory Service, H.J. Heinz Co. Ltd, Hayes Park, Hayes, Middlesex UB4 8AL
Milupa Ltd, Milupa House, Hercies Road, Hillingdon, Uxbridge, Middlesex
Robinson's Baby Food, Carrow, Norwich NR1 2DD

Toys

Early Learning, 45 Regent Street, Swindon, SN1 1LB (plus local branches)
Galt Toys, James Galt and Co. Ltd, Brookfield Road, Cheadle, Cheshire SK8 2PN
Hamleys of Regent Street Ltd, 188/96 Regent Street, London W1R 6BT
Offspring, E.J. Arnold and Son Ltd, Parkside Lane, Dewsbury Road, Leeds LS11 5TD

Clothing and equipment

Baby Relax Ltd, Rainham, Essex (*Nursery equipment*)
British Standards Institution Education Section, 2 Park Street, London, W1A 2BS
Knitting Craft Group, P.O. Box 6, Thirsk, North Yorkshire YO7 1TA
Nappy Advisory Service, 3 Elgin Road, Sutton, Surrey SM1 3SN
Persil Educational Leaflets, 50 Upper Brook Street, London W1Y 1PG
Robinsons of Chesterfield, Wheat Bridge, Chesterfield, Derbyshire S40 2AD (*Nappies*)

Books and education

Griffin Software for learning-computer tapes for children; BBC/IBA publications, children's
books – all available from W.H. Smith, Boots, etc.
Sainsbury's and Marks and Spencer publish their own books for children.
Ladybird Books Ltd, P.O. Box 12, Beeches Road, Loughborough, Leicestershire LE11 2NQ

Information covering various topics

Babyboots catalogue from local Boots stores
Health Education Council, 78 New Oxford Street, London WGA 1AH
Mothercare, Cherry Tree Road, Watford, Hertfordshire WD2 5SH
National Association for Maternal and Child Welfare, 1 South Audley Street, London W1Y 6JS
Sylvia Meredith Health Education Advisory Service, 3 Elgin Road, Sutton, Surrey
Wyeth Nutrition, Wyeth Laboratories, Taplow, Maidenhead, Berkshire

General information about local societies, health services, social services, etc., may be obtained
from your local public library, Citizens Advice Bureau, and Consumer Advice Centre. The
telephone directory gives names and addresses of local firms and services.

APPENDIX E   **Further Reading**

Useful books include:

The Complete Book of Babycare ed. Barbara Nash (St Michael)
The First Years of Life (Ward Lock, for the Open University and Health Education Council)
The Pre-school Child (Ward Lock, for the Open University and Health Education Council)
The Baby Care Book Dr Miriam Stoppard (Dorling Kindersley Ltd)
Child's Body: A Parents' Manual Diagram Group (Corgi Books)
A Child's Eye View and *Read Your Child's Thoughts* Mary Sime (Thames and Hudson)
The Science of Food and Cooking Allan Cameron (Edward Arnold)
Children's Rooms Mary Gilliatt (St Michael)

Useful booklets include: Magazines, Catalogues

Mind How You Go (Department of Transport)
Pregnancy Book (Health Education Council)
Play It Safe (Health Education Council and Scottish Health Education Group)

Useful catalogues include those from Mothercare and Boots, and the Galt Toy Catalogue.
Helpful magazines include *Mother* and *Mother and Baby*, and there is a relevant videotape,
The New Good Birth Guide by Sheila Kitzinger (Palace Videos).

APPENDIX F   Examination Techniques

Child Care and Development is a valuable subject in its own right, and will help and guide you in eventually bringing up your family. As many of you will also be studying this subject as an external examination course, the following points may be a helpful guide to you when you take the final theory papers.

1 Read the instructions on the cover of your paper. Do not answer more questions than are asked for, and select them from the correct sections. The examiner will put a line through any extra answers given.

2 Write as legibly as possible. The examiner cannot give marks for answers that he or she cannot read.

3 The examiner is looking for *facts*. Do not waffle, do not go off the point, and do not say the same things several times but in slightly different ways.

4 Read the questions carefully. Do not panic and think that there is nothing there that you can answer. Very often the information may be asked for in a different way from the one you are used to. Spare a few minutes to ask yourself what the question really means.

5 Plan your answer – on scrap paper if you can. Introduce your subject, put down all the important points, and draw them all together to set down a conclusion.

6 Illustrate your answer if possible. A clear, well-labelled diagram can sometimes explain your answer better than several wordy sentences.

7 Diagrams and drawings should be large, clear, neat and well-labelled. Use coloured pens or pencils sensibly for emphasis.

8 Try to divide out your time to give equal amounts to all your answers. If you have to miss out or rush the last question(s) you will be losing a large proportion of the marks.

9 Try to make some of your points original. Introduce personal experiences where the question allows for it. It makes your answers more interesting and shows the examiner that you understand your subject.

10 If you finish early, go over your paper carefully to see what you have missed out. Papers are planned to allow sufficient, but not too much, time for answering them.

11 Follow final instructions carefully. Tie your answer sheets together, put your examination number where indicated, fill in the box with the numbers of the questions you have selected.

12 When you have finished your examination and done your best, do not worry about it any more!

APPENDIX G A Specimen Examination Question and Answer Scheme

The copyright holders authorise ONLY users of this book to make copies of the examination question and answer scheme in this Appendix, for their own use in a teaching context. Copies must be used immediately and not stored for future use or re-use.

This question and the answer scheme were written for the 1984 West Midlands Examinations Board CSE paper.

Question

a What is contraception? Why is it used?   (2 × 2) marks

b *i)* What are the advantages and disadvantages of any *four*   (3 × 4) different methods of contraception?

ii) Use diagrams to illustrate *two* of the methods chosen.   (2 × 2)

                                                                      20

Answer scheme

This is the information used by the examiners to mark this examination question.

a *i)* Contraception means the prevention of conception or pregnancy, i.e. preventing the fertilisation of the ovum.   2

ii) Contraception is used to prevent a pregnancy, so that a couple may plan and produce a baby when their circumstances are suitable.   2

b Advantages and disadvantages of four methods:

1) **The natural (rhythm) method**

i) This method involves a close observation of the menstrual cycle to discover on which day the woman ovulates.

ii) The cycle begins on the first day of bleeding and for most women ovulation occurs about the fourteenth day.   (3 × 4) *iii)* To confirm this a temperature should be taken. On the fourteenth day the temperature drops slightly indicating ovulation.

   iv) The advantage of this method is that it is completely natural, with no chemicals or physical devices to be used.

   v) The disadvantages are that it is time-consuming to work out ovulation and the method is unreliable.

2) The sheath

   i) This prevents sperm from reaching the egg so that fertilisation cannot take place.

   ii) The sheath is worn over the man's penis and must be placed on when the penis is rigid.

   iii) The advantage of this method is that the contraceptive is only used at the time of intercourse.

   iv) The disadvantages are that the method may be uncomfortable or unreliable, as the sheath can be faulty or come off during intercourse.

3) The diaphragm or cap

   i) This is fitted in the vagina and traps sperm, preventing them from entering the cervical canal and reaching the ovum.

   ii) Spermicide cream or jelly should also be used on the cap.

   iii) The advantage is that the contraceptive is used only at the time of intercourse.

   iv) The disadvantages are:
     a) it may be fitted incorrectly.
     b) it may develop a fault.
     c) the cap has to be left in for eight hours after intercourse.

4) IUD

   i) Sometimes called the coil or loop.

   ii) Unlike the cap or sheath it allows fertilisation to take place, but because it acts as an irritant the egg is prevented from becoming implanted in the womb.

   iii) The egg dies and is expelled in the menstrual flow.
   iv) The coil has to be fitted by an expert.
   v) It consists of a plastic and copper device.
   vi) The disadvantages are:
     a) some women experience heavier periods or pain.
     b) occasionally the device is discharged or becomes embedded in the uterus.

5) **The pill**

i)   The combined pill contains oestrogen and progesterone, and the minipill progesterone only.

ii) The pill works by suppressing ovulation.

iii) As an egg is not dropped and therefore not available for fertilisation, the method has the lowest failure rate.

iv) Tablets start on the fifth day of bleeding and are taken for 21 days.

v)   A period usually follows in 3–4 days. (The minipill is taken every day.)

vi) The advantages are:
     a) it is 100 per cent effective (provided all the tablets are taken correctly).
     b) no premeditated device has to be used before intercourse.
     c) the woman has a light period.

vii) The disadvantages are its side-effects, including weight gain and increased risk of thrombosis after some time.

Illustrations (two diagrams to show two different methods):

neat, clear diagram	$\frac{1}{2}$		
correctly and well labelled	$\frac{1}{2}$ } 2 (2 × 2)		4
complete, correct diagram	1		
(part correct – $\frac{1}{2}$ mark)			(20)

APPENDIX H Further Activities

I Nursery activity

1   Shown here is a diagram of a small bedroom. Copy it into your project book, keeping the figures to scale.

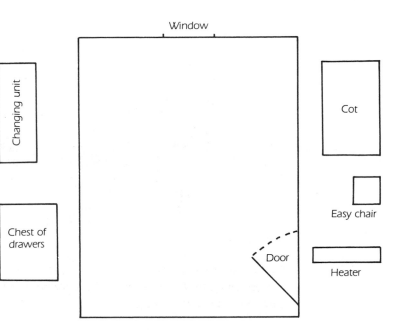

a) Place the various pieces of equipment in the room.

b) Collect suitable samples of wallpaper, paint, curtain fabrics, and floor coverings. (If you cannot get samples, get leaflets or make drawings.) Mount them neatly in your folder and explain why you chose them.

c) Explain how you would prepare a small unused room to make it clean and safe to use as a nursery.

d) Collect information about methods of heating and lighting your nursery, give details of running costs and efficiency.

e) Describe the additions you would make to your nursery to make it attractive, and to interest the child.

f) Below are some ideas for using various crafts to add interest and colour to a nursery. Make one or more of them, or use your own ideas.

Felt work mobile

Use a wire coat hanger for the top of the merry-go-round. Cover it with striped material or strips of felt. Cut simple shapes for the animals from brightly coloured felt. Attach the mobile to the roof with fine nylon thread so that the animals will move easily.

Felt mobile

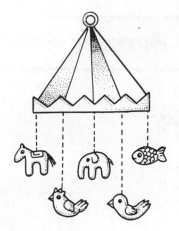

Appliqué number frieze

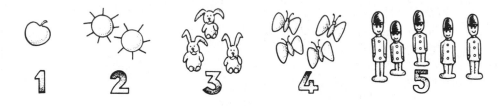

Appliqué number frieze

Use hessian or felt for the backing. Cut basic shapes from brightly patterned fabrics, and stitch them on to the backing with buttonhole stitch, or iron on with double-sided Vilene. Make the numbers very clear.

Knitted pictures

Knit a few squares or oblongs with scraps of knitting wool, string or cotton of various colours and textures. Knit small shapes for doors and windows. Stitch them on to canvas, hessian or any firm material. Pull the knitting to the shape you require, and chain-stitch on any details you wish.

Knitted picture

Window decorations

Cut outline shapes from stiff clear plastic. Using coloured foil or patterned cellophane (such as sweet wrappers) put decorations and features on the cut-out shapes. Attach fine nylon thread to the tops. When these are hung at the window the light shines through them.

Window decorations

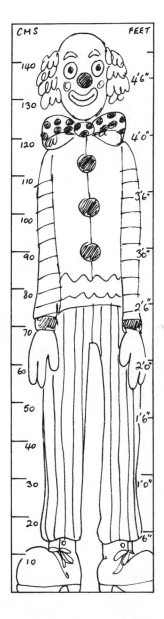

Paper-craft – Height chart

Use sheets of coloured sugar paper for the background. Measure off the long edges (one side in centimetres and one in feet and inches if you wish). Design a jolly figure which will amuse a child. Cut out each area in different patterned wrapping papers, foil, tissue paper or fluorescent paper. Stick the chart on the nursery wall. Children enjoy seeing how quickly they grow.

Paper-craft height chart

2 The pictures here show
articles of old furniture.
How could they be
adapted to make furniture
for a baby's room?

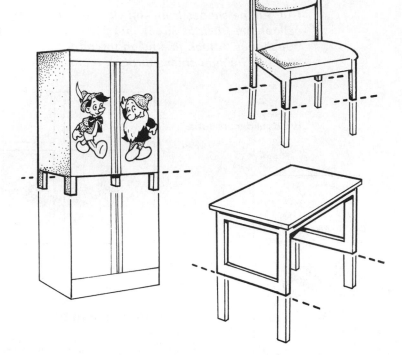

II Safety activity

1 Carry out an accident survey amongst your friends and relations. Draw up
a questionnaire similar to the one below. Leave sufficient space for the
answers between each question.

Accident survey

*1 Did you have any type of accident in your house before the age of five,
or can you remember an accident happening to an under-five in your
family?*
*(If the answer to this question is no, pass the questionnaire to another
person.)*

2 What type of accident was caused – burn, choking, cut, etc.?

3 Was it serious – did the child need to go to hospital?

4 What was the cause of the accident?

5 Could it have been prevented by more care and forethought?

6 What treatment did you receive, at home or at the hospital?

*7 Did the person who looked after you know what to do and what
treatment to give?*

8 Do you have a first aid kit at home?

9 How much do you know about first aid treatments?

10   *Has anything been done to prevent the same thing happening again?*

11   *Has this accident helped to make the family more safety-conscious?*

12   *Can you think of any areas in your house which could possibly be dangerous?*

Compare your findings with those of others in your group and draw up a chart of the main types of accidental injury and how they are caused.

Other questionnaires could be produced dealing with safety in the garden, on the roads, or in the playground.

2   This picture shows a number of potentially dangerous situations in the street. How many can you spot?

3 This is a poster produced by RoSPA. Do you think it would help to make you or a parent more safety-conscious?
Design a poster yourself which shows some aspect of safety.

Sweets or drugs?

**does your child
know the difference**

LOCK AWAY ALL MEDICINES

STOP HOME ACCIDENTS

4 What would you do in each of the following situations?

a) A child is found sitting on the floor holding an empty bottle of tablets, with some tablets in her hand.

b) A child is balancing on the window ledge of a half-open window on an upper floor.

c) A child has cut herself with garden shears.

d) A child is found face down in a shallow puddle of water.

e) A child has fallen off a table, has a large lump on her head and is semiconscious.

5 Draw a diagram of a normal small family garden, pointing out all the features that need attention to make it safe for small children.

III Playgroup activity

It is quite possible that your school or college will allow you to visit your local playgroup, as this is one of the best ways of gaining practical experience in looking after children and following their development. If you are studying a Child Development syllabus, it will recommend that you have as much experience of being with young children as possible, so even if it is not possible for your school to arrange playgroup visits, you could try to visit one during your holidays.

There are many different types of groups, catering for varied sections of the community, and you should try to get experience of several so that you can compare them. There are:

- village playgroups, often held in church halls, with plenty of open space.
- town playgroups where space may be limited, with lots of traffic and bustle near by.
- playgroups mainly for immigrant children or children from ethnic minorities, to help them to integrate into the larger community and/or learn about their cultural heritage.
- playgroups that cater for the needs of handicapped children.
- playgroups set up by the probation service, or Prisoners' Aid Society, which are there to give special assistance to the families of people who have broken the law.

Children who come into special categories, such as in the last three examples, are not being segregated from other children. Usually there is a mixture of children in these groups, but they all need special care and attention in their different ways, and sometimes a specially trained group-leader. It is essential that you try to get the utmost benefit from your playgroup visits. Most students think they are the most valuable and enjoyable part of the course, and they are a good indication of whether or not you will enjoy looking after children, if you are considering this as a career. However, you must remember several important things:

- you are a visitor and represent your school or college.
- you are there to work, not only to do the jobs you like.
- the children are the most important people there and their safety and comfort are of paramount importance.
- you must follow the instructions of the playgroup leader and the children's mothers. They have more experience than you.
- the playgroup will be depending upon your help. If you are ill or cannot go you must let your teacher know as much in advance as possible.
- do not attend playgroup if you are ill – you may pass on your infection, and you will not have the energy to do your job well.
- wear suitable clothing, such as jeans and a shirt or pullover and comfortable shoes.

- your visit should be for half a term or longer (five or six weeks at least). A visit of only one or two weeks only disrupts the work of the playgroup and is of little benefit to you.
- there should only be two or three students visiting at any one session. You should not spend time sitting and chattering with your friends, as it is more difficult for the playgroup leader to comment on your adverse behaviour – he or she is not your teacher.
- there should be a close contact between your school and the playgroup. This may be part of your course assessment and the group-leader may be asked to comment upon your work and attitude.

These are some of the things you may be expected to do at playgroup:

- getting out apparatus and putting it away. This involves being there before the children arrive and after they have left.
- tidying up and clearing up during the session.
- making up paste, powder paints, and playdough.
- helping to make up and give drinks and snacks to the children.
- helping the children to take off and put on outdoor coats and shoes, and helping them to go to the toilet.

You may be asked to supervise some play activity such as painting, water play, or the Wendy house, or to supervise the children on the large-scale equipment. You may be telling stories or leading the children in singing games or group activities. Remember not to try to take over when a child is trying to do something herself. She is there to learn and she will not do so if you cut out her picture or button her coat. Be prepared to show her, but not to do it for her. While you are there you will also be expected to observe, both the working of the playgroup and the behaviour of the children. Most schools or colleges will give you guidance about what to look for and how to behave. You will also be expected to keep a diary, make a report or fill in a worksheet. If you are not given a worksheet you can make one yourself, using the example that follows.

Sample worksheet

Playgroup routine

Make the following:

- children's timetable *from* 9.00 a.m. arrival *to* 12.00 noon departure
- students' timetable *from* 8.45 a.m. arrival and preparation *to* 11.45 a.m. clearing up and departure.
- a plan of the room and play area, with the main centres of activity shown.
- list of toys (small and large-scale), games, play activities such as water play, painting, etc.

Which of the activities and toys were the most popular? Which were the least popular? Which did the boys prefer? Which did the girls prefer?

Personal research

Is the playgroup well run and efficient?

Is the leader qualified in any way?

Is there sufficient help?

Are the room and play area large enough with sufficient storage space?

Are the kitchen and cloakroom arrangements satisfactory?

Is the heating efficient and safe?

Are the children kept fully occupied?

Are the activities varied with a balance of quiet and energetic periods?

How is the money raised to run the playgroup? Do they have outside help?

Do fathers help in fund-raising and making toys and equipment, or any other way?

Could you suggest ways of improving the organisation of the playgroup?

Would you alter the playgroup routine?

Would you try to obtain other toys or include other activities?

Safety

Are the toys and equipment checked and repaired regularly?

Is the floor non-slip and splinter proof?

Is the furniture child-size, stable, firm and splinter proof?

Are the doors always kept closed and locked if necessary?

Does the room open on to a busy road?

Is the outside play area well-fenced with no dangerous plants, steps, or uneven surfaces?

Have the windows got safety catches or bars?

Are the children kept away from the kitchen area?

Are the staff safety conscious? Is there first aid equipment and someone who knows how to use it?

Are there provisions in case of fire, with clear instructions what to do?

Have *you* spotted anything which could be dangerous?

Hygiene

Is the place kept clean and tidy?

Has it got easily cleaned surfaces and floors?

The atmosphere of the playgroup

Does it seem to be a happy place?

Are the staff keen to keep the children busy and integrate them?

Do they admit any handicapped children, or children with special needs?

Is the playgroup part of the community? Do they encourage visitors and organise jumble sales, parties and special activities?

Do the staff of the playgroup go on any special courses or try to keep up to date with information about children?

Child studies

- If possible observe a child who is new to the playgroup and note how long it takes her to settle down and how this is achieved – by her mother, the playgroup leader, and the rest of the staff.

- Compare a newcomer to the playgroup with a child who is just about ready to leave and start infant school. In what ways is the latter more mature?

- Study and compare two particular children who are very different in character and temperament. Choose one child who is shy, reserved and lacking in confidence, and one who is boisterous, noisy and aggressive. Try to assess the reasons why these children may be like this.

Ask the playgroup leader to sign your worksheet and to comment upon your attitude and method of handling children. Do not forget to thank him or her and express your appreciation.

Here are some ways in which your school could show an interest in the playgroup. Can you think of any more?

- Organise a Christmas party or pantomime for the playgroup children.
- Invite the playgroup staff to lunch in the Home Economics room.
- Make a set of play aprons in the needlework department.
- Design and make a special ramp for a child in a wheelchair.

APPENDIX J **Assignments**

The copyright holders authorise ONLY users of this book to make copies of the assignments in this Appendix, for their own use in a teaching context. Copies must be used immediately and not stored for future use or re-use.

Assignment 1 relates to care during pregnancy. *Assignment 2* relates to birth and the care of the new baby. *Assignment 3* uses the information given in the appendices.

Assignment I

Place a in the box(es) to indicate the correct answer.

1 A balanced diet will contain:

A *a mixture of fruit, vegetables and meat.*

B *plenty of good foods.*

C *a well-balanced mixture of all the nutrients, and water.*

D *roughage, water and protein.*

2 The following foods are not suitable during pregnancy if taken in large amounts:

A *fresh fruit and vegetables.*

B *spicy foods and pickles.*

C *milk and milk products.*

D *cakes and biscuits.*

3 Iron is found in the following foods:

A *cheese.*

B *offal.*

C *fish.*

D *chocolate.*

A shortage of iron in the diet will cause amnesia.

Right		Wrong	

4 Calcium is found in the following foods:

A *citrus fruit.*

B *fish with bones in.*

C *eggs.*

D *dairy produce.*

Calcium is needed for good teeth and bone formation.

Right		Wrong	

5 Which of the following should not be used during pregnancy without the doctor's consent?

A *Aspirin*

B *Travel sickness pills*

C *Cough mixture*

D *Laxatives*

E *All of them*

6 Which of the following are tests given during pregnancy?

Standard tests:

A *Urine test*

B *Blood test*

C *Intelligence test*

D *Balance test*

Special tests:

A *Amniocentesis test*

B *Saliva test*

C *Bone marrow test*

D *Fetoscope test*

7 Which of these minor complaints of pregnancy may only require a change of diet?

A *Constipation*

B *Backache*

C *Heartburn*

D *Pregnancy sickness*

E *Headaches*

8 The expectant mother who continues smoking during her pregnancy may affect the development of her baby.

True   False

9 Study the following statements. Put T (for True) or F (for False).

A *An abortion is the deliberate termination of a pregnancy.*

B *On average six fertilised eggs in every 24 will miscarry.*

C *The first 12 weeks of pregnancy are the time of most risk of a miscarriage.*

D *If the expectant mother has her bath too hot it will cause a miscarriage.*

E *A woman over 35 is more likely to have a miscarriage.*

10 Put the following statements about maternity wear in the order of importance that you think is correct. For instance, if you think B is the most important put a figure 1 in that box.

A *Fabrics should be cool in summer, warm yet light in winter.*

B *Underwear should be easily laundered.*

C *It should be inexpensive as the expectant mother may not want to wear it after the birth.*

D *The clothing should make the expectant mother look and feel pretty and feminine.*

E *Garments should not constrict the waist and abdomen. Fullness should come from the yoke.*

11 Tick the statements that are true.

A *Emotions are affected by hormone balance.*

B *If she is depressed the expectant mother is best left alone to get over it.*

C *Severe depression should be treated by the doctor.*

D *Depression is a normal aspect of pregnancy and the expectant mother will soon get over it.*

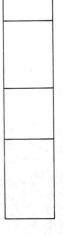

12 Decide which of the following you think are important in the relationship between prospective father and mother during the pregnancy.
For each, write in the box V (Very important), I (Important) or N (Not important)

A *The man should help his partner with household tasks.*

B *Physical lovemaking should continue.*

C *The man should help to cheer up his partner if she is depressed.*

D *They should both be able to discuss financial problems.*

E *They should go out together socially and meet friends.*

F *They should stand firmly together against interference from in-laws or relations.*

G *Both of them should give up social activities that do not include their partner.*

Try to sum up in one short paragraph what you think are the essentials of a happy and fulfilling pregnancy.

Assignment II

Place a ☑ in the box(es) to indicate the correct answer.

1 Put a tick in the box if you think the answer is true.

A *An obstetrician is a doctor who specialises in looking after new babies.*

B *The expectant mother should visit the post-natal clinic.*

C *The expectant mother should tell her midwife about any addictions she has to alcohol, smoking or drugs.*

D *The prospective father is not allowed to attend the clinic classes with his wife.*

E *Ultra scan is used to listen to the heart-beats of the foetus.*

F *The expectant mother will be taught how to breathe and how to relax at the clinic.*

2 Which of these things are essential when preparing a baby's nursery?

A *Make sure the room is not damp.*

B *Lay thick, pure wool carpeting.*

C *Put wallpaper on the walls.*

D *Only use lead-free paint.*

E *Have some form of indirect lighting.*

F *Have colourful roller blinds.*

G *Put safety catches on the windows.*

283

3 'Cotton, silk, rayon, linen, wool, are all natural fibres.'

False		True	

4 Which of the following points would you be looking for when choosing a cot?

A *It should be all made of metal.*

B *The mattress should fit the size of base.*

C *The bars should be 150–160 mm apart.*

D *It should have childproof catches.*

E *It should be stable.*

F *There should be pretty transfers on the side panels.*

5 Tick the ones that are correct.

 A *Wash programme for delicate fabrics*

B *Wash programme for articles with a special finish*

C *Programme for washing wool*

D *Use cool water*

E *Very cool iron*

6 Underline the names of the two fibres that are most flame-resistant

> nylon   cotton
> polyester   wool
> pure silk

Cotton can be given a flame-resistant finish by being treated with:

> Comfort Proban
> Chlorethylene Acrylic

(Underline the correct answer.)

7 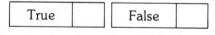 'This sign indicates that an article is safe and well-designed.'

True		False	

'It is issued by the Consumer Guidance Council.'

True		False	

8 Which of the following reasons should influence the expectant mother to decide to have her baby in hospital?

A *She is having her third baby.*

B *She has a history of miscarriage.*

C *She lives in a house without a bathroom.*

D *She is 32.*

E *It is a multiple birth.*

9 'The domino system is a method of delivery that involves home and hospital care.'

True		False	

10 Which of the following articles should the expectant mother pack in the case she is taking to hospital?

A *Front opening nightdresses.*

B *A watch.*

C *Clothing for the baby.*

D *Magazines and books.*

E *Nursing bras.*

F *Aspirins.*

G *Slippers.*

H *Bath towels and hand towels.*

11 Which of the following are true?

A *Breast feeding is best for the baby.*

B *Breast feeding encourages the uterus to shrink.*

C *The breasts will sag if the mother breast feeds her baby.*

D *Immunities in the mother will pass in her milk to the baby.*

E *Women with small breasts cannot breast feed.*

F *Colostrum is bad for the baby.*

G *Cow's milk has the same composition as breast milk.*

12 Which of the following are *not* normal characteristics of the newborn baby, and will need treatment?

A *A soft spot at the top and front of the baby's head.*

B *Sticky eyes.*

C *Fine hair all over the baby's body.*

D *Red blotches on the baby's head.*

E *A squint.*

F *Poor breathing.*

G *Jaundice.*

Assignment III

Most of the information needed to answer this assignment can be found in the Glossary at the end of this book.

Place a tick ☑ in the box(es) to indicate the correct answer to each question.

1 Complementary feeds are:

A *free samples given by food manufacturers.*

B *bottle feeds that top up breast feeds.*

C *feeds that are easy to digest.*

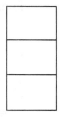

2 AID means:

A *artificial insemination with semen from a donor.*

B *artificial insemination carried out by the doctor.*

C *advanced insemination with semen from a donor.*

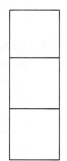

3 The fontanelle is:

A *a strawberry-shaped birthmark.*

B *the tummy button.*

C *the soft spot on top of a baby's head.*

4 Malnutrition means:

A *the study of food.*

B *a diet that is deficient in some nutrients.*

C *starvation.*

5 Colostrum is

A *the first fluid secreted by the breasts.*

B *the fluid in which the foetus floats during pregnancy.*

C *a pain-killing drug.*

6 Oestrogen is:

A a male sex hormone.

B the tissue that nourishes the foetus.

C a female sex hormone.

7 These services are available at a Family Planning Clinic:

A advice on birth control methods.

B advice on breast feeding.

C instructions on self examination of the breasts.

8 Child Guidance Clinics are:

A play centres for children.

B centres where advice on bringing up children may be obtained.

C centres where children with mental or emotional problems are treated.

9 A paediatrician specialises in:

A looking after children's feet.

B the treatment of children up to early teens.

C the care of the expectant mother.

10 NAWCH is an association which:

A is concerned with the welfare of children in children's homes.

B helps to improve the care given to children in hospitals.

C gives advice to couples who wish to adopt children.

11 RoSPA deals with:

A safety in public play parks and play areas.

B water safety.

C accident prevention.

12 Where could a couple with a young family, who had just moved to a new home in a new area, get information and advice on family and health matters? List ten places and/or people who could help.

APPENDIX K   How the Follow-up Exercises Link with the National Criteria Assessment Objectives

This is a condensed version of the assessment objectives from the national criteria for GCSE Home Economics. The key words are given in italics.

3.1　To *analyse* situations, *identify* human needs and material factors, *recognise* the interrelationships.

3.2　To *recall, seek out, select, record* and *apply* knowledge.

3.3　To use *investigative* procedures:
- i　to *test* and *compare*,
- ii　to *observe, measure* and *record*,
- iii　to *interpret* evidence in order to make *judgements* and *choice*,
- iv　to *justify* judgements and choice.

3.4　To *decide* and *plan* a *course of action* and *identify* priorities.

3.5　To *carry through* the course of action by *applying* skills.

3.6　To *assess* and *evaluate* the course of action.

The matrix lists the objectives that each question covers.

Matrix of assessment objectives

Follow-up Exercises	Assessment Objectives								
	3.1	3.2	3.3i	3.3ii	3.3iii	3.3iv	3.4	3.5	3.6
2　Pre-planned parenthood									
Question 1		•							
Question 2			•	•	•	•			
Question 3					•	•			
Question 4			•	•	•				
Activity								•	•
3　Basic physiology									
Question 1		•							
Question 2		•							
Question 3			•		•				
Question 4		•			•				
Question 5		•			•				
Question 6		•							

Follow-up Exercises		3.1	3.2	3.3i	3.3ii	3.3iii	3.3iv	3.4	3.5	3.6
3 (cont.)	Question 7		•			•				
	Question 8		•			•			•	
	Question 9		•		•				•	
	Question 10		•	•		•		•		
	Question 11	•				•	•	•		•
	Question 12		•	•	•	•				
	Question 13		•							
	Question 14	•				•	•	•		•
4 Development of the foetus	Question 1		•			•				
	Question 2		•							
	Question 3		•			•			•	
	Question 4		•			•	•			
	Question 5		•		•	•				
	Question 6	•	•			•				•
	Activity				•	•				
5 Care of the expectant mother	Question 1	•	•		•	•		•	•	
	Question 2	•	•			•		•	•	•
	Question 3	•	•	•		•	•	•	•	
	Question 4		•			•				
	Question 5		•							
	Question 6	•			•	•	•	•		•
	Question 7		•	•		•				
	Question 8	•	•			•		•		•
	Question 9		•			•	•	•		•
	Question 10	•				•				
	Question 11	•	•			•	•	•	•	•
	Activity			•	•	•				
6 Preparations before the birth	Question 1	•	•			•	•			
	Question 2	•	•			•	•			
	Question 3		•							
	Question 4		•	•		•				
	Question 5		•	•		•				
	Question 6	•	•	•		•		•		
	Question 7	•						•		•
	Question 8	•	•	•		•		•		•
	Activity 1	•						•	•	
	Activity 2	•						•	•	
	Activity 3	•		•	•	•		•	•	•

Follow-up Exercises	Assessment Objectives								
	3.1	3.2	3.3i	3.3ii	3.3iii	3.3iv	3.4	3.5	3.6
7 Birth									
Question 1		•			•				
Question 2		•							
Question 3	•	•			•	•			
Question 4		•							
Question 5	•	•			•	•			
Question 6		•			•				
Question 7	•	•			•	•	•		•
Question 8		•		•					
Question 9	•		•	•	•	•			
8 Looking after the newborn baby									
Question 1		•			•				
Question 2	•	•			•		•		
Question 3	•		•	•	•	•	•		•
Question 4	•				•				
Question 5	•				•		•	•	
Question 6		•							
Question 7	•	•			•				
Question 8		•							
Question 9		•			•				
Question 10		•			•				
Question 11	•		•		•	•	•	•	
Question 12	•				•		•		
Question 13	•	•	•	•			•		
Question 14	•						•	•	•
Question 15	•		•	•	•		•	•	•
Question 16	•	•			•				
Question 17	•				•	•	•		•
9 Stages of physical development									
Question 1		•							
Question 2		•							
Question 3		•			•				
Question 4		•			•				
Question 5		•			•				
Question 6		•			•				
Question 7		•		•					
Question 8				•					
Question 9		•		•	•				
Activity 1	•				•		•	•	
Activity 2	•			•	•		•	•	•
Activity 3	•			•	•		•	•	•

Follow-up Exercises	Assessment Objectives							
	3.1	3.3i	3.3ii	3.3iii	3.3iv	3.4	3.5	3.6
10 Conditions for physical development								
Question 1		•			•			
Question 2		•						
Question 3		•	•	•				
Question 4	•		•		•	•	•	•
Question 5	•		•		•	•		
Question 6	•		•	•	•	•		
Question 7		•						
Question 8	•	•	•		•			
Question 9		•						
Question 10		•						
Question 11		•						
Question 12		•						
Question 13	•	•			•			
Question 14	•						•	•
Question 15		•			•			
Question 16	•				•		•	•
Question 17	•		•		•	•		
Question 18	•	•			•	•		
Question 19		•	•	•	•			
Question 20		•			•			
Question 21	•			•	•		•	•
Question 22	•				•	•		
Question 23	•	•			•	•		
Question 24		•						
Question 25		•						
Question 26	•				•	•		
Question 27	•			•			•	•
Question 28	•	•						
Question 29	•				•	•		
Question 30	•		•	•	•			
Activity 1	•		•	•	•	•	•	•
Activity 2	•		•	•	•	•	•	•
Activity 3	•			•	•	•	•	
Activity 4						•	•	
11 Stages of intellectual development								
Question 1		•		•	•			
Question 2	•	•			•			
Question 3	•		•			•	•	•
Activity 1	•		•	•	•	•	•	•

Follow-up Exercises	Assessment Objectives							
	3.1	3.3i	3.3ii	3.3iii	3.3iv	3.4	3.5	3.6
12 Conditions for intellectual development								
Question 1		•	•		•			
Question 2		•			•			
Question 3	•		•		•		•	•
Question 4		•	•	•				
Question 5	•		•	•	•			
Question 6		•	•	•	•			
Question 7	•	•	•	•	•		•	•
Question 8	•		•	•	•		•	
Question 9	•	•			•			•
Activity 1	•		•	•			•	•
Activity 2	•		•	•	•	•	•	•
Activity 3							•	•
Activity 4							•	•
Activity 5	•				•		•	•
13 Social development								
Question 1		•			•	•		
Question 2		•			•	•		
Question 3	•	•			•			
Question 4	•	•			•			
Question 5	•	•		•	•	•		
Question 6		•	•	•	•		•	•
Question 7	•	•	•		•	•		
Question 8	•	•	•	•	•			
Question 9			•		•	•	•	•
Question 10	•	•			•	•	•	•
14 Emotional development								
Question 1	•	•	•	•	•	•	•	•
Question 2	•	•						
Question 3	•	•		•		•		
Question 4		•			•	•		
Question 5		•			•	•		
Question 6		•			•	•	•	•
Question 7		•			•	•	•	•
Question 8	•			•	•	•		
Activity		•	•	•			•	•

GLOSSARY

GLOSSARY

This gives an explanation of some of the specialist and unusual terms used in this book.

A

ABORTION   The loss of the foetus before the 28th week, either spontaneous (MISCARRIAGE) or induced (TERMINATION)

AFTERBIRTH   The discarded placenta and foetal membranes that follow the baby from the uterus.

AID   Artificial insemination with semen from a donor

AIH   Artificial insemination with semen from the husband

AMNIOCENTESIS   A test for abnormalities, which involves drawing off some of the amniotic fluid

AMNION   The inner layer of the membrane that forms the amniotic sac

AMNIOTIC FLUID   The 'waters' in which the foetus floats during pregnancy

AMNIOTIC SAC   The bag filled with amniotic fluid in which the foetus develops

ANALGESIC   A drug given for pain relief

ARTIFICIAL INSEMINATION   Method of fertilising the egg artificially

B

BONDING   The attachment formed between parent and child

BRAXTON HICKS' CONTRACTIONS   False contractions of the uterine muscles

BREECH BIRTH   A baby emerging with feet or bottom first

C

CAESAREAN SECTION   Cutting through the abdominal wall to deliver the baby

CERVIX   The neck or opening of the uterus

CHORION   The outer layer of the membrane that forms the amniotic sac

CHROMOSOMES   The fine thread-like structures, found in cells, that carry the GENES that give us our natural characteristics

COELIAC DISEASE   Intolerance to gluten, a protein found in cereals

COGNITIVE   To do with the intellect, reasoning and thinking

COITUS   Sexual intercourse

COLOSTRUM   The first milk secreted by the breasts, before the true milk arrives

COMPLEMENTARY FEEDS   Bottle feeds given to top up breast feeds

CONCEPTION   The fertilisation of the egg, and its implantation in the uterus

CONCEPTS   Patterns of ideas

CONFINEMENT   Delivery of the baby

CONTRACTIONS   Tightening of the muscles of the uterus to deliver the baby

CO-OPERATIVE PLAY   The stage of development when children play together

CROWN-RUMP LENGTH   The measurement from the top of the foetus' or baby's head to the base of the spine

D

DELIVERY   The birth of the baby and the placenta
DILATION   The width of the cervix during delivery
DOMINO SYSTEM   Domiciliary-in-out system of giving birth, which combines home and hospital care
DYSMENORRHOEA   Painful or difficult periods

E

EDD   The estimated date of delivery
EGGS   *See* OVA
EMBRYO   The name given to the fertilised egg from the time when the first cell starts dividing in the womb until 8 weeks
ENDOMETRIUM   The lining of the uterus
ENGAGEMENT   The stage when the baby's head enters the inlet of the pelvis ready for birth
EPISIOTOMY   A small cut made to the perineum to help the delivery
EXTROVERT   A person with an outgoing personality

F

FALLOPIAN TUBES   The tubes that connect the ovaries to the uterus, through which the egg cells travel
FERTILE   Able to conceive or father children
FERTILISATION   The sperm entering the egg
FHR   The foetal heart rate
FOETUS (FETUS)   The name given to the baby in the womb from 8–28 weeks
FONTANELLE   The soft spot at the top of the baby's head
FORCEPS   A metal instrument used to help the passage of the baby along the birth canal

G

GENES   *See* CHROMOSOMES
GENETICS   The study of heredity
GESTATION   The period of pregnancy

H

HORMONES   The chemicals that control growth and metabolism
HYPOTHERMIA A seriously low body temperature

I

INCUBATOR   A special care cot, where heat and humidity can be controlled
INDUCTION   Using artificial means to start labour early
INTROVERT   A person with an inward-looking personality

L

LABOUR   The process of giving birth
LANUGO   A covering of soft hair formed on the foetus
LAYETTE   A collection of first-size baby clothing
LMP   Last menstrual period

M
MALNUTRITION   A nutritional deficiency
MENSTRUATION   The female menstrual (monthly) cycle, which results in
    monthly bleeding (PERIOD)
MILESTONES   The stages by which physical and intellectual skills progress
MISCARRIAGE   *See* ABORTION
MULTIPLE PREGNANCY   The conception of two or more babies at the same
    time

N
NIPPLE SHIELDS   Covers used to draw out inverted (turned inward) nipples

O
OBESITY   Overweight
OESTROGEN   One of the female sex hormones
OVA   Egg cells (the female reproductive cells)
OVARIES   The two oval-shaped organs that produce and release egg cells
OVULATE   To produce eggs
OVULATION   The release of the ripened egg

P
PARALLEL PLAY   The stage of development when children play alongside
    rather than with each other
PATERNITY   The state of being a father
PEERS   A child's equals at school, playgroup, etc.
PERINATAL MORTALITY RATE   The number of stillbirths plus deaths of
    infants under one week old
PERINEUM   The skin and muscle between the rectum and the vagina
PERIOD   *See* Menstruation
PLACENTA   The tissue that nourishes the foetus, and forms the
    AFTERBIRTH
PLAQUE   The harmful substance that forms on the surface of the teeth
PMT   Premenstrual tension
PND   Post natal depression, a normal condition in the new mother after birth
PRE-ECLAMPSIA   *See* TOXAEMIA
PRE-TERM   A foetus born before the 36th week of pregnancy
PROGESTERONE   One of the female sex hormones
PUBERTY   The stage at which people become capable of reproduction
PUERPERAL PSYCHOSIS   Severe depression in the new mother after birth

S
SEMEN   The fluid that carries the sperm.
SEMINAL VESICLES   The organs at the base of the prostate gland that
    store sperm
SHOW   The discharge of blood-stained mucus that indicates birth has begun
SIBLING   A brother or sister.
SPERM   The male reproductive cells
STD (VD)   A sexually transmitted disease (venereal disease)
STERILITY   Inability to conceive or father children

T

TERMINATION   *See* ABORTION
TESTES   The male reproductive glands
TESTOSTERONE   One of the male sex hormones, secreted by the testes
TOXAEMIA (PRE-ECLAMPSIA)   High blood pressure and swelling at the end
   of pregnancy
TRIMESTER   The three three-month periods of a nine-month pregnancy,
   called the first, second and third trimesters

U

ULTRASCAN   An examination during pregnancy using an ultrasonic scanner
UMBILICAL CORD   The cord that attaches the foetus to the placenta,
   passing nourishment and protection against some diseases to the foetus
UMBILICUS   The navel or tummy button
UTERUS (WOMB)   The strong muscular bag that holds the developing foetus

V

VAGINA   The passage connecting the uterus to the surface of the body
VD   *See* STD
VEGANS   People whose diet does not contain any foods derived from
   animals
VENTOUSE DELIVERY   Suction delivery of the foetus
VERNIX   The waxy substance that protects the skin of newborn babies
VERTEX   The crown of the foetus' head
VULVA   The entrance to the vagina

W

WEANING   The gradual introduction of solid foods and reduction of milk
   feeds
WOMB   *See* UTERUS

Z

ZYGOTE   The single cell that is the beginning of the human baby

INDEX

INDEX

Abortion 7, 67, 69, 294
Abruptio placentae 49
Abstract thinking period 216
Acquired immune deficiency
    syndrome (AIDS) 21
Adrenal glands 18
Afterbirth 39, 294
Albumen 67
Alcohol 9, 55, 65, 67
Amniocentesis 30, 40, 50, 69,
    294
Amnion 40, 294
Amniotic;
    fluid 40, 69, 294
    sac 40-3, 100, 294
Anaemia 28, 47, 67, 69
Analgesic 294
Anoxia 31
Antenatal;
    classes 71
    clinic 66, 261
Antepartum haemorrage 49
Antisocial behaviour 255
Artificial insemination (AID, AIH,
    IVF) 24, 294
Asthma 185
Audiologist 153, 260
Autism 227
Automatic reflexes 110-11

Baby;
    baths 80
    bedding 78-9
    chairs 82
    characteristics of new born 118
    clinics 153
    clothing 133
    hygiene 125
    love and security 134
    slings or carriers 84
Baby's room 76-7
Bacteria 181
Bathing baby 126-7
Binovular 27
Bleeding (cuts) 192, 197
Blood;
    cells 28
    groups 28, 67
    pressure 49, 67, 99
Bonding 294
Bones, baby 147
Bottle;
    feeding 92-4, 121-5
    cleaning and sterilising 123
Bowel training 167-8

Braxton Hicks' contractions 99,
    294
Breast feeding 92-4, 119-20
Breasts 16, 32, 48, 61, 67, 69,
    107
Breech presentation 98, 99, 294
British Standards Institution (BSI)
    88
Bronchitis 185
Burns and scalds 192, 197

Caesarean section 89, 98, 104,
    294
Caffeine 56
Calcium 8, 60
Candidiasis 20
Carbohydrates 59, 60, 92
Carrycots and cots 79
Car safety 202-3
Casein 92
Centres for autism 261
Cerebal palsy 31, 227
Cervical;
    mucus 23
    smear test 67, 108
Cervix 14, 15, 22, 43-4, 57, 99,
    100, 294
Chicken pox 184
Childbirth Trust 89
Child Guidance Clinic 261
Choking 192, 197
Chorion 40, 294
Chromosomes 25-6, 29, 294
Citizens Advice Bureau (CAB) 88
Climax, male 6, 22
Clitoris 14, 15
Clothes;
    baby 85-6
    maternity 61
    toddler 172-9
Clubs for mothers 222
Coeliac disease 32, 294
Cognitive development 215-6,
    294
Coitus 21, 294
Coitus interruptus 6
Cold sore 185
Colic 117, 185
Colostrum 48, 69, 107, 294
Commercial baby foods, advant-
    ages and disadvantages 160
Community Health Council 89
Community midwife 65
Complementary feeding 120
Concepts 214

Concrete operational period 216
Confinement 90-2
Conjunctivitis 185
Condom 5, 6
Constipation 54, 186
Consumer Advice Centre 88
Contraception 4-6
Contractions 99-102
Convulsions 186
Co-operative play 245
Co-ordination;
    hand/eye 151
    manipulative 150-1
    muscular 150-1
Coughs 186
Cradlecap 186
Croup 186
Crown-rump length 41, 294
Curiosity 220
Cystic fibrosis 32

Delivery 100-4, 295
Dermatitis 131
Design Centre label 88
Development testing 152
Diabetes 59, 67
Diaphragm 5, 6
Diet, baby 146
Dilation 295
Diphtheria 182-3
Discipline 247-9
Domino system 89, 90
Down's syndrome 29, 30, 69
Drips 104-5
Drownings 197
Drugs, addictive 55
Dutch cap 5, 6
Dyslexia 227
Dysmenorrhoea 19

Earache 186
Ectopic pregnancy 48
Eczema 186
Eggs (see Ova)
Ejaculation 22
Electric shock 197
Embryo 38-9, 41, 69, 295
Emotions 252
Endometrium 18, 295
Engagement, prenatal 70, 295
Epidural block 103
Epilepsy 186
Episiotomy 104, 295
Erection 16, 23
Estimated delivery date 91

Exercises;
    antenatal 62, 72
    for young child 169
    postnatal 107
Expenditure, weekly 3
Extended family 116
Extrovert 247, 295

Fallopian tube 5, 14, 15, 21, 22,
    23, 47, 295
Falls 198
Family doctor 65
Family Planning Association 2
Family planning clinic 261
Feeding;
    equipment 165
    problems 166
Fertilisation 21–4
Fibroids 49, 105
First aid 195–8
Foetal monitoring 105
Foetus 26–8, 38, 39–44, 55, 68,
    69, 70, 295
Fontanelle 109, 118, 295
Food;
    child 161–4
    during pregnancy 58–60
    hygiene 158–9
    making attractive 164
Footwear, child 177
Forceps delivery 104, 295
Fractures, broken bones 197
Fresh air 169
Fungi
    disease causing 181
    poisonous 199

Gas and oxygen, analgesic 102,
    103
Genes 25
Geneticist 25, 260
Genetics 25, 295
Genito-urinary medicine 261
German measles, rubella 9, 31,
    182–4
Gestation 295
Gluten 157
Gonadotrophin 33
Gonorrhoea 20
GP (General practitioner) 260
    Unit 89, 90
Grand mal 186
Green Cross Code 201
Group play 245
Guthrie test III
Gynaecologist 66, 260

Haemoglobin 28, 47, 70, 167
Haemophilia 29
Haemorrhoids 54, 70
Health visitor 65, 71, 89, 260

Hearing 144
Heartburn 54, 58, 70
Heat strip 187
Height, baby 141
Heredity 25
Herpes 21
Home confinement 90
Homemade foods, advantages
    and disadvantages 160
Hormonal change triggering
    birth 98
Hormone drip 104
Hormones 4, 17–18, 33, 40, 48,
    62–3, 70, 93, 295
Hospital confinement 91
Hospitalisation of child 190–1
Hygiene 61, 63, 76, 182
Hypertension 49
Hypothermia 105, 132, 295
Hypothyroidism 32

Illness, 180–91
    symptoms of 184–7
Immunisation;
    of children 182–3
    prenatal 56
Immunity from disease 182
Incontinence 47
Incubator 106, 295
Induction 103–4, 295
Infection 181, 184
Infertility 22–4
Intra-uterine device (IUD) 5, 6
Intra-uterine transfusion 28
Introvert 247, 295
Intuitive period 215
In vitro fertilisation 24

Jargoning 226
Jaundice 28

Kitemark 88

Labia 14, 15
Labour 98–105, 295
Language development 225
Lanugo 42, 109, 295
Laparascope 24
Layette 85–6, 295
Lead 56
Lice 21
Locomotion 147–9
Low birth-weight baby 105

Maintaining children's clothing
    176
Malnutrition 167, 296
Marriage Guidance Council 2
Maternity;
    clothing 61
    unit 90

Maturation 214
Measles 182–4
Meninges 186
Meningitis 186
Menopause 19
Menstrual cycle 18–19, 22
Menstruation 4, 18, 296
Metazoan parasites 181
Midwife 67, 71, 99–102, 104–5,
    260
Milk;
    breast 92
    cow's 92
Minerals 60, 92, 167
Miscarriage 56–7, 67, 89, 296
Mixed feeding 157
Mortality, perinatal 53, 296
Mouth-to-mouth resuscitation 197
Mumps 185
Multiple pregnancy 26–7
Muscular dystrophy 29
Mutations 30

Nappies 128–9
Nappy folding 130
National Childbirth Trust
    (NCT) 71, 93
Natural childbirth 103
Negative emotions 252
Neonatologist 66, 260
Nightwear 173
Nipple shields 93, 296
Non-specific urethritis 20
Nose bleeds 186
Nuclear family 116
Nursery;
    layout 81
    schools 224

Obesity, in children 166, 296
Obstetrician 66, 260
Obstetric table 33
Oestrogen 4, 18, 40, 296
Opthalmologist 153, 260
Oral contraception 4, 6
Outdoor wear, children 175
Ova 15, 16, 18, 19, 21–4, 296
Ovarian cysts 49, 67, 105
Ovary 14, 15, 18
Overweight, mother 90
Oviduct 14, 15
Ovulation 4, 18, 296
Oxytocin 93, 102

Paediatrician 66, 153, 260
Pancreas 18
Parallel play 245, 296
Parasites, metazoan 181
Peer group 216, 296
Pelvis 67, 70, 90
Penis 15, 16, 22

Perineum 104, 296
Periods (*see Menstruation*)
Pethidine 102
Petit mal 186
Phenylketonuria (PKU) 31, 111
Phobias 255
Piaget, Professor Jean 214–16
Pincer grasp;
    mature 151
    primitive 150
Pituitary gland 18
Placenta 27, 38–44, 49, 57, 69,
    70, 102, 105, 296
Placenta praevia 49
Plants, poisonous 200
Plasma 28
Platelets 28
Play;
    clothes 174, 178
    groups 222–4
Pneumonia 187
Poisoning 197
Polio 182–3
Port wine stains 109
Positive emotions 252
Posseting 125
Postnatal clinics 261
Postnatal depression (PND) 108,
    296
Potty 84, 168–9
Prams 81–3
Pre-conceptual period 215
Pre-eclampsia 49
Pregnancy;
    sickness 54
    termination 7
Premature baby 105–6
Premenstrual tension (PMT) 19,
    296
Primary maternal preoccupation
    114
Progesterone 4, 18, 40, 57, 296
Proteins 60, 67, 92
Psychiatric social worker 257,
    260
Psychiatrist 257, 260
Psychologist 153, 257, 260
Puerperal psychosis 108, 296
Puerperium 108
Purées, preparation of 159
Pushchairs 82–3

Reflexes, automatic 110–11
Reproductive organ;
    female 14–15
    male 15–16

Rest, child 169–71
Resuscitation 197
Rhesus 28
Rhythm method 6
Rickets 147
Road Safety 201–2
Rubella 9, 31, 40, 67, 183

Safety harness 84
Safety;
    in the home 191–9
    of toys 236–7
    on water and ice 204
Scabies 21
Scarlet fever 185
Schools psychological services
    261
Semen 16, 22, 296
Seminal vesicle 15–16, 296
Sensorimotor period 215
Sexually transmitted disease
    (STD) 9, 20–1, 296
Sheath 5, 6
'Show' 99, 296
Siblings 116, 296
Sleep 132, 169–72
Smoking 40, 55, 65, 68
Socialisation 244–6
Social worker 66, 260
Soft spot 109, 118
Speech;
    development of 225
    therapist 153, 260
Sperm 21–2, 296
    tube 15–16
Spermicidal sponge 6
Spermicide 5, 6
Spina bifida 29, 30, 69
Sterilisation, vasectomy 5
Stillbirth 53–4
Stress, emotional 169
Suction delivery 104
Suffocation 198
Surgical induction 104
Surrogate motherhood 24
Syphilis 20, 67

Teats, bottle 122
Teeth, baby 145–6
Testes (testicles) 15–16, 18, 296
Testosterone 18
Test tube fertilisation 24
Tetanus 182–3
Thalidomide 31
Thermometer, clinical 187–8
Thrush 20, 187

Thyroid gland 18
Toiletry basket for baby 87
Toxaemia 45, 49, 67, 296
Toys;
    for physical development
    179–80
    for intellectual development
    232
Tracking 144
Transverse presentation 98–9
Trichomonases vaginalis 20
Trimester 38, 45, 296
Tuberculosis 182–3
Twins 26–7

Ultrasound scan 42, 50, 69, 296
Umbilical cord 38–9, 41–4
Umbilicus 296
Underwear, child 173
Uniovular 27
Urea 40
Urine 33, 47, 55, 67
Uterus 5, 14, 18, 22, 33, 47, 55,
    67, 70, 89, 100–2, 296

Vaccination, prenatal 56
Vagina 14, 15, 22, 47, 57, 99,
    296
Vaginismus 23
Varicose veins 55, 70
Vas deferens 15–16
Vasectomy 5
Vegans 58
Veneral disease 9, 20–1, 296
Ventouse extraction 104, 296
Vernix, 42, 296
Vertex presentation 43, 98, 296
Viruses 181
Vision 143
Vitamins 58, 60, 69, 92, 146,
    161, 167
Voluntary and other organisations
    262–3
Vulva 15–16, 296

Warts 21
'Water', amniotic fluid 99–100
Weaning 157, 161–6, 296
Weight;
    baby 141–3
    mother 8, 44–5
Whooping cough 182–3, 185
Withdrawal method 6
Withdrawn behaviour 255
Womb (*see Uterus*)

Zygote 22, 38, 296